BSHS MONOGRAPHS

— 12 —

TO SEE THE

FELLOWS FIGHT

TO SEE THE

FELLOWS FIGHT

Eye witness accounts of meetings of the Geological Society of London and its Club, 1822-1868

Edited by John C Thackray

THE BRITISH SOCIETY FOR THE HISTORY OF SCIENCE

© 1999 John C Thackray
and the British Society for the History of Science

First BSHS edition 2003

ISBN 0-906450-14-4

Transferred from the original text
by Optical Character Recognition techniques and typeset
in EFF Franek on the Acorn computer platform
by Geoffrey Bennett, Professional Office Services, 31 High Street,
Stanford in the Vale, Faringdon, Oxfordshire, SN7 8LH

Printed in Great Britain by Parchment (Oxford) Ltd

To Sue

Contents

Preface · iii

Introduction · v

Editorial Conventions · xiii

List of Abbreviations · xv

Acknowledgements · xvii

The Meetings, 1822-1868 · 1 - 222

Bibliography · 223

Name Index · 231

Subject Index · 243

Cover Illustration

A contemporary sketch of the Geological Society of London in session probably dating from the early years when the Society was housed in Somerset House. Members face each other across the table in parliamentary fashion. Leading figures take the front benches with others more faintly drawn behind. The president, flanked by the two secretaries, is at one end. Specimens to be discussed are on the table and a large drawing of a geological section hangs on the far wall. The artist is unidentified but may be Henry De la Beche, shown here as the spectacled figure on the left.

(Reference LDGSL 312. Courtesy of the Geological Society of London)

Preface

This book was all but completed when John Thackray died of cancer in May 1999. As many of his friends will recall he had been working on it for a number of years, a labour of love within the history of a subject that he also loved. The text was already submitted to the BSHS Monograph series. It has unfortunately taken much longer than the editors would have wished to bring to completion. However, it now stands pretty much as we hope he would have liked to see it. We – like so many of John's friends and colleagues – had great faith in John's understanding and knowledge of his subject matter and have therefore presented the material with as little interference as possible other than checking and standardising references and so on. We owe a particular debt to Dr Peter Wigley and Wing Commander Geoffrey Bennett who undertook to transfer the text into electronic form and thence into print. Geoff Bennett has provided very welcome publishing assistance in all regards.

John Thackray (1948-1999) was a much-admired and central figure for those with interests in the history of geology. Early in the 1970s he joined the Institute of Geological Sciences in South Kensington, London, as a Scientific Officer to the Geological Museum. In more recent years he was archivist of the Natural History Museum and honorary archivist of the Geological Society of London, two places from which much of the content of this monograph arises. He was greatly appreciated both here and abroad for his cheery enthusiasm for the history of geology and his astonishing knowledge of obscure books and pamphlets, manuscript letters, specimens, maps and all the other data essential for understanding early geological practice. He was a key member of the Society for the History of Natural History, serving as secretary and general fulcrum for 17 years. In 1975 he helped organise the Charles Lyell centenary symposium, appearing as Lyell in person to deliver a lecture derived from recently discovered archives. He was a longstanding member of the British Society of the History of Science and held an MSc in the history of science from Imperial College.

Full details of his career, his musical interests, his publications and book reviews, with his own fascinating "confessions", as a rare book and MSS collector can be found in *Archives of Natural History* (2000) 27: 1-22. While he would have been the first to protest that he was not a professional historian (modestly downplaying his professional qualifications), this monograph reveals not only John's scholarly appreciation of the subtle ways in which geology was shaped in the early nineteenth century but also his joy in unearthing those quirky details that – when put together – make something new and invaluable. Conversations are rarely recorded, and if they are, are invariably difficult to find. *To See the Fellows Fight* therefore presents a remarkable record of the early days of British geology at a learned society which had a proud record for the quality of its debates, as it appeared to the participants themselves.

Janet Browne, Jim Secord, Hugh Torrens

Introduction

The Geological Society of London was founded as 'a little talking geological dinner club' on 13 November 1807 (Woodward 1907, p10). It did not remain either little or a dinner club for very long, but developed into a formal society with members all over Britain and overseas, and a well articulated programme of cooperative research (Rudwick 1963). The Society fought for, and achieved, independence from the otherwise all-powerful Royal Society and, in 1811, published an impressive volume of *Transactions of the Geological Society*. The first twenty years were not uniformly productive or successful, and certainly in 1815 the Society was judged to be in a feeble state. [1] However the emergence of a Smithian approach to the study of regional geology using fossils to elucidate stratigraphy gave the Society a new lease of life, and the 1820s and 1830s saw new vigour in the Society's activities. From this date on, the Geological Society was the undisputed forum in London for the presentation and publication of geological research. A purely biological paper on fossils might still be read to the Linnean Society, and important memoirs were presented at the Royal Society if the author were hoping for the award of the Copley or Royal medals, but generally the Geological reigned supreme in its field.

The official record of the fortnightly 'ordinary' meetings, and the annual and special general meetings which made up the scientific and administrative business of the Society were published in the *Transactions* (1811-1856), the *Proceedings* (1826-1845) and the *Quarterly Journal*, later the *Journal*, (1845-present). This printed record is supplemented by manuscript minute books in the Society's archive. Between them these sources give details of, for the ordinary meetings, the nomination and election of new fellows, the receipt of gifts for the Library and Museum, the receipt of papers and letters, and finally an abstract of all papers read to the meeting prepared by the Assistant Secretary, and, where published, the author's complete text. This record, full though it is, gives no hint of the free and full discussions which generally followed the reading of a paper. Discussion of some sort seems to have been a feature of even the earliest meetings of the Society. The printed regulations for 1810 record that the ordinary meetings, to be held on the first and third Friday of every month from November to June, commencing at 8.00 pm sharp shall include the following business: 'to read such communications in geology as have been presented ... and to hear any observations which the reading of such papers may suggest'. [2] These discussions were formalised in 1827 when William Fitton was President, for we find the following in his Presidential Address for 1827-1828:

> I shall conclude, Gentlemen, by congratulating you on the good feeling by which the proceedings of this Society have always been characterized; and on the self-command that renders both agreeable and instructive the conversations, (I will not call them discussions – much less debates) with which it is now our practice to follow up the reading of memoirs at our table; and which have given to our evening meetings a character more like that of social intercourse in a private circle, than of the formal proceeding of a public body. This practice, I know, has been [a] subject of doubt, to many who wish well to our institution, and do not undervalue the personal character and disposition of our members. But, so long as our conversations are carried on with the urbanity by which they have hitherto been distinguished – while it is the wish of those who share in them to give or receive information, and not to shine – and the object is not victory but truth – there seems to be no reason to apprehend any very serious injury from the continuance of our geological warfare. (Fitton 1828, p61)

This emphasis on discussion is shown by a change to the Society's regulations. The 1827 edition states, as part of the order of business for the ordinary meetings: 'When other business has been completed, the persons present shall be invited by the Chairman to deliver aloud, from their places, their opinions on the communications which have been read, and on the specimens or drawings which have been exhibited at that meeting'. [3]

The Geological Society was unusual, if not unique, in permitting such discussions at this early date. At the Royal Societies of both London and Edinburgh, papers were listened to in dignified silence, while at the Linnean the titles of papers were not even announced before the meeting. Factual questions were permitted at the Astronomical Society, but there was no discussion of theoretical issues. The discussions were seen as a sign of the strength and vigour of the Society, and received approving notice in Babbage's *Reflections on the Decline of Science:*

> [The Geological Society] possess all the freshness, the vigour, and the ardour of youth in the pursuit of a youthful science, and has succeeded in a most dificult experiment, that of having

an oral discussion on the subject of each paper read at its meetings. To say of these discussions, that they are very entertaining, is the least part of the praise which is due to them. They are generally very instructive, and sometimes bring together isolated facts in the science which, though insignificant when separate, mutually illustrate each other, and ultimately lead to important conclusions. The continuance of these discussions evidently depends on the taste, the temper, and the good sense of the speakers. The things to be avoided are chiefly verbal criticisms – praise of each other beyond its reasonable limits, and contest for victory. The latter is, perhaps, the most important of the three, both for the interests of the Society and of truth. (Babbage 1830, pp45-46)

There were, however, problems, as Fitton had hinted in his Presidential Address. These problems related both to the science of geology itself and to the image of the science that geologists were keen to portray. The founder members of the Geological Society saw themselves and their out-of-town colleagues as being gatherers of geological facts which would, in the future, make the Society a mineral resource centre, and which would enable the production of a great mineral map of Britain. George Bellas Greenough, first President of the Society, was high priest of this approach, which stemmed from a general distaste for the unbridled theorising which was seen as characterising the eighteenth century, with its many fanciful 'theories of the Earth'. It was expected that the science of geology would progress by the steady accumulation of new facts, accompanied by the drawing of cautious and indisputable conclusions. These facts might be descriptive observations, specimens, drawings or other illustrations. The place for debate or discussion within such a scheme was clearly limited. A fact was a fact, either correct or incorrect. By the 1830s a new generation of geologists were running the Society, and there was a general appreciation that facts in themselves were not much use without a theoretical framework into which they could be set. However, old ideas died slowly, and the incoming President, William Whewell (76a [4]), pleaded forcefully for the primacy of facts in 1837. What happened in practice was that most papers read to the Ordinary Meetings of the Society were indeed primarily descriptive and fact-based, and it was the discussion that followed that set them within whatever theoretical debate or dispute was current at the time. A good example is R A C Austen's paper on a raised beach near Hope's Nose, in Devonshire (19 November 1834, 62), described by Adam Sedgwick as 'a plain matter of fact production', which nevertheless led to a heated discussion on the subject of elevation. At times the discussion clearly led well away from the subject matter of the paper itself. Dr Turnbull Christie's paper on certain younger deposits in Sicily (2 November 1831, 43) was used as a peg to hang a long discussion on a whole range of issues relating to earthquakes, elevation and the ideas recently put forward by Charles Lyell. Feelings ran high in 1834 when the facts put forward by Henry De la Beche on the geology of North Devon (3 December 1834, 63) were disputed on theoretical grounds by geologists who had never visited any of the localities. As Greenough put it, 'it was not our practice to give credit to the results of abstract reasoning when opposed to actual observation'. In this case, as in so many others, abstract reasoning eventually won the day.

The feeling was expressed from time to time that, although this was quite alright for the geologists, there was a danger that the 'johnny raws', as Roderick Impey Murchison described the general public, might be confused and think that after all these years, nothing had been decided, and that all was still debate and dispute. This may have been the reason why Council steadfastly refused to record or report the discussions; they were for internal consumption only, and were not to become part of the public face of science. Editors of both *The Athenaeum* (38a, 39a) and *The Geologist* (102b) had their knuckles rapped for mentioning discussions in print, both expressing their puzzlement at the decision. This is the reason that the only sources for the eye-witness accounts are to be found in the diaries, notebooks and letters of the participants. A change of heart on the part of Council in 1868 led to a very abbreviated record of contributions to discussions being printed in the Society's *Proceedings* and this year therefore forms the termination of the present collection.

The other perceived danger with the discussions was that the bounds of gentlemanly restraint and good manners might be passed and the whole thing descend into rowdiness and ill feeling. Opinions certainly varied about where the bounds should lie, with Fitton, for example, issuing a reprimand that a discussion in December 1834 (64a) had been 'too vifs', whereas Lyell felt that there was nothing to complain of in the debate (63c). Murchison certainly favoured an aggressive style in his speaking, and reported discussions in terms of military campaigns, with heavy artillery and sniper fire, although even he admitted to speaking 'more vehemently than I had intended' on one occasion (25 February 1852, 189b). Andrew Crombie Ramsay felt that this particular exchange was 'not an enlivening spectacle' (189a). Personal feuds and antagonisms undoubtedly existed within the Society's fellowship and from time to time these came out in discussion – Richard Owen and Gideon Mantell were unlikely ever to be civil to each other (168a), Murchison and Sedgwick were notorious, while Hugh Falconer and Lyell could usually be relied on to argue fiercely. Geologists as a happy band of brothers of the hammer was a myth that the Society fostered against the evidence of the case. Fitton might have disapproved, but many who attended the meetings as observers would have agreed with J S Lockhart, who declared: 'Though I don't care for geology, I do like to see the fellows fight' (Allen 1976, p70).

Polarisation into factions must have been encouraged by the layout of the Society's lecture theatre, which was on a parliamentary plan, with rows of benches facing each other across a large central table. The President sat at the head of the table, while senior fellows took the front benches and the more junior crowded in at the back. It is certainly tempting to imagine the opposing parties in, for example, the Great Devonian Controversy, facing each other from opposite sides of the table, each group making use of the specimens on the table and diagrams hanging on the walls to reinforce their points. However on at least one occasion Murchison and De la Beche actually sat next to each other (10 April 1839, 88a), so the point must not be over emphasised. The sketch of a meeting in progress (frontispiece), probably by H T De la Beche, seems to date from the Society's early years in Somerset House, sometime between 1828 and 1834. The room layout in later years at Somerset House is less certain, though Charles Lyell refers to 'a great horseshoe table' in 1838 (82a), and when the Society moved to Burlington House in 1874, it built a parliamentary-style lecture theatre which survived until 1972.

Two other important elements of the Society's life are included in the accounts that follow. The first is the annual Anniversary Dinner and Presidential Address, an occasion for the Society to show itself off to the world. Successive presidents vied with each other to assemble a yet more magnificent audience of lords, bishops, members of parliament and others, who would, by their presence, demonstrate the importance and high standing of the Society and the subject. These were both social and scientific occasions, as the dinner was followed by the Presidential Address, an exhaustive, and sometimes exhausting, summary of the achievements of the year. Also included are descriptions of meetings of the Society's Dining Club, which preceded the ordinary meetings. The Club had a restricted membership, and generally comprised the more senior and active fellows. Although it was principally a social gathering, the Club undoubtedly strengthened the grip that a small group of men had on the affairs of the Society, and provided a forum where Society business could be stitched up in advance where necessary. All was not always sober and serious, and Ramsay records scenes of 'wild and extravagant gaiety' on one occasion (170a).

What, then, is the historical value of these discussion reports? What do they tell us which would be hard, if not impossible, to gain from other sources? I suggest that the three main areas are in the Society's own workings and procedures; in the controversies which enlivened the science over the years; and in the personalities of the geologists involved.

The Society had its printed regulations to govern its proceedings, but there was also the way that things actually happened. Through the eye witness reports we can see the President juggling with the programme of the evening meeting to include a last-minute contribution from one of his friends (67a), or to include some item that he judges especially important. We can see him orchestrating the discussion itself, making sure that the front benches kept the lion's share of the action; we can see discussions being cut short or else being allowed to run late into the night, according to their perceived value. The late 1820s and the 1830s emerge as the Society's golden age, a time when meetings were well attended, when discussion was lively, and when all the 'great men' were in regular attendance. The Anniversary Meetings in particular attracted a glittering assemblage of the good and the great. By the mid 1840s there was a feeling that all was not so well. Meetings were often small, papers were trifling and discussion rambling or ill-informed (144). Sedgwick, William Buckland, William Conybeare and other players from the great days now attended less frequently, and there was a feeling of nostalgia for a past which was gone (151b and 201). There was even a move to make papers more accessible to a wider audience in order to boost numbers (228). Murchison's enthusiastic report on the reading of the Duke of Argyll's paper on 5 February 1868 reinforces the point: 'We had the grandest meeting last night which has been known in Somerset House for many a long year!!!' (236a).

Controversies, even long and hard-fought ones, have a habit of disappearing from the historical record. This is because the published books and papers which are their principal source material tend to be shorn of all personal feeling and controversy. There was a strong convention against any sort of personal attack in print, particularly in the pages of the publications of a learned society. Thus one could read through the publications generated by, for example, the Devonian controversy without getting any idea of the passions unleashed (Rudwick 1985). The Cambrian-Silurian controversy of 1843 to the 1860s is an exception to this rule, for here the printed record, even when written in the politest terms, makes the bitter argument between Murchison and Sedgwick pretty clear (Secord 1986). It is lucky this is the case, as surviving records of discussions do not help a great deal in reconstructing the dynamics of the long fight. Some key meetings are entirely unreported, while others receive just a few lines to show what a 'scrimmage' there had been (117a). The case is very different for the Devonian controversy of 1834 to the mid 1840s. Here there are long and detailed reports of the reception given to papers by all the main protagonists, from De la Beche's first letter on the anthracite from Bideford (63), to the contributions of Austen (80) and Parson Williams (88). We learn who supported who and where the battle lines were drawn. It also becomes abundantly clear that tempers frequently ran high and, to use Fitton's words, that this was real 'geological warfare'. Another controversy that was well reported was that over the evidence for glaciers in Britain which opened in November 1840 with papers by Louis Agassiz and Buckland (94). S P Woodward, the Society's sub-curator, provides a very detailed report of this and the following meeting, and the controversy can be traced on to Ramsay's papers on the glacial origin of lakes and the origin of the Permian boulder beds in 1862 (232).

The geologists of the Society's golden age may seem to us to have been giants, capable of all manner of heroic exploits, who shaped the very essence of geology, but to their contemporaries they were ordinary people, often with feet of clay. A multitude of comments in the discussion reports reveal how these men were seen. G B Greenough, one of the Society's founders and older than many of the other key figures, was the perpetual sceptic, always questioning and doubting, who, on one occasion, would not admit that the word 'sea' could be adequately defined (43a). William Buckland, from Oxford, who had been elected a fellow of the Society in 1813, was a witty and enter-taining speaker, but inclined to play the fool with strange anecdotes and allusions (1a and 152a). Adam Sedgwick, from Cambridge, just a year younger than Buckland, was a great orator, who could hold an audience spellbound for an hour or more (24d). He fell out with the Society, and disappeared from the record in the 1850s. R I Murchison, his one-time friend and later antagonist, was combative in debate, and always most anxious to win the argument. He could be 'awfully grand' (128b). Charles Lyell, a superb writer but a poor speaker, does not emerge as a clear personality in the 1830s, but later on was seen as devious and manipulative by the men of the Geological Survey (160b). Among the younger generation was Andrew Ramsay, whose almost painfully honest diary entries make clear his lack of self-confidence in the face of the Society and its 'great men' (118b).

These and many more emerge as real people from the reports of discussions, having their strengths and weaknesses, just like the rest of us. They ensure that the discussion reports, whatever their value in purely historical terms, are great fun to read.

Notes

1. Letter from Thomas Marcet to Leonard Horner, 18 November 1815, Lyell Mss at Kinnordy House.
2. GSL Business Papers, GS4.
3. GSL Business Papers, GS5.
4. References in bold typeface are to entries in 'The Meetings, 1822-1868'.

Editorial Conventions

The reports of meetings which make up the substance of this book are of two kinds: those which have been transcribed from the original manuscript, and those which have been taken from a secondary, generally printed, source. The former carry a reference to a manuscript collection, with references to books where the letter has been published; the latter have only the reference to a publication. They are chronologically arranged and numbered in sequence.

Reports transcribed from manuscripts retain the paragraph layout, capitalisation, spelling, underlining and abbreviation of the original document. Punctuation has been transcribed with some silent alterations where they seem helpful; the dash has frequently been replaced by a comma, semi-colon or full stop. Interlinear or marginal insertions have been silently brought into the text at the appropriate point, and deletions have been ignored. Text lost through tears, blanks left in the manuscript, and an illegible word or words are noted within < >. Editorial insertions, generally made to clarify a badly misspelled or drastically abbreviated name or locality, are enclosed within [ ]. Uncertain readings are immediately preceded by [?]. Additional information is given in footnotes, which are found at the end of each session. Sessions ran from November to June inclusive.

Reports taken from published sources are transcribed without alteration, and will generally represent a modernization of the original manuscript. Generally only those parts of a letter, diary or notebook entry relating to meetings of the Society and the Club have been included. Material omitted from within an entry is marked by ...

Each entry opens with a list of the papers read at the meeting. The titles have been transcribed without change from the minute book of Ordinary Meetings, 1822-1826; from the *Proceedings of the Geological Society of London*, 1826-1845; *Quarterly Journal of the Geological Society of London*, 1845-1856; and from the *Abstracts of the Proceedings of the Geological Society of London*, 1856-1868. All dates have been checked against C R Cheney's *Handbook of Dates* (2000), and corrected where necessary.

List of Abbreviations

Abbreviations used for manuscript sources are as follows:

ANS Taylor – Richard Cowling Taylor papers, Coll. 361, The Academy of Natural Sciences of Philadelphia, Ewell Sale Stewart Library, Philadelphia, USA.

APS Lyell – Lyell correspondence in the American Philosophical Society, Philadelphia, USA.

BGS Archives – British Geological Survey Archives, Keyworth, Nottingham, UK.

CMN Woodward – Correspondence of Samuel Woodward, Castle Museum, Norwich, UK.

CUL Fisher – Correspondence of Osmond Fisher, Sedgwick Collection, Add 7652, Cambridge University Library, UK.

CUL Sedgwick – Correspondence of Adam Sedgwick, Add 7652, Cambridge University Library, UK.

EUL Lyell – Correspondence of Charles Lyell, Special Collections, Edinburgh University Library, UK.

GSL Geikie – Correspondence of Archibald Geikie, LDGSL 789, Geological Society Archives, London, UK.

GSL Murchison – Papers of Roderick Murchison, Geological Society Archives, London, UK.

IC Ramsay – Papers of Andrew Ramsay, Imperial College Archives, London, UK.

MGA Dawson – Correspondence of J W Dawson, McGill University Archives, Montreal, Canada.

ML McCoy – Correspondence of Frederick McCoy, Mitchell Library, State Library of New South Wales, Sydney, Australia.

NHM Brickenden – Correspondence of L Brickenden, Palaeontology Manuscripts, Natural History Museum, London, UK.

NHM Owen – Papers of Richard Owen, General Library, Natural History Museum, London, UK.

NMW De la Beche – Papers of Henry De la Beche, Geology Department, National Museum of Wales, Cardiff, UK.

NUL Sopwith – Microfilm of the diary of Thomas Sopwith, Special Collections, Robinson Library, University of Newcastle, Newcastle upon Tyne, UK.

OUM Phillips – Correspondence of John Phillips, Oxford University Museum of Natural History, Geology Collections, South Parks Road, Oxford, UK.

RS Buckland – Correspondence of William Buckland, Library, The Royal Society of London, London, UK.

RS Herschel – Correspondence of John F W Herschel, Royal Society Library, London, UK.

SAS Mantell – Typed transcript of the diary of Gideon Mantell, Sussex Archaeological Society, Lewes, Sussex, UK.

SCA Sorby – Sorby correspondence, Sheffield Archives and Conservation Unit, Central Library, Sheffield, UK.

TC Whewell – Papers of William Whewell, Trinity College, Cambridge, UK.

TL Mantell – Gideon Mantell, Mantell Family papers. MS–Papers–0083, Alexander Turnbull Library, Wellington, New Zealand.

Acknowledgements

I received a great deal of help and encouragement during the ten or more years that I have been working on this project. First I must thank the archive and library staff at all the places cited in the list of abbreviations. All have responded cheerfully to my enquiries, helping me with their catalogues and indexes, and supplying photocopies when requested. Tom Sharpe of the National Museum of Wales, Ann Barrett of Imperial College, and the staff of the Alexander Turnbull Library, Wellington, New Zealand, deserve special mention in this respect. Robert Sopwith generously gave me access to the diaries of Thomas Sopwith. I must also thank the staff of the libraries where I have used printed sources: Cambridge University Library, The Geological Society, The Natural History Museum and The Victoria and Albert Museum.

I have received help with particular problems from Martin Guntau, R H B Lane, Colan MacArthur, Ian Rolfe, Susan Sheets-Pyenson, Richard Wilding and Leonard G Wilson. But above all my thanks go to Janet Browne, Martin Rudwick, Jim Secord and Hugh Torrens, who have all been involved in the project since it started and have contributed to it in ways too numerous to mention.

The institutions and libraries listed in the Abbreviations have generously given permission to quote from their collections.

John Thackray

The Meetings, 1822-1868

The Meetings

Session 1821-1822

1. 1822, February 1

Annual General Meeting, at which William Babington was elected President.

1a. Charles Lyell wrote to Gideon Mantell on 8 February:

> The Professors of Cambridge [1] & Oxon [2] were present at our dinner & Buckland was called upon to explain the vast quantities of bones which he found in the summer in a cave at Kirkdale in Yorksh. [3] of wh. he had a large bag-full with him – innumerable jaws of hyaenas, teeth of Elephant, Rhinoceros, &c., unmineralized like those in the limestone-caves in Gemany full of bears. He produced some light balls or pellets wh. he said he brought to town at first doubting what they cd. be. Dr. Wollaston (I think) first pronounced they were like some calculi sometimes found in some species of Canis. Upon being taken to Exeter Change [4] by Dr. Fitton the man there recognised the production & exclaimed, "Ah that is the dung of our hyaena!" On analizing it they find it composed of carbonate & phosphate of lime, the same as hyaena's dung, which being an animal it seems of an ossiphagous appetite, has always its dung proportionately more ossified than any other. Buckland in his usual style enlarged on the marvel with such a strange mixture of the humorous and the serious, that we cd. none of us discern how far he believed himself what he said, take the following as an example of the whole.
>
> "The hyaenas, gentlemen, preferred the flesh of elephants, rhinoceros, deer, cows, horses &c., but sometimes unable to procure these & half starved they used to come out of the narrow entrance of their cave <u>in the evening</u> down to the water's edge of a lake wh. <u>must</u> once have been there, & so helped themselves to some of the innumerable water-rats in wh. the lake abounded – thus you see the whole stalactite & the other bones stuck over with the teeth of water-rats."

TL Mantell, f60; quoted in Lyell 1881, 1, p115 and Wilson 1972, p95

Notes, 1821-1822
1. Professor the Rev Adam Sedgwick.
2. Professor the Rev William Buckland.
3. The story of the discovery of Kirkdale Cave is told in Rupke 1983, pp31-41.
4. A menagerie off The Strand, London, managed by Edward Cross.

Session 1822-1823

2. 1823, June 20

A notice was read on some fossil bones of an Ichthyosaurus from the Lias near Bristol, also on two new species of fossil teeth, by George Cumberland, Esq., Hon.Mem.G.S.

A letter was read accompanying some specimens from Stonehenge by Godfrey Higgins, Esq. An extract of a letter was read from Lieut. J. Short, Royal Engineers, addressed to & communicated by Dr. Babington, Pres.G.S., containing remarks on the Isle of Bourbon.

A notice was read respecting the Pebbles in the bed of clay which covers the Red Sandstone in the S.W. of Lancashire by Dr. Bostock, V.P.G.S.

A paper was read on the Geology of Rio de Janeiro by Alex. Caldcleugh, Esq., M.G.S.

A paper was read containing a description of a section of the Crag strata at Bramerton near Norwich by Richard Taylor, Esq., communicated by John Taylor, Esq., Treasurer G.S.

2a. Charles Lyell wrote to his father on 21 June:

> We had a very full meeting of the Geological last night; many foreigners at our club [1] dinner, who were very entertaining. Professor Oersted, of Copenhagen, pronounced the following eulogium of our scientific dinners of which, as it was spoken in English, you may imagine the ludicrous effect. 'Your public dinners, gentlemen, I do love, they are a sort of sacrament, in which you do beautifully blend the spiritual and the corporeal!!'
>
> A Mr. Underwood dined with us, who was so long a *detenu* in France that he now resides there, preferring it to England. He said, 'The Bourbons are becoming much more arbitary than before the Revolution; the prisons are full of political offenders. A looker-on sometimes sees more than those who are actually engaged, and my opinion of the French people is, that they are much too *corrupt* for a free Government, and much too enlightened for a despotic one.'
>
> Lyell 1881, 1, p122

Note, 1822-1823
1. The Geological Society Club was not formally constituted until November 1824.

The Meetings

Session 1823-1824

3. 1824, February 20

A notice was read of the discovery of a perfect skeleton of the fossil genus hitherto called Plesiosaurus, by the Rev. W. D. Conybeare, F.R.S., M.G.B.

A notice was read on the Megalosaurus or great Fossil Lizard of Stonesfield, near Oxford, by the Revd. Wm. Buckland, F.R.S., F.L.S., President of the Geological Society of London & Professor of Mineralogy & Geology in the University of Oxford, &c., &c.

3a. William Buckland wrote to William Vernon a few days later:

We had a great meeting in Bedford Street [1] on Friday last, the largest I ever remember. The great attraction was the entire Plesiosaurus which I have purchased for the Duke of Buckinghan [2] and of which Mr. Conybeare on that evening read a description; the specimen is nearly entire, and, though a young animal, is ten feet long; when full grown it must have been twenty feet at least. The neck has the very unusual number of forty vertebrae, head like a lizard, neck like a snake, body of a crocodile, paddles like a turtle and two feet long, tail very short, nearly equal to the length of a saddle; its neck (double as long in proportion as the swan) is an anomaly as yet unique. I had also a paper on the Stonesfield Megalosaurus; so that with two monsters of such a kind, and so crowded an audience, my first evening of taking the chair as President was one of great *eclat*.

Gordon 1894, p84, and Harcourt [1880-1905] 13, p198

3b. William Conybeare wrote to Henry De la Beche on 4 March:

Friday's dinner at the Geol. was one of the pleassantest public meetings I have ever attended. Buckland as the new Pres. was put to his oratory, some dozen of us talked in our turn, but in place of the usual trash on such occasions every one had some interesting facts connected with the management of the Society or the progress of the science to communicate. We adjourned to the Society's rooms at 1/2 past eight, & there I lectured on my Mstr. [Monster] & Buckland on the Stonesfield bones. Afterwards a somewhat animated discussion arose between B. & the Botanists whom the former charged with great inattention to the interests of science in neglecting the fossil plants. This led to the appointment of a delegation to wait on Browne [Robert Brown] & invite his assistance. This was given readily enough & active measures are in progress on this subject. Another interesting feature of our Geol. meeting was the determination there fomed by Mr. Taylor (the great mining man) to institute a regular school (for Geology, the elements of mathematics, mechanics &c.) for the Cornish miners. [3] Attending also to his engagements in the Mexican mines he quoted a letter to Humboldt who pays this country the compt. of saying that they can only be worked as they ought by the Spirit & skill of Englishmen.

NMW De la Beche

Notes, 1823-1824
1. The Society had its rooms at No 20 Bedford Street, Covent Garden, from 1816 to 1828.
2. The specimen was discovered by Mary Anning of Lyme Regis. *See* Torrens 1995; and Tickell 1995.
3. Taylor published *Prospectus of a School of Mines in Cornwall* in 1825. *See* Burt 1977, p 66.

Session 1824-1825

4. 1825, January 7

The paper entitled, "On a recent formation of freshwater rock marl in the County of Forfar, with some remarks on the origin of shell marl", by Charles Lyell, Esq., Sec.G.S. was concluded.

4a. Roderick Murchison wrote in his notebook:

At the meeting of Friday the 7th took my seat & shook the hand of our President Professor Buckland.

A paper read by Mr Lyell one of the Secretaries upon the calcareous marl which he had found in & round certain small lakes in Forfarshire N[orth]. B[ritain] [1] considered by him to have been formed by the decomposition & deposition of molusca as found in it – also as a Post diluvian formation & by a process still in action, yet affording a curious parallel between it & the fresh water formation of the Isle of Wight (whilst the latter is considered antidiluvian tho' of the highest & most recent order & over the London Clay & Chalk being only subjacent as to the Diluvial

Gravel & the alluvial deposits). Queries in his paper as to the cause as above, or if the deposition (sometimes 20 feet thick of marl, carboniferous & testaceous) could be accounted for by the tufaceous deposit of calcareous springs forming carbonate of lime in their passage thro' sand & testacea?

Professor Buckland quitted the Chair & elucidated the Paper; his observations drew out Mr Greenough the Vice President, who was somewhat sceptical as to the marl being post diluvian, & observed that the lines of demarcation between the recent & old formations which he had always considered as fixed were now about to be unsettled, & that it gave him pain to witness this after all their labours – comparison with the travertine of Italy & tufaceous Mediterranean deposits as instituted by Buckland were doubted by him. gravels he had looked upon as settled – now again open to cavil & doubt. Mr Buckland replied & endeavoured to prove the whole a post diluvian fomation – peat bog under the marl. beaver remains found in it prove its recent formation, that animal not being extinct in Gt Britain until the period when wolves were destroyed.

Mr Warburton made some sensible observations & reconciled the 2 modes of accounting for the formation of the marl by attributing it to <u>both</u> the causes assigned, viz. To the decomposition & petrifaction of the molusca of themselves & by the action of the water occasioning calcareous deposits. Old Mr Guillemard, a Swiss, stated a chemical objection to the water carrying more than a certain quantity of Carbonic acid & therefore it could only act in that proportion.

Tea & toast followed with a very agreable conversazione in little groups. my Rhinoceros now roused Professor Buckland – none found fossilized in Scotland – that in Museum in Edinb being a hoax detected by him. 2

GSL Murchison N143, f45

4b. Charles Lyell wrote to Gideon Mantell on 8 January:

I have just been reading a longish paper of mine entitled "On a recent formation of freshwater rock marle in Forfarshire (Scotland) with some remarks on the origin of shell marle." I was much flattered with the manner in which the memoir was received & discussed.

TL Mantell, f60

5. 1825, January 21

A paper was read entitled, "On the Freshwater formations recently discovered in the environs of Site (Cette) at a short distance from the Mediterranean & below the level of that sea", by M. Marcel de Serres, Prof. of Min. & Geol. to the Faculty of Sciences of Montpelier.

5a. Roderick Murchison wrote in his notebook:

Professor Buckland in the chair. a long & curious paper was read upon the stratification in the neighbourhood of <u>Cette</u> [3] in France by Mons <u>Serres</u> of Nice [4] & sent to the Geological Society. The section exhibited by sinking 3 wells was detailed very minutely by which it appeared that there was an alternation 1st of Fresh Water formation with correspondent shells, 2d Marine Formation above the level of the Mediterranean & the adjoining salk lake, & 3dly below that another <u>fresh</u> water formation which extended <blank> yards <u>below the level</u> of the Mediterranean, and further that organic remains of land animals were found as snails < > <u>helices</u> <blank> below the first fomation. This occurred in one of the wells, whilst in another at some little distance there was no fresh water formation so low, nor any terrestrial remains but several <u>lacustrine</u> deposits.

In the debate which followed Mr. Buckland observed that altho' the paper gave an excellent detail yet that we required a more <u>general</u> description of the country & the <u>localities</u>, which he hoped some of us would afford in describing the neighbouring hills & mountains, the circle of the beds, the nature of the adjoining lake &c. he observed that the alternation of fresh water & marine formations were very frequent, occurring in Isle of Wight, Paris basin, Germany, interior of Africa, in Asia &c, & that marine remains in fresh water formations such as fish in our Stonesfield Slate – the same in hard calcareous deposits as our Portland Stone. That in the Isle of Wight formation at <blank> the fresh water formation dipped considerably beneath the level of the sea &c.

That with respect to terrestrial animals being found in the detritus he always accounted for that phenomenon by the local floods, and he alluded to a lake on the borders of the Baltic at <blank> which at this day was alternately filled with salt water & then by fresh water when the currents of the adjoining rivers overflowed & carried out the salt water leaving a fresh water lake. and if sufficient time elapsed in each of these stages he presumed that upon examination of the alluvium there the admixture of terrestrial remains with those of fresh & water might be found also. he thought that Mons Bendon [? Baudon] had written a paper to prove that terrestrial & fresh water animals might be [?] inured by degrees to exist in quondam marine strata & vice versa. he instanced the Thames as depositing in its high floods cakes of <blank> & other terrestrial animals – these might be imbedded amidst other strata before they were decomposed. <u>Travertine</u> was found of two different epochs & there was certainly some of Ante as well as of Post Diluvian fomation. What are called diluvial beds frequently contained specimens of all ages. Thus in Italy (as Dr. Fitton & others had well observed) the mixture of the old trap or volcanic remains were rounded & mixed [with] those of the tertiary fomations. This would depend upon the strata which happened to be upper most in that district when acted upon by water – no one maintained that there never existed a hiatus in stratification or that no 1 never was found on no 4, but only that no 4, where the stratification & deposition were regular, never was found <u>above</u> no 1.

Mr Greenough regretted that the Travertine should not be assigned to one distinct formation & said that we had much to examine on this point.

a young member Mr Gray talked unintelligbly about snails, estuaries, ditches in neighbourhood of Tilbury & fresh water channels flowing into the Thames, but which being brackish never contained terrestrial animals but only a mass of beings such as periwinkles <blank> which were known to prevail indiscriminately in such situations. Mr Warburton supported Buckland. Mr Lyell made some observations.

Mr Buckland at length turned the discussion to the subject of one of his <u>new Caves</u> near Torquay Devon [5] to which he was going next day, & in which had been found bones of Rhinoceros, Elephant, Hyaena &c, [of] which he exhibited but the tooth of a horse which his friend at Torquay [6] had sent him as being found with the others, [but which] he pronounced to be no Fossil but the grinder of a very respectable old waggon horse certainly of great age. Mr. B. said he did not pretend that this newly discovered cave would prove to be one of Hyaenas like that of Kirkdale, & then adjourned the meeting to tea toast & conversazione.

We then examined the presents of the Evening: – Sir A. Crichton's minerals chiefly Siberian; volcanic productions, porphyries, pitch stones &c from Sardinia collected by Mr P Thomson Scrooppe (to whom I was introduced) – the gradations & affinities in these were very curious; also specimens from Lake Huron by Sir H Davy containing <blank> & <blank> in calcareous deposits; also specimens of Labrador by Mr. Morrison.

GSL Murchison, N12

Session 1824-25

6. 1825, June 17

An extract of a letter was read from and for John Kingdon, Esqr., communicated by Jos. Townsend, Esqr., F.G.S.

A paper was also read entitled, "Observations &c. on a walk from Exeter to Bridport", [by Mr. Woods].

6a. Roderick Murchison wrote in his notebook:

Paper of Mr Woods read upon the neighbourhood of Exeter. Alluding to a stratum of [?] pure flints at <blank> near <blank>, he stated that it was useless to suppose that a stratum of chalk existed there as Professor Buckland had done, & that it had been washed away leaving the flints, for that the formative <illegible> have been plastic clay. He further stated that the Quartz pebble in the <blank> of the neighbourhood were the same as those of the London basin cum multis aliis [7] [?] &c.

Having quitted the Chair our Professor begged to put Mr Woods right on one or two points. The district of Exeter & Coast has been fully & ably detailed & figured by Mr de la Beche, [8] one of the Society, to whom B[uckland] referred us & exhibited his drawings. as to Quartz pebbles in gravel, B. explained that they were to be found here and there all over the world, proving the action of the diluvium (he believed in America & he hoped soon to learn in India &c), but that the gravel of the London Basin was almost exclusively made up of Chalk flints from the surrounding strata, therefore Mr Woods' comparison was incorrect. and as to the substitution of Plastic Clay for the Chalk, it was only doing that of which he, Mr Woods, accused the Professor, viz Placing a stratum there in order to get rid of it, for not one morsel of Plastic Clay exists there now. B gave the rationale of the adoption of this term of Plastic Clay. He introduced it as a superstratum to the Chalk to preserve the identity of our Isle of Wight & London Basins with that of Paris, & because the leading distinction of these sands consisted in that reddish soapy clay. [9] The difficult points still for examination on this part of the coast of Devon were still <blank>

Mr B. recapitulated the effects of the storm of last November upon the town of Sidmouth [10] the barrier of gravel silt which formed the barrier on the beach had been washed into the lower storey of the houses, & carried with it fish pans & all apparatus into the cellars below. when the storm subsided the inhabitants descended into their cellars which now resembled his Caves,

The Meetings

containing masses of mud & gravel with all these extras mixed with them, out of which the pots & pans were fished. Thus was it he supposes in his dens or caves. hence he calls the lower part of them the <u>scullery</u>, into which all the apparatus & bones of the beasts were washed & deposited by the deluge. The case of the post & rails with <u>the bars of iron</u> being torn up carried into an upper window & found twisted & convoluted (as occurred at Sidmouth) was given as a striking effect of water.

In allusion to the fossil Bones presented on this occasion by Mr Townsend from <blank> Chipping Norton Oxon, [11] Mr Buckland stated them to be the most curious specimens which he had ever received as coming from the <u>oolite fomation</u>. the half vertebra, which entire must have measured 14 inches in diameter, Mr Clift had examined & declared to be larger than that of any animal existing or fossilised except perhaps an extraordinary <u>whale</u> to which they referred it. one bone resembling a tongue is quite beyond discovery.

Specimens of the Paris formation to fill up chasms in our series presented by Lyell. – remark the Gris de Fontainbleau with its two varieties of crystals in the mass of marly sand, & its deposited bunch of grape appearance in botryoidal clusters. observe also the <u>menilite</u> (menil montant) siliceous concretion round & pressed into the marl, also the mill stone Chert or Grit of Mendon [? Meadon] – high price of these mill stones & their rare occurrence in nature.

GSL Murchison N143, ff11-7

Notes, 1824-1825

1. The background to this paper is given in Wilson, 1972, pp131-134.
2. This appears to be a wrongly labelled specimen rather than a hoax (Buckland 1825, pp309-311).
3. Sete, 10km north of Montpelier, France.
4. De Serre's paper was received, in French, on 3 December 1824.
5. Kent's Hole, or Cavern, near Torquay, Devon, was first excavated in 1824 by Thomas Northmore, see [Northmore, T], 1825.
6. Almost certainly Thomas Northmore.
7. 'along with many others'.
8. In a paper read on 5 March 1819 (De la Beche, 1822).
9. First used in England by Buckland in a paper read on 6 January 1816 (Buckland 1817, p277). Buckland adopted it from Cuvier and Brongniart's 'Argile Plastique'.
10. The storm hit Sidmouth on the night of 22/23 November 1824 (Hutchinson, 1843, p67).
11. These fossils were described in a letter of Mr Kingdon that was read to the meeting, but they do not appear in the list of donations for the evening. They are now recognised as bones of the sauropod dinosaur *Cetiosaurus*.

Session 1825-1826

7. 1825, November 4

A paper was read entitled, "An Account of some Geological Specimens collected by Captain P. P. King in his Survey of the coasts of Australasia; and by Robert Brown, Esqr. on the shores of the Gulf of Carpentaria during the Voyage of Captain Flinders", by William Henry Fitton, M.D., V.P.G.S., &c.

7a. Gideon Mantell wrote in his diary:

> Went to London by the Lewes coach; dined at the Thatch'd House Tavern in St. James' Street; met Mr Lambert, M. Adolphe Brongniart, Buckland, Chantrey, Bailey etc. Attended the first meeting of the Geological Society.
>
> SAS Mantell, quoted in Curwen, 1940, p56

8. 1826, February 3

A paper entitled, "Remarks on some parts of the Taunus Mountains in the duchy of Nassau", by Sir Alexr. Crichton, Vice Pres.G.S. was read in part.

8a. Roderick Murchison wrote in his notebook:

> Debate upon Sir A Crichton's paper on the Taunus Mountains & the Geology of Nassau – Dr Buckland accounted for all the fresh water formations of the valley & sides of the hills, viz "The upper freshwater of Paris", by supposing the Rhine to have been dammed up in its course – "give me (said the Dr) 3,000 men & in a week I will again convert the whole of that district into one fresh water lake".
>
> He observed that similar repetition of the several geognostic features to those mentioned by Sir A Crichton were to be seen all along the Rhine between Bonn & Bingam [Bingen]; recommended Mr. <illegible>, a dealer in minerals & fossils of these parts at <blank>, as being able to supply the cabinet of any future Geologist or collector, and the work of a young man whose name he had forgotten as the best guide. [1]
>
> A long discourse upon the volcanic remains or <u>trap</u> of the district followed; some of the plaines to the north of this district Dr B described as resembling a crowd of Ant or Mole Hills which were evidently but the remnants of volcanic peaks peeping out thro

The Meetings

the crust of trap, tufa & soil, & their iregularity he resembled to haycocks half tossed about & dipping in every possible direction.

Respecting the Grawacke slate of Sir A's District of Wisbaden [Wiesbaden] & Nassau he said that the analogous was to be seen on Snowdon in Wales altho not exactly similar, yet all over Germany. Instanced the mountains of Eisen miejer, and appealed to Mr Greenough, as containing not only all the <u>bivalves</u> in the present collection but also univalves & <u>turbinated</u> shells which were never observed in the same rock in England.

Touching the <u>charring</u> of the brown coal or lignite he remarked at length upon the inconsistency of Werner who with a vast breadth of this coal at <blank> so near to Freyburgh & which is overlaid by a mass of volcanic rock or basalt yet never <u>would</u> see that the latter was of igneous origin & had fairly charred the lignite – handled specimens of real <u>charcoal</u> which marked. 2

Dr B burned a piece & begged gentlemen to observe the analogy between stink & sublimity – Burke having said that a "stink was sublime". 3

GSL Murchison, N29, ff5-7

Notes, 1825-1826

1. Buckland had visited the Rhineland in 1816 and 1817.
2. A G Werner (1743-1817) maintained in his lectures that basalt was an aqueous precipitate. Charring of coal deposits by basalt was used as evidence of its igneous origin in Playfair, 1802, p73.
3. This is probably a reference to Burke 1759, pp156-9.

Session 1826-1827

9. 1826, November 17

A notice was read, "On some beds associated with the magnesian limestone, and on some fossil fish found in them", by the Rev. Adam Sedgwick, Woodwardian Professor, F.G.S.

A paper was read entitled, "Observations on the bones of hyaenas and other animals in the cavern of Lunel near Montpelier, and in the adjacent strata of marine formation", by the Rev. W. Buckland, D.D., Professor of Mineralogy and Geology in the University of Oxford.

9a. Roderick Murchison wrote to William Vernon on 20 November:

Last night we had a lively and amusing paper of Buckland's upon the hyaena cave near Montpellier, with the information that it does not contain the bones of *Camels*, as was reported, but merely the remains of Abyssinian hyaenas, who appear to have been much fatter, and to have deposited finer cakes of album Graecum than the 'starvelings of the Kirkdale Cave'. [1]

We had also a prefatory letter of Professor Sedgwick's last night upon certain beds in the magnesian limestone in which the fossil fish occur in Cy [County] of Durham; this is to be followed by a grand *clearance* of all the obscurity which has hitherto enveloped this cap of the coal measures, and a general comparison between it and a very distinct continental strata.

Harcourt [1880-1905], 13, pp208-209

10. 1827, January 5

A notice was read, accompanying some specimens from the Hastings-Sand Formation, with a copy of a work on the fossils of Tilgate Forest, by G. Mantell, Esq., F.R., L. and G.S. in a letter to R. I. Murchison, Esq., Sec.G.S.

The reading of a paper was commenced, entitled, "On the coal-field of Brora, in Sutherlandshire, and some other stratified deposits of the North of Scotland", by R. I. Murchison, Esq., Sec.G.S., F.R.S.

10a. Roderick Murchison wrote to Gideon Mantell on 5 January:

I should have replied before now to your obliging letter of 1 Jany, had I not been exceedingly occupied by incessant councils of the Geol. Society, and in preparing my own paper for its last reading, which took place on Friday last when we had a very full meeting (including Professor Sedgwick fresh from Paris & full of news, [2] and 2 very able young Prussian Geologists Messrs Oeynhausen & Dechen who are acquiring our language and our geology with equal rapidity). The subject matter of my memoir being novel seemed to attract a good deal of notice, and the approbation of Dr. Buckland & Prof. Sedgwick is an ample recompense for my travels thro the Hebrides, Orkneys &c.

According to the strict letter of our rules neither your specimens could have been exhibited nor your notice could have

The Meetings

been read until the affairs in hand were concluded, but I put aside my own paper on that evening & if you had offered a premium for encomium you could not have desired any thing more gratifying than the eloge which Dr. Buckland passed upon your works.

TL Mantell, f74

11. 1827, February 16

Annual General Meeting, at which William Henry Fitton was elected President.

11a. Gideon Mantell wrote in his diary:

Anniversary of the Geological Society. Dined with the Fellows at the Free Mason's Tavern; [3] and afterwards went to the Society's House in Bedford St. Covent Garden: called on Mr Lyell who was confined to his room by illness.

SAS Mantell

12. 1827, March 2

A paper was read, "On the volcanic district of Naples", by G. Poulett Scrope, Esq., F.G.S., F.R.S.

12a. Roderick Murchison wrote to William Vernon on 6 March:

Our last meeting was enlivened by a most amusing debate upon Scrope's Paper on the Volcanoes of the Phlegraean fields; he differs toto caelo from Daubeny, Von Buch and Brieslap [Breislak]. Little Daubeny came up from Oxford, so that the rival fires met. [4] Greenough, Herschel, and Fitten [Fitton] spoke well. We go on famously with our new President, and his conversaziones are most agreeable.

Harcourt [1880-1905], 13, p212

13. 1827, March 16

A paper was read, "On the Geology of the vicinity of Pulborough, Sussex", by P. J. Martin, Esq.

13a. Roderick Murchison wrote to Gideon Mantell a few days later:

I went carefully over all the memoir [by Martin] with Mr Greenough & Dr. Fitton & prepared it for our last meeting when it was read – and as all the previous authorities including yourself were brought forward in illustration an animated discussion followed – I have since made an abstract which will appear in the Annals of Phil for April. [5]

TL Mantell, f74

Notes, 1826-1827

1. Buckland had visited the caves at Montpelier in September 1826, on the tour which followed his marriage.
2. Sedgwick's visit to Paris is described in a letter to Dr Ainger (Clark and Hughes, 1890, 1, pp270-272).
3. The Freemason's Tavern, Great Queen Street, London. The Society held its inaugural meeting here in November 1807.
4. Scrope and Daubeny were authors of rival books on volcanos (Scrope 1825, Daubeny 1826).
5. No abstract of Martin's paper appeared in the *Annals of Philosophy*.

Session 1827-1828

14. 1828, February 16

Annual General Meeting at which Dr. W. H. Fitton was re-elected President and read the Anniversary Address.

14a. Charles Lyell wrote to Gideon Mantell on 17 February:

I had hoped you might have been at the Anniversary which was well attended in spite of the snow. On Fitton's right & left were the Presidents of the Royal & Astronl. Socys. [1] The 2 Professors of Oxfd. & Cambridge also attended [2] & & others of the best men. The Eveng. discussion on the Ava bones was improving. [3] Buckland reconciled all to his diluvian hypothesis, as what facts would he not? But be his theory wide of the mark or not, he is always worth hearing.

They think the remains thus hastily picked up belonged to from 10 to 20 individuals of the genus Mastodon to begin with, a pretty

The Meetings

good haul. It was larger & quite different from the largest European Mastodon. The rest of the menagerie is rhinoceros, hippopotamus, ox, deer, gavial alligator (very large) trionyx – turtle (gigantic) horse? doubtful, shells supposed to be a cyrene & very like a species now living in the Estuaries of India, nay in rivers. Buckland gets over the shells by saying that Crawfurd is not clear they were in the same continuous stratum. The associated wood is monocotyledinous & dicotyledinous all the former is silicified or agatized, very little of the latter, but this is converted into carb. of lime. Their theory being that there is much silex naturally in cones palms &c & this attracts silex.

The Mosaic deluge of course did all this. none of the species are positively identified yet with any known diluvial animal. The bones are never silicified. They are overcharged with hydrate of iron. not more so it seems than some diluvial bones possessed by Buckd & Sedgwick. Be it so, then modern postdiluvial causes as you suggest can do every thing, at least as far as mineralogy is concerned.

TL Mantell, part quoted in Wilson, 1972, p186

14b. Richard C Taylor wrote in his notebook:

Minute of Professor's description of the Fossil bones from Ava – at the Geol. Society 15th Feby 1828.

The first time that fossil bones have been discovered in Southem Asia, from nr the Petroleum springs on the banks of the Irewaddy River. Those produced consist of 2 species of Crocodile – the gavial & alligator.

Tortoise – Trionyx – also a fragment either of an enormous tortoise or of a crocodile.

Mastodon – New species. The teeth showing 10 rows of tubercles while the American & European Mastodon has only 4

Rhinoceros, Hippopotamus, Deer, Horse, Ox.

Portions of the Trunks of Palms, or fibrous ditto of wood or timber.

Dr Buckland remarked the singular circumstance that all the monocotyledonous plants were agatized but that all the Dicotiliginous were in a state of Carbonate of lime.

These were found in Tertiary beds.

Cyclas, the freshwater shell like those at Woolwich in great abundance in fine marle.

<u>Breccia</u> resembling the Hertfordshire Puddingstone. Traces of the Plastic Clay.

London Clay – like those of Sheppey – Teredo, also like Bognor Rock, or Palermo.

Springs of Petroleum occur always in the Tertiary beds.

Gypsum & large crystals of selenite, same place.

Dr B. considers that Tertiary beds have now been discovered in all parts of the Globe. The plants & animals they contain seem to denote an almost universal climate all over the world.

ANS Taylor

15. 1828, April 18

A paper was read, "On the fossil remains of two new species of Mastodon, and of other vertebrated animals, found on the left bank of the Irawadi", by William Clift, Esq., F.G.S., F.R.S., conservator of the Museum of the Royal College of Surgeons.

A paper was next read, "On a collection of vegetable and animal remains, and rocks, from the Burmese Country, presented to the Geological Society by J. Crawfurd Esq", by the Rev. W. Buckland, D.D., V.P.G.S., F.R.S., &c.

15a. Richard C Taylor wrote in his notebook:

Additional minutes same subject, chiefly Dr Buckland's observations.

Strata analogous to our Plastic Clay, London Clay & Crag in ava, & resembling our Woolwich Clay beds. Mr Clift considers these specimens exhibit 2 new species of mastodon, in addition to the 6 named by Cuvier. The cast of the Teeth of the Grand Mastodon of Cuvier is much smaller than that of the Irewaddy. The thigh bones of the Mastodon are flattened [sketch]. The Mastodon occurs in marine formations in France, & associated with marine remains; its bone was sought for & worked by jewellers for the phosphate of iron.

Baron Cuvier presented several casts of bones amongst which was the skull of the Great Bear, of enormous magnitude. Similar ones exist in this country, found in a cave at Torquay & other places.

A cast of an enormous tooth of a bear also from France. Other bones from the freshwater formations of Paris.

Dr Buckland produced two enormous vertebra of some unknown saurian animal from the Green Sand, within 1 mile of Thame nr Oxford. 4 times the size of the Mastodon & double the size of the Great Lizard of Tilgate Forest & Stonesfield. Indeed it must have belonged to an animal "large enough to have swallowed up a Mastodon". [4]

The Meetings

Dr Fitton suggested that the Crag was diluvial merely, and its fossils of diluvial origin likewise.

Dr Buckland contended in reply, that the Crag was a tertiary formation, and that diluvium rested <u>over</u> the Crag.

Mr Warburton supported Dr Fitton's view, & considered the Crag to be precisely the same as the Diluvium, but there were intervals of repose in the deposits, as marked by the series of beds. These beds of peat, with trunks of trees standing as they grew, alternate with beds of gravel with fossil shells & bone. The gravel is in no ways to be distinguished from the gravel of acknowledged diluvium, & is only mixed with shells.

Dr Buckland stated Phosphate of Iron occurs in the Diluvium of St Catherine's Docks [London], forming a blue crust on stones & in lumps of a foot thick.

2 specimens of Teeth encrusted with Iron Pyrites – teeth called Golden Teeth by Pennant. [5]

ANS Taylor

15b. Charles Lyell wrote to Gideon Mantell on 21 April:

There was a crowded meeting on Friday; more than £400 subscribed towards the expenses of moving into Somerset House. [6]

Clift's papers on the Ava Bones & drawings magnificent best thing of the kind I have seen in Engld. Shaft's [Scharf's] lithography infinitely superior to Ad. Brongniart's. Buckland's paper on same & his discussion or lecture excellent; too much of the unfortunate diluvian theory mixed up with the Ava bones.

TL Mantell, f60

16. 1828, May 16

The reading was begun of a paper entitled, "On the Old Conglomerates, and other secondary deposits of the north coasts of Scotland", by the Rev. Adam Sedgwick, Woodwardian Professor, Cambridge, V.P.G.S., &c. and R. I. Murchison, Esq., For.Sec.G.S. and F.R.S.

16a. Richard C Taylor wrote in his notebook:

Fossil Fish.

From the highly bituminous & micaceous Schist of Caithness and the Orneys [Orkneys], overlying the best Roofing Slate. In the specimens presented by Professor Sedgewick & Mr Murchison, Mr Pentland identified <u>two</u> new genera.

One resembling the Bony Pike (Erox)

Baron Cuvier conjectured them to be freshwater, and this opinion is confirmed by their being accompanied by remains of Testudo, and no marine remains were observed. There are differences between these & those in the Copper Slate of Thuringia.

It is not yet determined by the authors whether this Schist & the fossil fish appertain to the Old or the New Red Sandstone.

Dr Buckland said the new Red Sandstone was not sufficiently indurated to form flagstones, while the Old Red Sandstone only contains flagstones.

It is often extremely difficult to distinguish the Old from the New, but the nodular Limestone, called Cornstone, accompanies & seems to Characterise the Old.

Prof. Sedgwick stated that the Conglomerate Sandstones were of vast thickness in Scotland, and mentioned that mountains 3000 feet thick were composed of old Red Sandstone Conglomerates.

That the fossil fish of the North of Scotland materially differed from those of the Magnesian Limestone & of the Copper Slate of Thuringia, and [?] believes this to [be] a perfectly distinct freshwater formation, situated between the old and the new Red Sandstones. [7]

It contains Trionyx

Mentioned finding the Weald Clay, full of its peculiar shells in the North point of the Isle of Arran, by Prof. Sedgewick & Mr Murchison.

Mountain Lime

Enormous Orthoceratites presented from Scotland by same Gentlemen, accompanied by Nautilites & Producta Scotica.

Mr Conybeare said the Radii of Balistes [8] occured in the Transition Limestone nr Bristol.

Fossil Bones from Brentford

Many portions of Rhinoceros, Hippopotamus, Elephant, Horse, Ox, and Bear, also what is very interesting, as observed by Buckland, the teeth of Hyenas. The third place where they have been found in Diluvium – 1 near Maidstone, the other near Rugby in Gravel.

White Balls, or concretions, like small Septaria also found with them, and abound in the Marle accompanying these bones near London. Dr Buckland observed them in great abundance near Prague in Bohemia.

He thinks that all the animals whose remains have been seen in Caves will be traced in the diluvial gravel.

The Meetings

Fossil Crocodiles
Mr Conybeare gave a lecture on the fossil Crocodiles and Gavial, illustrated by Casts. [9]

He enumerated 11 or 12 species in the Secondary Strata, 9 of which are well ascertained, and 2 others occur also in England.

From the examination he has made, & so far as evidence can be obtained, he considers that reasonable ground exists for viewing all that exist in different formations as distinct species.

The 1st or lowest in the Geol. series is the crocodile of the Avon, so distinguished by Mr Conybeare, occurs in the New Red Sandstone of Guys Cliff.

2nd. in blue Lias
3. Inferior oolite of Caen, in Normandy
Cornbrash
Kimmeridge Clay above the Coral Rag
Portland Rock
Sands of the Weald of Kent
Lower Chalk – on the Continent only
London Clay – described by Mr Parkinson & Mr Greenough

12 geological sites are thus enumerated, & Mr C thinks there were as many species.

Mr Conybeare went on to observe that the recent species of Crocodile and gavial are natives of tropical climates, therefore an important inference is drawn that these fossil species were also inhabitants of hot climates, and other circumstances seem to shew that all fossils originally existed in warm climates.

Dr Buckland conceived that no inference can be drawn to the contrary of what had been urged on the subject of fossil animals of hot climates, from the fact of the remarkably preserved mammoth of Siberia having been discovered clothed with hair, because the camel & even the lion has hair or long wool.

To this Mr Greenough objected that it was the flesh & not the hair which proved the fact of the climate being then cold when the animal died. The flesh preserved & enveloped in ice, is conclusive of its being then a cold climate.

Tortoises approach colder latitudes somewhat, certainly than crocodiles, but are not then abundant. A gentleman stated that they abounded in Lake Erie & Lake Superior, which were very cold in winter, & even in the Mediterranean.

Mr Greenough said that the Diluvium in some parts of Switzerland was 600 feet thick and often not to be distinguished from the Conglomerates or even from the oldest granite.

ANS Taylor

17. 1828, June 6

The reading of the paper of Professor Sedgwick, and R. I. Murchison, Esq. begun at the last Meeting, was concluded.

A paper was read by the Rev. Dr Buckland, on the Cycadoideae, a new family of fossil plants, specimens of which occur silicified in the Free-stone quarries of the Isle of Portland.

A letter to the President was read, from Gideon Mantell, Esq., F.G.S., &c. enclosing a list of fossils of the county of Sussex.

17a. Richard C Taylor wrote in his notebook:

Presented a French geological work in which is a comparative Table of the Places & the different natures of the beds in which fossil Bones are found. [10] 17 animals in England.

a paper from Dr Buckland on the fossil plants in the Limestone of the Isle of Portland, with specimens presented by himself & Mr Webster.

Approaches to the cycas, commonly called petrified Birds' nests. Mr Brown the naturalist, on examination considers these plants allied to Cycas, & appear to be the lower part of the stem of that genus, or of Zamia. Mr Brown considers it forms a link between the coniferous plants & the cycads & apparently of tropical vegetation.

Concludes by stating his conformity with the suggestion of M. Brongniart that in the entire series of fossil vegetation, from the coal measures upwards to the Tertiary, a gradual approach is made from vegetation of the very hottest climates to that now existing: exhibiting in part a gradual cooling. and if we revert to the violent heat which must have existed at the period of the formation of the primeval, the difference of the earth's temperature must be immense.

Mr Mantell contributed a Catalogue of all the fossils of the Sussex formations.

He mentions as remarkable that the Unio of the Coal measures occurs in the Tilgate Stone.

Professor Sedgewick objected to the term Lacustrine as applied to the freshwater formations in the Weald, & the great deposits of the Shanklin Sands, by Mr Mantell. These formations contain beds of oysters, which are never known in freshwater. Therefore they were intermixed beds. Both Mr Sedgwick & Mr Webster considered that they were rather more similar to the deposits at the mouth of a large river, than those of a lake.

The Meetings

Mr Greenough asked, if this be the mouth of a large river what direction that river took, and where is it to be traced?

Mr Sedgewick in reply said that it would be as futile to expect at the present day to find the footsteps in the sand of the builders of the Pyramids, as to find any accordance with the present surface & that of a former world. So great had been the degradation to which the beds in some places had been subjected, as may be seen in the western isles of Scotland.

Mr Stokes suggested that a Delta or the mouth of a River on a large scale like that of the amazon approaches more to the circumstances which are afforded by these formations than any other, & that the mixed accumulation of marine, terrestrial & fluviatile bodies could not be accounted for so well in any other way.

The larvae of <u>Libellula</u> [11] are found in a recent state deposited in Deltas.

A gentleman shewed that we are ignorant of the nature of the water in which any of these remains formerly existed. for instance the Chalk contains no chemical proof of having been deposited in salt water – it affords no traces of muriate of soda.

ANS Taylor

17b. Adam Sedgwick wrote to Roderick Murchison on 25 June:

Our paper on the conglomerates increased to such a size that it was obviously too large to be taken in at one meeting. When all the details were left out and almost every portion of the two coast-sections of Caithness, there was enough remaining to produce that peculiar oscillatory motion in Fitton's lower extremities which you have often marked on like occasions. All went off well and ended with the dish of Caithness fish which were beautifully cooked by Pentland and much relished by the meeting. [12] Greenough, Buckland, Conybeare, and all the first performers were upon the boards. The account of the Conglomerates of the Murray Firth & the old red of the N.W. coast, together with certain speculations & corollaries, were put off till the following meeting.

GSL Murchison S11/23; quoted in Clark & Hughes 1890, 1, p321 and Geikie 1875, 1, p144

18. 1828, June 20

A paper was read, "On the Geology of Bundelcund, Boghelcund, and the districts of Saugor and Jabalpoor in central India", by Captain James Franklin, of the Bengal Army, F.R.S., F.A.S.

An extract was read of a letter from Samuel Hobson, Esq. to Dr. Roget, F.G.S., Sec.R.S., &c. (dated at New Orleans, 6th April, 1827,) and enclosing an account of some gigantic bones, by Samuel W. Logan, M.D.

An extract was read of a letter from his Grace the Duke of Buckingham, to Professor Buckland, V.P.G.S. dated at Naples, 3rd April 1828, giving an account of certain phaenomena, which attended the late eruption of Vesuvius.

A letter was read from Charles Stokes, Esq., F.G.S., F.R.S. to W. J. Broderip, Esq., Sec.G.S. explanatory of three drawings of Echini.

18a. Richard C Taylor wrote in his notebook:

With reference to the fossil fish of Caithness Schist, it is observed by Mr Sedgewick & Mn [Murchison] that they are unaccompanied with a single shell or zoophite. Dr Buckland concurred in the opinion that they were dissimilar to those of the Copper Slate & the dificulty appears to be to what geological era to assign them. He considers them to belong to the Transition rocks; but there is only one other instance where fish occur in formations of such antiquity ...

Zamia. Dr Buckland brought a fine specimen of the recent Zamia of the Cape of Good Hope by which to compare & illustrate the fossil plant of Portland, called petrified Bird's Nests. Mr Brown considers the latter to form an intemediate link between the Pines or coniferous plants and the Zamia.

Mr Mantell list of Sussex fossils to the number of 400 species, of which 70 are in the London Clay

13 Plastic Clay
263 Chalk &c
43 Hastings Clay
22 are freshwater

Capt James Franklin map & paper on the geology of a part of Central India
a large portion of India is covered with Trap rocks. Trap rocks derive their names from the appearance of steps or traps, assumed in the forms of the mountains of that substance.
Capt. Franklin thinks the Lias Limestone occurs in this district, but has no fossils thence.

The Meetings

Mr Greenough stated that the Society possessed a series of specimens from India of ammonites which are objects of adoration or worship with the Hindoos, & an examination of them wd shew if they belonged to Lias. They are found on the S.W. side of the Himalah Mountains and fall from a height beyond the reach of man & above the limit of perpetual snow. They are only thus obtained by natives & then religiously preserved, so that the Europeans seldom known of them, and are carefully concealed from their knowledge. [13]

Mr Sowerby considers the species as peculiar. Mr Stokes says there are 3 species of sacred ammonites in this collection.

In a letter from the Duke of Buckingham on some observations of the elevation of the column of smoke in a late eruption of Mount Vesuvius, that its height was 3½ times that of the mountain, or as 14 to 4.

ANS Taylor

Notes, 1827–1828

1. Davies Gilbert and J F W Herschel.
2. Professor William Buckland and Revd Professor Adam Sedgwick.
3. These were specimens from the banks of the Irrawaddy River presented by Mr J Crawfurd. *See* Clift's paper read on 18 April 1828.
4. These were the bones of the sauropod dinosaur *Cetiosaurus*.
5. This reference to Pennant has not been identified.
6. The Society held its first meeting in Somerset House on 5 December 1828. £923 - 8s - 6d was subscribed to cover the cost of refurbishing the rooms.
7. The Caithness fish beds are now ascribed to the Middle Old Red Sandstone.
8. The fin spines of a fossil shark.
9. This lecture is not recorded in the Society's minute books.
10. De Chabriol & Bouillet 1827, p83.
11. A dragonfly.
12. J B Pentland and A Valenciennes studied the specimens and attempted to identify them (Sedgwick & Murchison 1829, p143).
13. These may be the 'Ammonites from the southern face of the Mana Pass in the Himalaya Mountains' presented by H T Colebrooke to the Society on 17 November 1825.

Session 1828-1829

19. 1828, November 7

The reading of a paper, "On the Geology of Nice", by H. T. De la Beche, Esq, F.R.S., L.S. & G.S. was begun.

19a. Richard C Taylor wrote in his notebook:

A paper commenced from Mr De la Beche on the Geology of the Environs of Nice. Where he observed the analogous formations to the Green Sand & oolite fomation.

Mr Greenough sd that no two countries could be more dissimilar than Nice & the oolite districts of England, Yet an accurate observer would perceive the fomations were the same.

Spoke of the want of agreement in the London Clay fossils, in the clay in difierent parts of England, that the fossils of <u>Sheppy</u> are found no where else, but the clay fossils are very similar to the <u>Calcaire Grossiere</u>

<u>Osseous Breccia</u> occurs in depositions & even in veins near Nice. Mr Greenough said that osseous breccia occur all along the shores of the Mediterranean, on each <u>side</u> from Spain to Constantinople.

Sub-fossils mentioned by Mr De la Beche, agreeing with those in the seas, but at a higher level.

ANS Taylor

20. 1828, November 21

The reading of Mr. De la Beche's paper, "On the Geology of Nice", was concluded.

20a. Richard C Taylor wrote in his notebook on 24 November:

Mr Greenough observed that Magnesian limestone was always disturbed, & placed irregularly, & commonly in the vicinity of <u>trap</u> rocks. The opinion of Von Buch was that it was caused by a similar process to that of trap formation, viz an <u>injection of the magnesia</u>.

Dr Fitton was glad to hear Mr Murchison confirm an opinion he had entertained that diluvium was of different epochs.

Mr Murchison having stated that <u>Nummulites</u> were peculiar to Tertiary strata, Mr Greenough said that he thought they would be

The Meetings

found to exist in the <u>Green Sand under the chalk</u> as he had them sent from Devizes, but could not personally vouch for the fact.

Mr Murchison stated that Gryphites were <u>tertiary fossils</u>.

ANS Taylor

20b. William Buckland wrote to Henry De la Beche on 26 July 1829:

When your paper [on Nice] was read I was informed, but was not present to hear, that it was contended that what you had called Green Sand is all Tertiary. This opposition has been heard no more of since.

NMW De la Beche

21. 1828, December 5

The reading was begun of a Paper,[1] "On the Excavation of Valleys, as illustrated by the Volcanic rocks of Central France", by Charles Lyell, Esq., V.P.G.S., F.R.S., &c. and R. I. Murchison, Esq., For.Sec.G.S., F.R.S., &c.

21a. Roderick Murchison scribbled in his notebook:

"Greenough" Considered the Diluvial Doctrine as one of the <u>Fundamental</u> principles of geology – torrential rivers only in Auvergne which have diluvial action.

<u>Wandsford, Thessal</u> &c & any partial deluges.

Soulavie & other Abbés tend to introduce the doctrine of modern causes but were all silenced.

Diluvium of Nice for example – rush of water <u>from Alps</u> could not carry boulders to Nice equally as to plains of Rhone because [of] steep escarpment at the fomer.

<u>Buckland</u>. Rivers usual obs.

I reply that valleys do not contain a single <u>extraneous</u> rock in Auvergne. To his query respecting tumbling <illegible> & <u>rotten</u> granite, I answer that Gneiss in Auvergne is not decomposing – <u>sides</u> are now hard as well as bottom.

Buckland states that the Diluvium is <u>universal</u> & <u>beneath</u> the basalt – I answer if so then Auvergne proves too much & establishes <u>several</u> diluviums. Why is no diluvium ever found <u>on</u> any of the older basalts, say I – no answer – B. praises the account of the Thyets stream upwards & allows it happened. <u>Perrier</u> – all <u>diluvial</u> – all the <u>trap</u>. Friends in France make 500 divisions into 300 formations.

[?] Lineur – gravel in all parts of the hill.

Album Graecum [2] was not sausages digested when the animals were drowned; bones not gnawed <u>on both sides</u>. no proof.

Warburton. Large boulders on plains are debacle not torrents.

Mezzo terraine not alluded to by GG & B [George Greenough and Buckland] – viz large blocks scattered have been contended for as proving universality of deluge, but whence came the <u>water</u>? & where has it gone!? Lithophage [3] had time to eat their holes, giving proof of great time – surface of Mendips – water in state of rest – admit portion of earth surface – Look to disturbances of earth & see causes still in action to raise earth from the present level of water – therefore account for diluvial action over all <u>periods of earth</u>

GSL Murchison N43, f98

22. 1828, December 16

Messrs Lyell and Murchison's paper, begun at the last Meeting, was concluded.

22a. Roderick Murchison wrote in his notebook:

Reply to Fitton – Paper is not on the Diluvium of Europe, quite misunderstood. Greenough – Great events from little cancers – small causes – torrential rivers not suficient – capable of mensuration – no barometers in other countries – These great rivers carry only large bodies of water & no bolders with them – (mistake of Greenough, I did not cite Humboldt).

Volcanic countries can alone offer barometers & therefore [were] chosen.

What evidence of pebble beds in Auvergne not being like those of Charlton (or other Tertiaries) in Kent

Currents not proceedings from Craters.

Scrope's reply of the ink stand. [4]

Water (greater quantity not required) – change of position only if water required or earth to stop.

Warburton – coast of America (observations on) not to be overthrown by old letters of saints (as quoted by Greenough) relating to old eruptions of Vesuvius.

pebbles only on <u>shores</u>, do not extend to the <u>deep</u>, hence all conglomerates were formed on Coasts, & deep seas are incompatible with small rolled stones. Thinks the [illegible] elevation en masse of solidified rocks (probably borne out by the Section of Bassano)

Sedgwick – I defend Poets of Greenough no great [illegible] –

deteriorations – Lisbon – protruded masses – Sabrina – Chili vindicated – playing on surface of things – surface of nature stagnant – mountains not on edge – agents of great violence then as reconcilable to our own senses. <u>Secondary</u> Limestones of Alps. either acknowledge our utter ignorance to agents of greater activity – <u>monstrous</u> theory of Werner – Volc agency the <u>vera causa</u> – good logic. – no drivilling of [illegible] or poets – <u>reality</u> of crystalline solutiveness – Granitic mountains raised en masse – Arran. Epochs of [illegible], & conglomerates <u>responding</u> to each <u>elevation</u>

Buckland – Will not say that the water was from whence or where – Boulade or Perrier – Ice berg may as well be said to have found an ancient valley –

GSL Murchison N43, ff113-118

22b. George Poulett Scrope wrote to Charles Lyell on 23 December:

I came up to hear the conclusion of your paper and witness, and in small way share in the hot discussion that ensued. Greenough, driven to extremities to deny that modern waters have any excavating forces, refused to believe the lavas of the Vivarais contemporary with the craters & cones. I put it to him that if he were, on returning home, to find a pool of ink on his library carpet, and trace it up to a broken inkbottle in the corner, he would hardly think me in my senses if I argued that the breaking of the bottle and the spilling of the ink belonged to different epochs, and were wholly unconnected with each other. Buckland gave in quoad the Vivarais vallies but talks of the softness of the granite & basalt. We shall soon see the Mosaic geologists quite change their note and exaggerate the power of the present excavating forces in order to get it all done within the proper Newtonian chronological periods.

APS Lyell

22c. Charles Lyell wrote to his sister on 21 January 1829:

My letters from geological friends are very satisfactory, as to the unusual interest excited in the Geological Society by our paper on the excavation of valleys in Auvergne. Seventy persons present the second evening, and a warm debate. Buckland and Greenough furious, <u>contra</u> Scrope, Sedgwick, and Warburton, supporting us. These were the first two nights in our new <u>magnificent</u> apartments in Somerset House.

Lyell 1881, 1, p238

23. 1829, February 6

A paper was read, "On the discovery of a new species of Pterodactyle; and also of the Faeces of the Ichthyosaurus; and of a black substance resembling Sepia, or Indian Ink, in the Lias at Lyme Regis", by the Rev. W. Buckland, D.D., F.R.S., Professor of Mineralogy and Geology in the University of Oxford.

A paper was read, "On the Oolitic district of Bath", by William Lonsdale, Esq. of Bath-Easton.

23a. Richard C Taylor wrote in his notebook:

A paper by Dr Buckland describing an animal to which he has given the name of Pterodactylus Dorsetiensis, discovered in the Blue Lias of Lyme in Dorsetshire. Not before observed in this Country & only seen in the Tertiary beds of Paris.

Since investigating the structure of this animal it has recurred to Dr Buckland that the bones at Stonesfield which have hitherto been assigned to birds belong to this singular animal. The same remark applies also to those of the Tilgate Forest. Dr Buckland therefore agrees with Mr Miller in the opinion that they may be expected in many formations between the Chalk & the Lias.

Another paper in which the same author describes the frequent existence of bodies in the Lias which he now attributes to the faeces of Ichthyosaurus. They are called Bezoar stones [5] at Lyme, & are embedded in the Lias both there & at Whitby. on examination both externally & in forming transverse sections, they are found to contain scales of fishes & vertebra, even of the young Ichthyosauri.

Thinks that indications of similar substances exist in the Tilgate beds. as to the interesting question of how so many animals are found in such excellent preservation, he thinks the Ichthyosauri were destroyed suddenly, perhaps smothered in the mud.

Remarks that in the Lias Pentacrinites are found adhering to wood at Lyme.

Dr Buckland read a paper on some animal apparently a Sepia, producing a black substance allied to Indian Ink also from Lyme.

<u>Mr Lonsdale's Sections nr Bath</u>

Prof. Sedgewick. general remarks on the Section as compared with that of the same formations at the Yorkshire Coast. observed that to a certain extent all form[ations] were local, or had <u>local characters.</u>

The series of Oolite strata on the Yorkshire coast has a perfect resemblance to a Coal formation, particularly the Lower oolite.

The Meetings

There it possesses the characters of a Coal formation from the top of the Oxford Clay to the Lias. They only in this particular differ from the upper in the section nr [?] Hutton. Near Bath no such characters prevail.

The Calcareous grit is beautifully exhibited in the Yorkshire cliffs, & abounds with fossils & the same is repeated at Weymouth.

Mr Conybeare observed that the Sandstones & sands East of Northampton had not yet been sufficiently studied, but he conjectured that they would be found to assimalate more than was expected to the Yorkshire Oolitic Coal formations!

ANS Taylor

24. 1829, February 20

Annual General Meeting at which W. H. Fitton read an address and the Rev. Adam Sedgwick was elected President.

24a. Roderick Murchison wrote in his notebook:

> To correct Fitton on following points on his discourse
> 1st as to date of Montlosier's work (if he chooses to digress);
> 2dly to remark on omission of my paper, on the very slight allusion to Sedgwick's Magn Limest [Magnesian Limestone] [6], & on the almost omission of our very long & laborious conglomerate whilst pages are devoted to short notices. Sedgwick can never notice his own productions & therefore so much more incumbent on the Pres. (Fitton) to notice them.
>
> GSL Murchison N45

24b. Roderick Murchison wrote to William Buckland on 21 February:

> You should have been present yesterday to have heard Sedgwick blazing away – His invocation to Herschel "May Virgo go before him & Gemini follow after him" produced peals of laughter.
>
> RS Buckland

24c. Charles Lyell wrote to his sister on 26 February:

> Sedgwick quite astonished them, it seems, in the chair at the general meeting, which was very full. Among innumerable good hits, when proposing the toast of the Astronomical Society, and Herschel, their president, he said, alluding to H's intended marriage (for he is just about to marry the daughter of a Scotch clergyman) [7], 'May the House of Herschel be perpetuated, and, like the Cassinis, be illustrious astronomers for three generations. May

all the constellations wait upon him; may Virgo go before, and Gemini follow after'. Poor H., notwithstanding his confusion, got up after the roar of laughter had continued for three minutes, and made a famous speech.

Lyell 1881, 1, p251

24d. Charles Lyell wrote to Gideon Mantell on 23 March:

I was not at the dinner, not being returned. altho' not advertized 70 to 80 persons came – never before so many. All agree that the Chair at a scientific convivial meeting had never been so well filled as by our new President Sedgwick, who offhand sported an inexhaustable number of bright & original ideas in innumerable speeches. On coming to the Prest of the Astronl. Socy, Herschell, he made fine play about his intended marriage, for H. has since married a beautiful & accomplished Scotch lassie aged 18. He talked of the House of Cassini having been illustrious for 3 successive generations in astronomy so might that of Herschell prove &c. "Gentlemen may the House of Herschel be perpetuated, may all the constellations wait on them, may 'Virgo' go before & 'Gemini' follow after, & may their offspring resemble the stars of heaven in number & brilliancy &c." this was received by a roar of laughter for 3 minutes and H tho' at first put out of countenance recovered & made an admirable speech.

The Society & the subject has gained vastly in strength & following with the last 2 years.

TL Mantell, f61

25. 1829, March 6

An account of a remarkable fossil-plant in the coal-formation of Yorkshire by John Lindley, Esq., F.G.S., F.R.S., &c. and Professor of Botany in the University of London, was read.

The reading of a paper, "On the remains of Quadrupeds which have been discovered in the Marine and Freshwater Formations of the Peninsula of Italy", by J. B. Pentland, Esq. was begun.

25a. Richard C Taylor wrote in his notebook:

Mr Lindley's description of a fossil plant in a nodule of argillaceous iron ore. It exhibits the frond of a plant to which he gives the name of <u>Trichomanes roduntatus</u> and does hesitate to identify with that which is now only known recent in the deep forests of New Zealand.

The Meetings

    Mr Pentland's paper describing the Tertiary strata of the Sub-appenines.

    His assertion that the beds were horizontal & proved a retiring level of the sea was contradicted by Messrs Lyell, & Murchison who state that those beds were highly inclined.

ANS Taylor

26. 1829, March 20

A paper was read, "On the Tertiary and Secondary Rocks forming the Southern Flank of the Tyrolese Alps, near Bassano", by Roderick Impey Murchison, Esq., Sec.G.S., F.R.S., &c.

26a. Richard C Taylor wrote in his notebook:

    Murchison on the same district [the Sub-Appenines]
    Produced Nummulites & other multilocular shells above the chalk at <u>Bassano</u>. Shells like those of the London Clay.
    The Tertiary beds there are as pinnacled & serrated as the secondary or primative, being often nearly perpendicular.
    The Plastic Clay is absent in Italy & [he] considers it a local estuary deposit, not a freshwater generally & extensively. Not freshwater even throughout England, as the Isle of Wight. Therefore there is no evidence of an interval of repose with a general accumulation of terrestrial & freshwater remains, between the Secondary & Tertiary order as the French considered. [8]
    In this Mr Greenough concurred, that this law is not general, & that the theory is wholly given up and refuted, so far as the French originally thought to carry it.
    The Tertiary rocks are often confused in Italy by the interposition or protrusion of Rocks of igneous origin as amygdaloidal trap.
    Mr Greenough argued on the small agreement of formations at considerable intervals, & that [they] varied even from quarry to quarry in the same formation, contending that those divisions have been carried too far.
    Dr Fitton objected to the separating the formations into Tertiary & Secondary. They were thought to possess many distinct characters, particularly by having beds of freshwater shells, and by being unconformable to the chalk, which latter is not the fact, & the former is not peculiar to the upper beds, the inferior beds having also freshwater shells.

Session 1828-29

To this Mr Lyell objected that although all or most of the Genera may have been traced in both classes, yet the species are decidedly different. No species in the tertiary are repeated in the secondary.

Mr Stokes added that no <u>volutes</u> are seen in the Secondary strata, and no <u>belemnites & ammonites</u> in the tertiary.

Professor Sedgewick wholly denies the doctrine of Mr Greenough about the limited space occupied by fomations. He only wonders that so many points of agreement may be found so widely. Admitted there is no such thing as an Universal formation, but that it is modified in different places. Mr Sedgewick thinks the Crag of Suffolk resembles the shales of Bourdeaux. Amongst others it contains the <u>Murex contrarius</u>.

The Woolwich beds are extremely doubtful.

ANS Taylor

27. 1829, May 15

The reading of a paper, "On the Hydrographical Basin of the Thames, with a view more especially to investigate the causes which have operated in the formation of the valleys of that river, and its tributary streams", by the Rev. W. D. Conybeare, F.G.S., F.R.S., &c., &c. was begun.

27a. Charles Lyell wrote to Gideon Mantell on 16 May:

A splendid meeting last night. Sedgwick in chair. Conybeare's paper on valley of Thames directed against Messrs. Lyell & Murchison's former paper [9] was read in part. Buckland present to defend the 'diluvialists' as Conybeare styles his sect & us he terms 'fluvialists'. Greenough assisted us by making an ultra speech on the impotence of modern causes. No river he said within times of history has deepened its channel one foot! It was great fun for he said – our opponents say " give us Time & we will work wonders, so said the wolf in the fable to the lamb [10] – why do you disturb the water – I do not you are further up the stream than I – but your father did – he never was here – then your grandfather did so I will murder you. give me <u>time</u> & I will murder you, so say the fluvialists!" roars of laughter in which G. joined agt. himself. What a choice simile! M & I fought stoutly & Buckland was very piano. Conybeare's memoir is not strong by any means. He admits 3 deluges before the Noachian! & Buckland adds God knows how many <u>catastrophes</u> besides, so we have driven them out of the Mosaic record fairly.

TL Mantell, f61; quoted in
Wilson 1972, p264 and in Lyell 1881, 1, p252

27b. Charles Lyell wrote to Gideon Mantell on 23 May:

> Broderip & I misbehaved at the R.S. [Royal Society] on Thursday by giving way to a fit of laughter during the seance, on overhearing that old twaddle Josh Smith F.R.S. talking to a friend about our last Geol. debate. He said "I was glad they argued so temperately for that was quite right, for you know Sir the facts are all against Moses & <u>Mr Greenough</u> proved in an impressive speech that 'Time can do everything!!' but they (the G.S.) shewed I think that they do not wish to <u>abrogate</u> the Xtian <u>dispensation</u> as some might think!!"
>
> TL Mantell, f61

28. 1829, June 5

The reading of a paper on the Valley of the Thames, by the Rev. W. D. Conybeare, F.G.S., F.R.S., &c., &c. (begun at the last meeting,) was concluded.

28a. Charles Lyell wrote to Gideon Mantell on 7 June:

> The last discharge of Conybeare's artillery served by the great Oxford engineer against the fluvialists, as they are pleased to term us, drew upon them on Friday a sharp voley of musketry from all sides, & such a broadside at the finale from Sedgwick as was enough to sink the Reliquiae Dil for ever & make the 2d. vol shy of venturing out to sea.[11] After the memoir on the impotence of all the rivers which feed the 'main river of an isle' & the sluggishness of Father Thames himself, 'scarce able to move a pin's head', a notice by Cully, land-surveyor was read on the prodigious force of a Cheviot stream, 'the College', wh. has swept away a bridge & annually buries large tracts under gravel. Buckld. then jumped up like a council [counsel], said Fitton to me, "who had come down special."
>
> After his reiteration of Conybeare's arguments, Fitton made a somewhat laboured speech. I followed & then Sedgwick, who decided on 4 <u>or more</u> deluges & said the simultaneousness was disproved for ever, &c. &c., & declared that on the nature of such floods we should at present 'doubt and not dogmatise'. A good meeting.
>
> TL Mantell, quoted in Lyell 1881, 1, p253

28b. Charles Lyell wrote to John Fleming on 10 June:

> Of course, in defining the Fluvialists, they (for Buckland wrote half the memoir) took care to build up their man of straw, and triumphantly knock him down again. But in the animated discussion which followed the reading of the first half of the essay, at the Geological Society, we made no small impression on them. And when, last Friday, the remainder came on, we had a hot rencounter. Buckland came up on purpose again, and made a leading speech. But after we had exposed him, and even Greenough, his only staunch supporter, had given in on many points, Sedgwick, now president, closed the debate with a terribly anti-diluvialist declaration. For he has at last come round, and is as decided as you are. But you must know that Buckland now, and Conybeare, distinctly admit three universal deluges, and many catastrophes, as they call them, besides!
>
> Lyell 1881, 1, p254

Notes, 1828-1829

1. The background to this important paper is given in Wilson 1972, pp191-203 and 262-263.
2. Calcareous fossil faeces; a term used in materia medica.
3. A rock-boring bivalve.
4. See following extract.
5. So-called from their resemblance to the stomach stones of oriental goats, renowned as an antidote to poison (Adams 1938, pp104-106).
6. Sedgwick's paper on this formation was read on 7 March 1828.
7. Herschel married Margaret Brodie Stewart on 3 March 1829.
8. See, for example, Prevost 1828.
9. Read on 5 December and 16 December 1828.
10. This is loosely based on Aesop's fable of the 'Wolf and the Lamb'.
11. Buckland 1823. A second volume was widely expected, but never published.

Session 1829-1830

29. 1829, November 20

The reading of a paper, "On the Tertiary Formations which range along the flanks of the Salzburg and Bavarian Alps", being in continuation of the memoir, "On the Valley of Gosau", by the Rev. Adam Sedgwick, Pres.G.S., F.R.S., &c. and Roderick Impey Murchison, Esq., Sec.G.S., F.R.S., &c. was begun.

The Meetings

30. 1829, December 4

The reading of the paper by the Rev. Adam Sedgwick, Pres.G.S., F.R.S., &c. and Roderick Impey Murchison, Esq., Sec.G.S., F.R.S., &c. begun at the last meeting, was concluded.

A paper, "On the discovery of the bones of the Iguanodon, and other large reptiles, in the Isle of Wight and Isle of Purbeck", by the Rev. William Buckland, D.D., V.P.G.S., F.R.S., &c., &c. was then read.

30a. Charles Lyell wrote to Gideon Mantell on 5 December:

> We were all disappointed at your not being here yesterday, for Murchison told us you were to have been here. Sedgwick & his wind up on the Alps went off splendidly in a full meeting. You & the iguanodon treated by Buckland with due honours, when exhibg. some great bones of a little toe from Purbeck – he greatly amazed my friend Sir T. Phillips, not <u>Dick</u> your friend, by his humour about the size of the sd. giant, compared to the small genteel lizards of our days.
>
> TL Mantell, quoted in Lyell 1881, 1, p258

31. 1829, December 18

A paper was read entitled, "Observations on part of the Low Countries and the north of France, principally near Maestricht and Aix-la-Chapelle", by William Henry Fitton, M.D., F.G.S., &c.

31a. Gideon Mantell wrote in his diary:

> Dined at the Crown and Anchor [1] with Professor Sedgwick, Dr Buckland, Mr Chantrey etc. Attended the meeting of the Geological Society in the evening: a very full attendance. Passed the evening most delightfully.
>
> SAS Mantell, quoted in Curwen 1940, p73

32. 1830, January 15

A paper was read, entitled, "On the Fossil Fox of Oeningen, with an account of the Lacustrine Deposit in which it was found", by R. I. Murchison, Esq., Sec.G.S., F.R.S., &c.

32a. Richard C Taylor wrote in his notebook:

A fossil Fox exhibited by Mr Murchison, the first carniverous animal that had been discovered in the lacustrine deposit of Oenengen on the Rhine. Mr Mantell conceives it to be strictly resembling the common European fox, Vulpes communis. These quarries have also produced numerous grassiverous animals – Reptiles, Birds, fishes, tortoises, insects and immense numbers of vegetable impressions, which much resemble the plants of Europe.

Dr Buckland thought that the presence of Testudo would indicate a warmer temperature than European. It was observed that they are found in the Lakes of N. America.

Mr Lyell says we know too little of the shells in the European seas & cannot therefore positively determine what may be considered extinct in these collections.

ANS Taylor

32b. Roderick Murchison wrote to Gideon Mantell on 19 January:

The Fox had very fine play & gave us an excellent run. Buckland told one of his old stories about hounds, hunters, fox & all nearly ending their days in an unexpected hollow in Essex, where they might have been potted & petrified – the thing was only told as a joke, because he gave high praise to the memoir, but alas many of the Johnny Raws who come to S.H. [Somerset House] to gape & laugh, went away I doubt not in the belief that my beast might have been a Vulpes hunted into a hole & not a true fossil which B. really never meant to imply. Your description is exceeding good, but by the way, your term "Genus" Vulpes elicited subsequent remarks from Dr. Horsfield & other naturalists who I presume are not aware of Fred Cuvier's distinctions.

TL Mantell, f74

32c. Charles Lyell wrote to Gideon Mantell on 5 February:

Murchison's paper was well drawn up, the meeting full, the discussion unusually animated & your description & summing up of evidence recd. excellently & full of a sort of Caution which is deplorably wanting in Buckland's last paper on the Iguanodon toe. [2] He can swear to a genus from a rolled vertebra in Swanage bay whereas Cuvier cannot when he saw 20 from Loxwood & a femur &c. &c. [3] Your anatomical description of the fox <illegible> not have been read at our meeting.

TL Mantell, f62

The Meetings

33. 1830, February 19

Annual General Meeting at which Adam Sedgwick was re-elected President and read the Anniversary Address.

33a. Gideon Mantell wrote in his diary:

> Dressed and went to dinner with Mr Lyell at the Crown and Anchor. the anniversary of the Geological Society. Sat next to Lyell and Delabeche and near Murchison – very pleasant party – Prof. Sedgwick in the chair – famous chairman rather too lengthy in his speeches. Adjourned at nine to Somerset House; Sedgwick read his address; an admirable one. Took tea and gossiped till twelve with Buckland and Lyell Principally.
> SAS Mantell, quoted in Curwen, 1940, p74

34. 1830, April 2

The reading of a paper on the Geology of Weymouth, and the adjacent parts of the coast of Dorsetshire, by the Rev. William Buckland, D.D., F.G.S., F.R.S., &c. and Henry Thomas De la Beche, Esq., F.G.S., F.R.S., &c. was begun.

34a. Roderick Murchison wrote to Gideon Mantell on 3 April:

> We had Buckland & De la Beche's long expected memoir last night on the Weymouth Coast. on the whole it is a well worked up concern, tho' I opened as smart a fire as I could (in the subsequent discussion) upon several minor points in it. The breccia at the base of Tertiary & filling up the cracks & swallows in the Chalk they call "Breche à place" – "<u>no more Diluvium</u>" – with allusions to "Craie Chloritée" instead of wholesome plain English "Upper G. Sand" &c. all these gallicisms they will no doubt abandon, for they are exclusively "De la Bechian" & quite unworthy of <u>English</u> Geologists, who are looked to as the "types" & where names are established all over the continent as Classical. [4] The Portland rock and Kimmeridge Clay we found fully illustrated in the museum at Strasbourg from the adjoining Department &c.
>
> There was a <u>collateral</u> subject introduced viz the <u>Iguanodon</u> bones & this way: alluding to the thinning out of the Weald Strata before they reach the Weymouth Coast, Buckland not only told of Bartlett's toe, [5] but introduced a fine story about some more of the same animal with which the table was covered by an arrival from the I. of Wight sent by Mr Vine (near Brook in the Hasting's

Sands). some of these vertebrae (of enormous size certainly) the Doctor insisted were of your Iguanodon on account of their quadrangular form. I objected a little to [the] conclusiveness of his reasoning, & fairly beat him I think out of the toe bone case. whether the vertebrae be really those of Iguanodon no one short of yourself can predict, but quoad the old toe, there is no more proof of its having been part of that animal than my great femur. I presume that even in the case of the vertebrae you rest for the present satisfied with probabilities that is, until you can find more parts of the animal conjoined &c.

TL Mantell, f74

35. 1830, April 16

The reading of a paper on the Geology of Weymouth, and the adjacent parts of the coast of Dorsetshire, by the Rev. William Buckland, and Henry Thomas De la Beche, Esq., begun at the last meeting, was concluded.

35a. Charles Lyell wrote to Gideon Mantell on 5 February:

His [Buckland's] & D. la B.'s on Weymouth read last time – good, but some diluvial heresy tacked on at which I fired a shot. The iguanodon's bones brought by them from Isle of Wight are rolled, ugly, unmeaning pebbles, save one 'sub-quadrangular vertebra,' as Dr Buckland says, which he declares proves it to be an iguanodon. Even that is imperfect.

TL Mantell, f62

36. 1830, May 7

A paper was read, entitled, "Sketches explanatory of Geological Maps of the Archduchy of Austria and of the South of Bavaria", by Ami Boué, M.D., For.Mem.G.S., &c.

36a. Charles Lyell wrote to his sister Eleanor on 11 May:

>Murray of Simprim asked me to take him to the Geological Club. As luck would have it, he sat next Buckland, with whom he was much delighted, as with a most entertaining lecture delivered by him afterwards, at a full meeting of the Geological Society, on Bones of the Mastodon brought by Basil Hall from N. America, and by Beechey & Co. of Extinct Elephants from Behring's Straits. [6] Also on my Angus Kelpie's feet, which were so much admired, that when I offered the Professor one, he would not accept, saying he

The Meetings

should rob the Geological Society, for each differed from the other in something. 7

Lyell 1881, 1, p267

37. 1830, June 4

A paper was read, entitled, "On the Geological Relations of the South of Ireland", by Thomas Weaver, Esq., F.G.S., F.R.S., M.R.I.A., &c.

37a. Richard C Taylor wrote in his notebook:

Mr Weaver's paper. numerous organic remains occur in the Grauwacke Slate and Transition Slate series of Ireland.

Transition Coal or Anthracite of Kerry, all the coal & culm in the County of Cork is anthracite. The measures contain abundant vegetable remains, Calamites &c.

Professor Sedgewick. Had observed in Russia abundance of Coal Plants in the Transition beds. Observes that even in this country, Yorkshire for instance, beds of coal are worked beneath the Carboniferous series.

Mr De la Beche – as to the definition Transition, never could find out the difference between Transition & Carboniferous series.

Mr Lyell also doubted the propriety of making that distinction, as the same fossils are found in each. Dr Fleming found fish scales in Old Red Sandstone.

Mr Murchison thinks the distinction is correct & allowable as applied to English & Irish Rocks, because the Old Red Sandstone intervenes.

ANS Taylor

Notes, 1829-1830

1. The Society held its annual meetings at the 'Crown and Anchor', just off The Strand, from 1832 to 1846 (Whittet 1983).
2. See Lyell's comments on the meeting of 4 December 1829.
3. These specimens were discovered by J King and presented to the Society by R I Murchison (Murchison 1826, p104).
4. The gallicisms make only a fleeting appearance in the published paper (Buckland and De la Beche 1835, p10).
5. 'Bartlett's toe' refers to the supposed toe bone of an iguanodon sent to Buckland by the Rev T O Bartlett and described by him at a meeting on 4 December 1829.
6. These are recorded as donations to the Society's museum, and were presumably described by Buckland at the meeting.
7. A 'kelpie' is the name given in the Lowlands of Scotland to a water spirit that frequently takes the form of a horse. The specimens are described in Babbage 1837.

Session 1830-1831

38. 1830, November 3

The reading of a paper entitled, "Remarks on the Formation of Alluvial Deposits", by the Rev. James Yates, M.A., F.G.S., F.L.S. was begun.

38a. *The Athenaeum* reported:

The first meeting of the Society for the present season was held on Wednesday evening; Professor Sedgwick in the chair. The Secretary read the minutes of the last meeting, and a very numerous list of presents both in books and specimens. The chairman, in moving the thanks of the Society to the different donors, very justly dilated on the liberal additions both to the library and museum, and congratulated the meeting on the great interest that was taken in the objects of the Society ...

A paper by Mr. Yates, on the subject of alluvial deposits, was read; when the author addressed the meeting in support of his theory, and Mr. Greenough made a few remarks in reply; – but the more general discussion of this subject, the fertile topic of dispute amongst geologists, was postponed until the ensuing meeting.

The Athenaeum, 158, pp697-698, 6 November 1830

39. 1830, November 17

The reading of the paper on the Formation of Alluvial Deposits, by the Rev. James Yates, begun at the last meeting, was concluded.

39a. *The Athenaeum* reported:

The Society held their second meeting on Wednesday evening; but it has been intimated to us that the Council do not wish the proceedings of their meetings published;[1] and after the liberal manner in which we have been introduced, we feel ourselves bound to yield to their wish; in doing so, however, we trust we may be allowed to express our surprise at this resolution. We had imagined, that the diffusion of knowledge in *these days*, was a matter highly to be wished, and that the desire to do so was worthy of encouragement. We are convinced, however, some good reason must exist for this apparently strange determination.

The Athenaeum, 160, p730, 20 November 1830

40. 1830, December 15

A paper was first read, entitled, "An Explanatory Sketch of a Geological Map of Transylvania", by Dr. Ami Boué, For.Mem.G.S.

A paper was then read, "On the Astronomical Causes which may influence Geological Phenomena", by J. F. W. Herschel, Esq., F.R.S., F.G.S., &c., &c.

40a. William Fitton wrote to John Herschel on 16 December:

> Your paper was read last night &, as I am told, with great approbation, & an excellent speech was made in illustration of it by Sedgwick, who came in half a dozen coaches from Cambridge, & got in at 8 1/2 just as the meeting had begun.
>
> RS Herschel, HS7, p231

41. 1831, March 2

A paper was first read, "On the rippled markings of many of the forest marble beds north of Bath, and the <u>foot-tracks</u> of certain animals occurring in great abundance on their surfaces", by George Poulett Scrope, Esq., F.G.S., F.R.S.

The reading of a paper, entitled, "A description of longitudinal and transverse sections through a portion of the carboniferous chain between Penigent and Kirkby Stephen", by the Rev. Adam Sedgwick, F.G.S., F.R.S., Woodwardian Professor in the University of Cambridge, was begun.

41a. Roderick Murchison wrote in his notebook:

> lst: Scrope's memoir "on the Forest Marble or Stonesfield Slate with ripple & foot marks" &c. Too much said of ripples to show it was an ancient shore because the phenomenon is almost universal. The author's view of its affording support to gradual elevation from W to E good; his theory of alternations of convex & concave waves. The animal foot marks referred by him to no one tribe, whether Crab, Mollusc, Bivalve, Bird or quadruped! a third claw discovered by Vigors in the indented paste – ergo probably a <illegible>.
>
> Greenough said a few words on the universality of the ripple in sand.
> Fitton spoke at some length explaining the value of the paper.
> Vigors spoke, Broderip do, Clift examined.

De la Beche rose several times to say various.

Mr. Yates spoke of the ripples in Grauwacke in the Alps.

Mr. Strutt said a few words.

Old Smith talked con amore of the <u>uphill</u> movements of sand, & sand infilled westerly by wind & wave; believed that no stratum had ever been moved since its deposit; that the overlapping at the escarpments was due to overflowing; called attention to the N-E. & S-W. direction of the great series of ripples as harmonizing with the general direction of the Strata in England; of the universality of the ripple. [2]

At dinner Mr. Smith recalled several curious details – 1st as to some of the earliest boroughs in England being made <u>for</u> foreign manufacturers to the exclusion of the natives. Spoke of the old charter of a borough in Wales where no Welchman could be a burgess. this led him to speak of the earliest iron workers whom he described at <blank> in Wales & the first iron wire drawers by <u>machinery</u> at Tintern Abbey – previous to which all iron wire was pulled out by manual labour.

First alum works in England introd. by Sir J. Chaloner a Yorkshireman who [?] pinched the mode of manufacture from Italy (the Papal states) – where is the Alum Shale there? [3]

2nd Sedgwick's memoir of detail of his native region from N to South (section by de la Beche) was read in part. the structure of the country only described, & the accuracy of <u>local geological horizons</u> found to be <u>good</u> across wide valleys – even the beds of particular shale & limestone being persistent for many miles. The great Scar limestone, which from the South to N. of Yorkshire is non metalliferous, becomes interlaced with Coal seams in Northumberland.

GSL Murchison N58, ff2-5

41b. Charles Lyell wrote to Gideon Mantell a few days later:

Scrope has been reading a paper on the ripple-marked oolite sandstone of age of cornbrash with lots of long worm marks or things thrown up by burrowing animals & on the same slabs the most clear foot marks of an animal – what no one knows. [sketch] a slight mark in the middle where the tail or body touched seemingly. There being only two marks is a puzzle, but had there been 3 it cd not be a bird because they don't leave 2 lines.

TL Mantell, f62, incorrectly dated 1 Dec 1830

The Meetings

42. 1831, March 30

A paper was read, entitled, "Geological remarks on the vicinity of Swan River and Isle Buache or Garden Island, on the coast of Western Australia", by the Rev. Archdeacon Scott, F.G.S.

42a. Charles Lyell wrote to Gideon Mantell on 31 March:

> I did the honours of your skull & read an extract from our letter on the homo diluvii testis to the satisfaction of a numerous meeting last night [4] – which told the better as there was a very short paper only read by Archdn Scott on Swan River. [sketch]
>
> The whole Paper was in a few words a sienite range & primary inland a few miles & near the shore blown calcareous sand like Cornwall converted into rock &c. &c. & including petrified trees or as some will have it stalactites – I rather think the sand & carb. of lime does form round trees & their branches, that there is a solution of carb. of lime by rain water acting on fine dust from shells comminuted & which containing animal matter give out carb. acid gas on putrefying.
>
> TL Mantell, f62

Notes, 1830-1831

1. There is no direct reference to this in the Council Minutes, but on 15 December 1830 the Secretary was directed to supply regularly *The Athenaeum* and *The Spectator* with a notice of the papers read, names of the authors, and also the name of the President in the chair, the fellows elected at the meeting and the most remarkable presents. By implication, details of the discussion were not to be supplied (Geological Society Archive, CM1/3).
2. William Smith's ideas are briefly discussed in Laudan 1976, pp213-215.
3. The early history of the Yorkshire alum trade is given in Young 1817. Smith was living at Hackness near Scarborough at this date.
4. The reading of Mantell's letter is not recorded in the minutes.

Session 1831-1832

43. 1831, November 2

A paper was read, "On certain younger deposits in Sicily and on the phaenomena accompanying their elevation", by Dr Turnbull Christie, F.G.S. and communicated by the President.

43a. Charles Lyell wrote to Miss Horner the following day:

Dinner at Club of Geol Socy, as usual an agreable meeting. Murchison in the chair, agreed to meet on Friday & tell me lots of names. Greenough, Broderip, Pringle, Stokes, Basil Hall his brother – or "the muffler" as Sedgwick calls him in Cumberland phraseology for it means a dabbler in all things – and strangers. Basil Hall brought his newly purchased autograph of the 'Antiquary,' by Sir Walter Scott, and two pages of preface lately written by Scott at Portsmouth, in his own handwriting, giving his reasons to Basil Hall why he liked the Antiquary better than all his novels.

... A paper of Dr. Turnbull Christie's on Sicily led Murchison to call me up & I had the field much to myself. I told you that a temporary cloud came over me in Edinburgh at seeing the controversial storm gathering agt [against] me in the horizon; but I must say it was dispelled by this meeting, for never [even] on the first meeting after my first vol. appeared did I hear it so much spoken of. Fitton declared to the meeting his conviction that my theory of earthquakes wd. ultimately prevail. Greenough made one of his ultra-sceptical speeches saying that once he only doubted what 'stratification' meant but now he was quite at a loss to conceive the meaning of the term 'sea' in Geology & he thought no one could explain what 'the sea' meant. Fitton gave him some hard hits for thus fighting shadows, & 'assisting the cause of darkness' by doubting elementary truths. B. Hall with more humour said as a sailor that he felt alarmed at hearing the existence of a great mass of waters (for he wd. no longer give offense by talking of 'the sea') called in question, &c. He then eulogised my book, and after the meeting two American gentlemen came up to be introduced, and poured out a most flattering comment on its popularity in the United States; [1] but what was much more to the purpose than this sort of incense, they gave me many facts bearing on my theories respecting part of North America. I did not get back till near one, and then a great fire in Holborn, which was too grand a sight to lose, detained me three-quarters of an hour.

Kinnordy Mss, transcribed by L G Wilson.
Lyell 1881, 1, p349; quoted in Wilson 1972, p326

43b. Roderick Murchison wrote to William Whewell on 14 November:

Our campaign Geological opened well, with an excellent memoir of Dr Christie on the Bone Breccia of the Coasts of Sicily

The Meetings

showing subdivisions of it most clearly marked & having been put together posterior to the creation of many existing species of shells &c. – in short the dissection of Diluvium in its grosser sense.

TC Whewell, Add Ms a 209/91

44. 1831, November 16

A paper was read, "On a large species of Plesiosaurus in the Scarborough Museum", by John Dunn, Esq., V.P. Scarborough Philosophical Society, and communicated by Roderick Impey Murchison, Esq., P.G.S.

A letter was then read, addressed to the President and Fellows of this Society, "On the ancient and present state of Vesuvius", by Count de Montlosier, For.Mem.G.S., President of the Academy of Clermont Ferrard, &c., &c.

44a. Charles Lyell wrote to Miss Horner on 17 November:

We had yesterday an excellent meeting, both at the Club of the Geological Society and at Somerset House. A paper of Count Montlosier on Somma and Vesuvius excited much interest; we had a famous discussion. Buckland, Greenough, Fitton, De le Beche, and I began, but Necker, on being invited, spoke half an hour most capitally. I never heard a better lecture.

Lyell 1881, 1, p352

44b. Roderick Murchison wrote to William Whewell on 17 November:

We had a <u>capital</u> meeting last night. 1st, a memoir on the Gigantic Plesio [Plesiosaurus] of Scarbro. 2d, Old Montlosier on Vesuvius, which drew out a long & lucid explanation from Necker (de Saussure); Lyell, Buckland, Fitton, Greenough, De la Beche, & others being orators. Buckland filled up all the parts wanting in the Plesio, & perfected a monster for those who in a snowy Nov. night were disposed to nightmare.

TC Whewell Add Ms a 209/92, quoted in Geikie 1875, 1, p195

45. 1831, November 30

A paper, "On the geology of the Southern Provinces of Spain", by Capt. Edward Cook, R.N., F.G.S. was begun; and a communication containing extracts from the memoirs published by M. de Buch in the Preussische Staats Zeitung, "On the new volcanic island in the Mediterranean, and its connection with the extinct volcanic island of Pantellaria, and the hot springs of Sciacca on the coast of Sicily", by Leonard Horner, Esq., V.P.G.S. and addressed to the President, was read. [2]

45a. Charles Lyell wrote to Miss Horner on 2 December:

I had a hard task yesterday to keep my resolutions of severe temperance, for Murchison was so unwell, that he asked me to preside at the Geological Society club dinner, and take his friend Colin Mackenzie to it; so I was obliged to push about the bottle, and to sham taking a fair quantity of wine. Our numbers were thinned by the Royal Society Anniversary and by rain, but it went off well, and in the evening brilliantly. A sort of geographical paper, long and dull, and really of no value whatever, was to have been read by my travelling companion Captain Cooke, now again in Spain. [3] We had staved it off till we had read out the others. But when your father's letter to the President came about the new isle north-east of Pantellaria, we determined to shove Cooke's into the coal-hole without ceremony. So when Turner had read some passages, Murchison (for he was recovered enough to take the chair) said to the meeting that it would not be doing justice to Captain Cooke to go on, since there were certain maps and illustrations which ought to accompany, not yet arrived: that it was begun, just that it might keep its place, &c. I then officiated as secretary, Broderip being ill, and read Hoffman's paper, which produced animated discussion, into which I entered largely. The structure of Pantellaria, the wasting away of the new isle, the par-boiled fish, the floating cinders, the clefts at Sciacca, &c., all afforded subjects for Fitton, myself, De la Beche, Dr. Babington, Murchison, and others to dilate upon ...

After the paper of Hoffman's was over, old Whishaw came up to me and said he never heard one more interesting, and he thought Horner had drawn it up with great clearness and judgement.

Lyell 1881, 1, p354

46. 1831, December 14

A letter was first read, "On the influence of Season over the Depth of Water in Wells", from William Bland, jun., Esq., of Hartlip, near Sittingbourne, and addressed to the Rev. William Buckland, D.D., V.P.G.S., &c.

The Meetings

A paper, "On the stratiform Basalt associated with the carboniferous formation of the North of England", by William Hutton, Esq., F.G.S. was begun.

46a. Charles Lyell wrote to Miss Horner soon after:

> Dined at the Geological Society club. Majendie [Magendie], the famous French physiologist, sent by the Institute to Sunderland about cholera, dined with us. [4] He complains of the public hospital. Agrees well with the opinion which you sent me about Mittau, that in general the less you do, the more you leave it to nature, the better. A pleasant club. Stokes, Greenough, Buckland, Lord Cole, Broderip, and a few more. Murchison was pheasant-shooting in the country, but cut in for the meeting. A short paper on Springs, and another by Mr. Hutton on the Whin Sill of Yorkshire, drew up Buckland, Greenough, Fitton, Murchison, and De la Beche; and as they seemed much disposed to go on for ever, Buckland speaking five times, but not once too often, I was glad to sit quiet, having held forth at such length on the new isle, &c. last time.
>
> Lyell 1881, 1, p357

47. 1832, January 18

An essay, "On the geological structure of the Crimea", by Baron Stanislaus Chaudoir, communicated by Sir Alexander Crichton, K.W.S., F.G.S., F.R.S. was read.

47a. Charles Lyell wrote to Miss Horner on 19 January:

> We had a very full meeting at the Geological Society, Henslow being there, and his famous paper on Anglesea incidentally alluded to. [5] Conybeare got up, and quoted some lines from Pindar on the feats of the infant Hercules, as he observed that Henslow's first paper was such a masterpiece. At which 'the first of men' [6] rose, and begged to observe, that as mythological allusions were introduced, he must inform them that Henslow was making his first tour with <u>him</u>, his master in geology, when he went off on that expedition; so that, like Minerva, he had sprung full-armed from the head of JOVE!
>
> Lyell, 1881, 1, p366

48. 1832, February 1

A paper was read, "On the deposits overlying the carboniferous series in the valley of the Eden, and on the north-western coasts of

Cumberland and Lancashire", by the Rev. Adam Sedgwick, F.G.S., F.R.S., Woodwardian Professor in the University of Cambridge, &c.

48a. Charles Lyell wrote to Miss Horner on 3 February:

> Just returned from the Geological Society, having dined at the club, and since taken an active part in a debate, with Sedgwick, Conybeare, De la Beche, Fitton, Greenough, and others – which was prolonged unusually till half-past ten o'clock – 'on the old and new red sandstone', and other dryish subjects, which Adam made entertaining. The paper was by him. The attendance was quite splendid, very numerous, and all the best men there.
>
> Lyell 1881, 1, p368

49. 1832, February 17

Annual General Meeting at which Roderick Murchison was re-elected President and read the Anniversary Address.

49a. Charles Lyell wrote to Miss Horner on 19 February:

> On Friday I went to the General Meeting and the Anniversary Dinner of the Geological Society, at the Crown and Anchor – a splendid meeting. Near the President sat Lords Milton, Morpeth, Cavendish; Sir John Malcolm, Sir J. Herschel, Sir J. Johnston, M.P., Sir R. Vyvyan, Sir C. Lemon, and other M.P.s. Literature represented by Hallam, Lockhart, Sotheby, &c. Geologicals – Buckland, Conybeare, Fitton, Greenough, Sedgwick. Then from Cambridge, Whewell, and many other good men. All the best geological residents in town. Murchison was ill, but got through the fatigue very respectably indeed. All the speeches were short, and many of them able. I was glad when mine was over, but Murchison made my reply easy, by giving me something to say off-hand, as he told them he should say nothing of my book till the evening; and I told them I should follow the President's example, in thinking that they would have enough of me if they heard of me once in a day. Hallam asked to be introduced, and talked of Bonn friends. Ferguson of Raith asked me to walk with him from the tavern to Somerset House, and asked after you all. There were about one hundred and thirty at the dinner, and a hundred of them picked men.
>
> Lyell 1881, 1, p372

The Meetings

50. 1832, March 14

A paper was read which described:
1st. The structure of the Cotteswold Hills and country around Cheltenham,
2nd. The occurrence of stems of fossil plants in vertical positions in the sandstone of the inferior oolite of the Cleveland Hills, by Roderick Impey Murchison, Esq., P.G.S., F.R.S., &c.

50a. Joseph Prestwich wrote in his diary:

At 1/2-past 8 went to the Geological Society; heard a very animated and interesting discussion on the Oolitic fomations. Messrs Murchison, Conybeare, Sedgwick, De la Beche, Lyell, Greenough spoke; asked Dr Turner to propose me as a member.
Prestwich 1899, p35

51. 1832, June 13

A paper was first read, entitled, "Observations on the London Clay of the Highgate Archway", by Nathaniel Wetherell, Esq., F.G.S.

A paper was afterwards read giving, "An account of the discovery of portions of three skeletons of the Megatherium in the province of Buenos Ayres in South America", by Woodbine Parish, jun. Esq., His Majesty's Charge d'Affaires and Consul General at Buenos Ayres, followed by a description of the bones by William Clift, Esq., F.G.S., F.R.S., &c., &c.

51a. Charles Lyell wrote to Gideon Mantell on 14 June:

Buckland was really powerful last night on the Megatherium, a lecture of an hour before a crowded audience, only standing room for a 3d. Lots of anatomists there, paper by Clift, gigantic bones exhibited & still to be seen but likely to be removed by & by. Try by all means to get to G.S. and see them. Buckland made out that the beast lived on the ground by scratching for <u>yams</u> & <u>potatoes</u>, & was covd. like armadillo by a great coat of mail (it exhibd. on table) to keep the dust from getting into his skin as it threw it up. As it was as big as an elephant the notion of some that he burrowed underground must be abandoned. "We may absolve him of the imputation of having been a borough-monger indeed from what I before said you will have concluded that he was rather a <u>radical</u>". He concluded by pointing out that the structure of the sloth was beautifully fitted for the purposes to wh. he was intended so Megatherium from his habits. Buffon therefore & Cuvier even in describing the sloth as awkward & C the Mega-error – They are as admirably formed as the gazelle. &c.

TL Mantell, f62

Notes, 1831-1832

1. The only visitors recorded on this night were Mr Goodhall jun, Mr Henry Harton and Dr Wight.
2. The Society's manuscript minutes attribute the memoirs to Professor Hoffman of Berlin, not Von Buch. This is confirmed by Lyell's report.
3. Lyell and Cooke left London in June 1830 and travelled through France to the Pyrenees, Cooke pressing on into Spain when Lyell returned to England (Wilson 1972, pp294-303).
4. François Magendie was sent to England by the Acadèmie des Sciences to investigate the cholera outbreak which afflicted Sunderland from late October 1831. He arrived in Sunderland on 2 December, was back in London by 14 December, and returned to Paris for Christmas (Olmsted 1944, pp181-191).
5. Henslow 1822.
6. Adam Sedgwick.

Session 1832-1833

52. 1832, November 7

A paper entitled, "Notices on the geology of the North-west of the Counties of Mayo and Sligo", by the Venerable Archdeacon Verschoyle, and communicated by Roderick Impey Murchison, Esq., P.G.S., was begun.

53. 1832, November 21

The reading of Archdeacon Verschoyle's paper, begun at the meeting held on the 7th of November, was concluded.

A communication was then read from the Rev. Adam Sedgwick, V.P.G.S. and Woodwardian Professor in the University of Cambridge, respecting certain fossil shells overlying the London clay in the Isle of Sheppey.

The Meetings

53a. Charles Lyell wrote to Gideon Mantell on 26 November:

Last Wedy. we had a notice by Sedgwick on the discovery of a bed of recent shells resting on the London Clay at the height of 140 ft. above the level of the sea in Sheppey; 5 or 6 species – turbo littoreus, ostrea edulis, cardium edule, buccinum antiquum & some others of our coast. They think it not crag because recent shells, but I doubt, for I fancy they are all common to the crag & so few wd show nothing as to proportion. But at all events it is important, & Capt Kater seems to have found a similar deposit near Ramsgate on London clay, 6ft. high above beach. But I have not yet seen his specimens.

TL Mantell, f62

54. 1832, December 5

A paper was read, entitled, "Observations on the Remains of the Iguanodon, and other fossil Reptiles, of the Strata of Tilgate Forest in Sussex", by Gideon Mantell, Esq., F.G.S., R.S. and L.S.

54a. Gideon Mantell wrote in his diary:

To Somerset House and prepared for the evening's lecture. Dr. Buckland joined me to whom I read the principal parts of my paper and pointed out the characters of my new fossil. At eight joined the Society; a very full meeting; all my friends there – my kind friend Mr Bakewell, though infirm had even ventured out; Chassereau and Weekes too were present. I was allowed to read my paper, but was directed to curtail it one-third lest it should be too long, which was a great annoyance, at so short a notice. However all passed off very well, and at the conclusion I had the painting let down, which very much gratified the greater part of the audience. [1] After this, to my great astonishment, Dr. Buckland commented on many parts of my statement, and assumed that he had suggested that the spines belonged to the back of the animal, and in a strain so wholly unlike the candid and liberal manner in which he had always acted towards me, contended that there was not the least doubt of the fact, although in truth nothing could be more perplexing than to explain how this could have been effected; as Mr. Clift, Owen and all the comparative anatomists present agreed. I replied to Dr. B's arguments and from the applause which followed my address I believe satisfactorily. My kind friends Mr Lyell and Dr Fitton successively addressed the Society in a too partial strain in my favor. On the whole I had every reason to be

Session 1832-33

highly gratified with the reception my discovery met with: but I was hurt beyond measure at the treatment, the unmerited treatment, I received from Dr Buckland, whose wishes I had always endeavoured to fulfil, and had that very morning sat up till past three to assist him!

SAS Mantell, quoted in Curwen 1940, p110

54b. Gideon Mantell's biographer recorded:

Bakewell had never joined any of the scientific societies and the only meeting of the Geological Society he attended was the one at which Mantell read his account of the discovery of the Hylaeosaurus, and showed the fossil bones from Tilgate Forest. Bakewell on that occasion was so carried away by his kindly feelings towards the author, that, contrary to the etiquette of the Society, at the close of the address he applauded loudly, and others then joined in.

Spokes 1927, p153

55. 1833, January 9

An Essay, entitled, "Observations on Coal", by W. Hutton, Esq., F.G.S. was first read.

A communication, "On Ophiura found at Child's Hill, to the N.W. of Hampstead", by Nathaniel Thomas Wetherell, Esq., F.G.S. was then read.

55a. James Mitchell wrote to Samuel Woodward a few days later:

The most interesting paper read at the Geological Society was on the 9th instant from Mr Hutton about coal. By the aid of the microscope the grand fact that coal is of vegetable origin has at last been fully & undeniably made out. and further the structure of the coal is ascertained to be exactly the same as that of the canes and cactuses found in the coal formations plants within the tropics or a little to the north of the tropics. It is important to have question set at rest & the fact established on such a solid foundation that it may be built upon.

CMN Woodward, 1833, f1

The Meetings

55b. Charles Lyell wrote to Gideon Mantell a few days later:

Last Wedy. we had a paper by Hutton shewing that every vein of Newcastle coal retains its vegetable structure! when you cut thin slices & magnify them.

TL Mantell, f62

Note, 1832-1833

1. This was a large painting by Mr Warren Lee of the restored hind limb of the Iguanodon (Curwen 1940, p110).

Session 1833-1834

56. 1834, January 22

A paper was read, "On the structure and classification of the Transition rocks of Shropshire, Herefordshire and part of Wales, and on the lines of disturbance which have affected that series of deposits, including the valley of elevation of Woolhope", by Roderick Impey Murchison, Esq., F.R.S., F.G.S., &c.

56a. Roderick Murchison wrote to Sir Philip Egerton on 3 February:

By accident I had a very good dress circle on my second night, for besides Buckland, Warburton, Lyell, De la Beche and performers who <u>could</u> understand it, the President of H.M. Council, the M. [Marquis] of Lansdowne, dined with me at the club, having quitted a Colonial Council to do so, and he sat it all through the evening.

Geikie 1875, 1, p221

57. 1834, February 21

Annual General Meeting, at which George Bellas Greenough read the Anniversary Address and was re-elected President.

57a. James Mitchell wrote to Samuel Woodward on 30 September:

I have been infomed that Mr Mantell of Lewes, or rather Brighton, is not a little displeased that Mr Greenough did not mention his discoveries in his last address. All together public societies though useful are all much perverted to feed the wants of a narrow junta, who in each several case get into the administration. Hence they bring forward themselves, employ the funds in publishing their own lucubrations & smother other men all that they can. Such is human nature – so we must submit to it.

CMN Woodward, 1834, f 121

58. 1834, February 26

A paper, "On the quantity of solid matter suspended in the waters of the Rhine", by Leonard Horner, Esq., F.G.S., F.R.S. was first read.

A paper was next read, entitled, "Observations on the geological structure of the neighbourhood of Reading", by J. Rofe, Esq., and communicated by Robert Hunter, Esq., F.G.S.

58a. Charles Lyell wrote to Leonard Horner on 26 February:

> Your paper is positively to come on to-night – first my Pyrenees, then you, then Egerton. I stood out for this arrangement, as we had priority by right. The answering was a heavy business. Greenough not in spirits, Buckland heavy, no Sedgwick. [1] I communicated some information received the same day from Boué about the Strasbourg meeting, and the Stuttgart reception of the savans, which the King of Wurtemburg is preparing. [2] I also took occasion to recommend those who were going to the Continent to visit Germany, and praised their geologists, and stated how interesting the geology of Germany was in relation to our own. Lastly, I gave a rapid sketch of the controversy about the level of the Baltic and rise of Sweden, and announced that I was going there.
>
> Fitton's short speech was the only one which made them laugh. Dublin and Fitton was the toast. He descended on Antrim, and said that Playfair told him that when he (Playfair) visited the Giant's Causeway the sea was rough, a swell, what in Ireland would be called a state of <u>agitation</u>. The boatman proud, as all Irishmen are of their country, and annoyed that the stranger gentleman should be disappointed, after two ineffectual attempts to get to the Causeway, said, 'Your honour sees that it's not the sea that is out of humour: the sea (say) would be quiet, your honour, if the wind would but let her alone'. The speakers were Greenough, Buckland, Sir T. Ackland, Sir J. Johnston, Murchison, Fitton, De la Beche, Lyell, J. Taylor, Dr. Turner. Fitton's account of Greenough's speech

was that more than half of it was employed in pelting Lyell with nonsense, and at the end summing up in his favour.

Lyell 1881, 1, p404

59. 1834, March 12

A paper was read, entitled, "Observations on the Temple of Serapis at Pozzuoli, near Naples; with Remarks on certain Causes which may produce Geological Cycles of great extent", in a Letter to W. H. Fitton, M.D. from Charles Babbage, Esq.

59a. Charles Lyell wrote to Roderick Murchison on 15 March:

> I quite agree more especially from what I heard at the Brit. Mus. yesterday from some of their folk who were at G.S. last Wedy that the false impression made on the novices by the opposition of G [Greenough] is most injurious & that we cannot too often impress upon them, more especially when the P. [President] is not in the chair, that the denier & doubter of <u>all</u> elevation is in a minority of <u>one</u>, absolutely of <u>one</u> if we enumerate <u>all</u> our working & thinking geologists. You are perfectly right in thinking that the audience, such is the weight of G's name as author of the map, 3 are perfectly bewildered & think that nothing is agreed.

GSL Murchison, L, 17/16

60. 1834, April 9

A paper was first read, entitled, "A short notice of the Coast Sections from Whitstable in Kent to the North Foreland in the same County", by William Richardson, Esq., F.G.S.

A paper was afterwards read, "On the several Ravines, Passes, and Fractures in the Mendip Hills and other adjacent Boundaries of the Bristol Coal-field, and on the geological Period when they were effected", by the Rev. David Williams, F.G.S.

60a. James Mitchell wrote to Samuel Woodward on 30 April:

> At last meeting but one at the Geological Society I had an opportunity of expressing my sentiments on the subject of what is called the London Basin. I denied its existence in toto as being a mere figment of the imagination having not one single proof in its support, and quoted my experience in my researches in all the

Counties round London. The attempt at a defence of the term Basin was exceedingly feeble – In fact it was all but abandoned.

Where an attempt has been made to lay it down on paper it is a mere piece of guessing.

Another member defied them to find any thing like a boundary to the so called Basin in any one place whatever. I am sure they cannot, and it is one of the dreams of the Geologists of the beginning of this century which will be laughed at & quite out of faith before 1850 if be not nearly so already.

CMW Woodward, 1834, f61

Notes, 1833-1834

1. Lyell is here describing the Club dinner, held before the Society meeting.
2. The annual meeting of the Versammlungen deutscher Naturforscher und Ärzte was held in Stuttgart in September 1834. King Wilhelm I of Wurtemberg, a liberal man interested in cultural and scientific questions, presumably held a soirée in connection with the meeting. The Strasburg meeting has not been identified.
3. Greenough 1820.

Session 1834-1835

61. 1834, November 5

A paper was read, "On a new classification of fishes, and on the geological distribution of fossil fishes", by Prof. Agassiz, of Neuchatel.

61a. Charles Lyell wrote to Gideon Mantell a few days later:

Agassiz's paper went off famously at Geol. Socy. He has given us a great excitement to obtain a knowledge of the vertebrata, & I bought a good skeleton of a hedgehog on which he gave a most interesting lecture. I am getting Flower to make up some fish skeletons.

TL Mantell, f63

61b. James Mitchell wrote to Samuel Woodward on 28 February:

Dr Buckland spoke in raptures of the paper as affording a new guide to geologists, and enabling them by means of the fishes to determine the identity and the age of the strata. It appeared to me

The Meetings

that he was over sanguine, which I believe is to a considerable degree his natural temperament – Fishes occur too seldom to be of great utility as a Geological guide, even if their indications were more conclusive and intelligible than I apprehend them to be.

CMN Woodward, 1835, f30

62. 1834, November 19

A paper was first read, entitled, "An account of the raised beach, near Hope's Nose, in Devonshire, and other recent disturbances in that neighbourhood", by Alfred Cloyne Austen, Esq., F.G.S.

A paper, entitled, "Some facts in the geology of the central and western portions of North America, collected principally from the statements and unpublished notices of recent travellers", by Henry Darwin Rogers, Esq., F.G.S. was then begun.

62a. Adam Sedgwick wrote to Henry De la Beche on 17 December:

I happened to be present when Austen's paper was read, & I do not remember that he [Lyell] made any allusion to your former paper. [1] This, at least, I am certain, that no remarks were made in an offensive form. It was a plain matter of fact production in which he dwell't at considerable length upon a raised beach. Why then your informant supposed this to be personal to <u>De la Beche</u> I know not. They called on me to speak, whether I would or no, for I had not been in the meeting room for twelve months before in consequence of my accident last year. I attacked Greenough right & left on the subject of elevation, & then, for fear of going too far on this tack, turned round to compliment him by saying that we were on the subject of these Devonshire limestones <u>coming back to his old opinions</u> &c. &c. In short, as far as I remember what passed, there was not either in the paper or the debate afterwards a single syllable which need hurt your feelings. Indeed I do not remember that your paper was alluded to: but in this I may be mistaken.

NMW De la Beche

63. 1834, December 3

The reading of Mr Roger's paper was resumed and concluded.

A letter was then read from H. T. De la Beche, Esq., F.G.S. and addressed to the President, on the anthracite found near Biddeford [sic] in North Devon. [2]

A paper was afterwards commenced on the physical and geological structure of the country to the west of the dividing range between Hunter's River (lat. 32 south) and Moreton Bay (lat. 27 south), with observations on the geology of Moreton Bay and Brisbane River, New South Wales, by Allan Cunningham, Esq. and communicated by William Henry Fitton, M.D., F.G.S.

63a. George Greenough wrote to Henry De la Beche on 4 December:

Your Bideford paper gave rise yesterday evening to a very animated discussion. Murchison led the attack, and expressed his astonishment that so experienced a Geologist should have fallen into so great a mistake as to fancy that the specimens on the table had anything to do with transition rocks. As no one offered to speak on the other side, I ventured to affirm that you had not committed the mistake attributed to you, adding that Murchison had confessedly never seen the country, & that you had examined it attentively, that it was not our practice to give credit to the results of abstract reasoning when opposed to actual observation, that the strata in the north of Devon were well laid open to view, & that for miles together &c.&c. Lyell then rose, being equally ignorant of the country and supported Murchison's view with so much spirit as to excite the cheers of several of his hearers. Turner answered him, and Yates, who had also spoken on the side of Murchison; saying that the rocks in the neighbourhood of Bideford had all the mineralogical characters at least of Greywacke & had been generally considered as such, and if the specimens now on the table did not exhibit those characters, the probable reason was that you had not anticipated the doubts which had been expressed, and consequently had thought it unnecessary to send specimens of well characterized Greywacke. Murchison repeated his conviction that you had made a mistake confounding things essentially different & supposing the Coal plants to be regularly interstratified with the Greywacke when in point of fact they formed a separate series resting on its edges. This I denied, as far as I could rely on my own observations made some years since indeed but perfectly present to my mind, and stated that the Bideford culm beds were traceable for miles together running parallel to the other beds of the Greywacke formation, which instead of lying over the Ludlow series as Murchison fancied, reminded me strongly of the Beds with which he was well acquainted at Can's office, [3] lying low down in the Welsh series. I added with a view to pacify my opponents that in the neighbourhood of Tenby there were beds alternating with Coal, so like Greywacke, that Buckland & myself were for a long time deceived into a belief that we were looking at transition rocks, & I suggested a possibility that these Tenby beds might perhaps be related to the Bideford and both to the Coal Measurers of Kanturk in Ireland described by Weaver. I instanced the Calvados case [4] to shew that the position you had assigned to the Bideford coal was not so unexampled as had been stated & asked whether it was likely that such practised observers as you & Weaver should both have fallen into the same error, if the error were one as clear as my opponents, reasoning wholly upon what ought to be, not what was, assumed. these remarks produced a new attack from Murchison. Could it have been imagined that such a line of argument should have been taken by the President? with great respect of the chair he differed from him toto caelo. was it to be endured that at this time of day & in this room they should still hear mineralogical characters relied on as tests of geological position? Was greywacke to be called greywacke because it had the external characters of greywacke? had not Mr. Agassiz taught us only a fortnight ago that black was white? that the Glarus slate was good honest chalk &c. &c. – so ended the conflict. Murchison declared he would never use the Word Greywacke again so long as he lived, and departed. All this was very amusing but such discussions I am sure will not tend to the benefit of science or to the credit of the Society, & had I not myself been a party to that which took place yesterday, I should have expressed that sentiment publicly.

NMW De la Beche

63b. Edward Turner wrote to Henry De la Beche on 7 December:

You will have heard from Greenough how your discovery of Coal & its fossil in the Greywacke was last Wednesday turned topsy turvy without scruple; but I think it also as well that my account of the adventure should also be sent. Murchison, in fact, said that he had never seen the Country, but would nevertheless take upon himself to affirm, so identical were the fossils with those of the ordinary coal fields, that your coal also belonged to the carboniferous beds. Certainly no man could speak more positively on the subject. I asked as soon as Murchison ceased whether he supposed the coal to be an accidental deposit in the Greywacke, or that the rocks generally along the Coast of Devon were not Greywacke but belonged to the Carboniferous series. He supposed the fomer. Greenough defended you as well as he could, his argument lying chiefly on th ground that there was nothing unreasonable in the expectation that coal should occur in Greywacke. Lyell then spoke, more guardedly then Murchison, but inclined to the same side. Then, seeing that no one had any thing more to say, I said as much as I could for an absent man. I argued that the rocks in that coast of Devon were so well exposed and so regular that a Geologist of your practice could not be so far deceived as to suppose the Coal of the same age with the interstratified Greywacke when it was not so. I said that the only error which appeared to me possible, was the supposition that you had erred along with the President and all other Geologists who had seen North Devon in mistaking for Greywacke, rocks of the Carboniferous series. I was unable to prove from fossils what the age really was, but affirmed that the mineralogical characters were well pronounced, admitting at the same time the possibility of deception by mere mineralogical character. The Society obviously leaned to the side espoused by Murchison.

NMW De la Beche

63c. Charles Lyell wrote to Henry De la Beche on 2 January 1835:

There was nothing for you to complain of in the debate, but Greenough got nettled, perhaps with reason, tho' I don't plead guilty. He used some of his two-edged arguments & was put down in an over careless way, especially for a chairman.

NMW De la Beche

64. 1834, December 17

The reading of a paper, "On the physical and geological structure of the country to the west of the dividing range between Hunter's River (lat. 32 south) and Moreton Bay (lat. 27 south), with observations on the geology of Moreton Bay and Brisbane River, New South Wales", by Allan Cunningham, Esq., and communicated by W. H. Fitton, M.D., F.G.S. begun on the 3rd December, was resumed and concluded.

A paper was next read, entitled, "An account of land and freshwater shells found associated with the bones of land quadrupeds beneath diluvial gravel, at Cropthorn [sic] in Worcestershire", by Hugh Edwin Strickland, Esq., F.G.S.

The Meetings

A paper was afterwards read, "On the bones of certain animals which have been recently discovered, in the calcareo-magnesian conglomerate on Durdham Down, near Bristol", by the Rev. David Williams, F.G.S.

A paper, "On the chalk and flint of Yorkshire, compared with the chalk and flint of the southern counties of England", by James Mitchell, LL.D., F.G.S. was then read.

A notice, "On the want of perpendicularity of the standing pillars of the Temple of Jupiter Serapis near Naples", by Capt. Basil Hall, R.N., F.G.S. was afterwards read.

64a. Roderick Murchison wrote to Henry De la Beche on 19 December:

The President after reading out in a most <u>impressive</u> manner your rejoinder, interdicted all observation thereon. [5] Upon this our impartial Censor, Fitton gave <u>us all</u> (from the President downwards) a solemn flagellation. The President catching it for his interdict & the stoppage of free discussion, your opponents for having been too <u>vifs</u>. We had an interesting paper from young Strickland on his case of 23 species of lake & fluviatile shells under Diluvium to the discussion of which we gave ourselves up and I journeyed home in the President's carriage.

NMW De la Beche

65. 1835 January 21

A paper was first read, "On an outlying basin of Lias on the borders of Salop and Cheshire, with a short account of the lower Lias between Gloucester and Worcester", by Roderick Impey Murchison, Esq., V.P.G.S.

A paper was afterwards read entitled, "A general view of the new red sandstone series, in the counties of Salop, Stafford, Worcester, and Gloucester", by Roderick Impey Murchison, Esq., V.P.G.S.

A letter was also read from Thomas Weaver, Esq., F.G.S. addressed to George Bellas Greenough, Esq., P.G.S.

65a. Roderick Murchison wrote to Adam Sedgwick on 22 January:

Last night I gave the Society 2 memoirs the first of which was on my basin 10 miles by 5 miles broad in North Salop, 50 miles from the <blank> The Second was on the New Red Sandstone of

Gloster, Worcester, <blank> Stafford & Salop. The novelty in this paper consisted in shewing on many points powerful trappeous conglomerates like the <blank> at the base line of the formation in Worcestershire near certain Trappean rocks hitherto undescribed (Abberley, Rosemary Rock, <blank> Warshill &c) as well as on some points south of the Malverns ... I wish much you had seen them for no one present understood any thing about it & Greenough from the chair said there was little new matter. If he had had I have encountered in working out these facts he would not have so spoken.

CUL Sedgwick, transcript in Add 7652, IIID, 7

66. 1835, February 20

Annual General Meeting at which George Greenough read the Anniversary Address and Charles Lyell, Esq. was elected President.

66a. Charles Lyell wrote to Gideon Mantell on 21 February:

The dinner went off famously, more than a hundred persons. After the toasts had been given of the King, Royal Fam, Geol. Socy, late Prest, & Prest, I gave you. I send you a copy of my speech almost word for word as delivered & on looking over my notes I found I had not omitted any of the material points which I had intended to speak of. I assure you I had the feeling of the meeting with me & in some respects it produced a better effect than if you had been there. It was by far the longest toast given but I am sure they were not tired. Ld. Lansdowne who was on my left hand asked all about you. I got him to give Oxford & Buckland. Fitton gave Cambridge answered by Sedgwick. Sedgwick the R.S. [Royal Society] answered by Lubbock. Buckland the Linnaean. I the Astronomical answered by Baily. Greenough the Geographl answered by Murchison. We then drank Burnes the traveller who made a good speech. Warburton also held forth as Vice Pres. & I wound up by a eulogium on Lonsdale which I did con amore, & it was received with enthusiasm. We adjourned late to hear Greenough's address, a matter-of-fact abstract of the proceedings of last year. As a specimen of the extracts from it which he read, he read a list of all the sixteen elementary substances of which De la Beche supposes the earth's crust to be made!! On my right hand at the dinner I had the Belgian minister, Van de Weyer. Among others there were Hallam, Stokes, Lord Cole, Sir Charles Lemon, Duncan of Oxford, Sir A. Crichton, Ingham, M.P., Drinkwater, &c. &c.

TL Mantell, f63/116, partly quoted in Lyell 1881, 1, p447

The Meetings

67. 1835, June 10

A paper was first read, entitled, "Note on the Trappean Rocks associated with the (New) Red Sandstone of Devonshire", by Henry T. De la Beche, For.Sec.G.S.

A memoir was next read, "On the range of the Carboniferous Limestone flanking the primary Cumbrian Mountains; and on the Coalfields of the N.W. Coast of Cumberland, &c.", by the Rev. Adam Sedgwick, F.G.S., Woodwardian Professor in the University of Cambridge and Williamson Peile, Esq., F.G.S. of Whitehaven.

A paper was afterwards read, "On the occurrence near Shrewsbury of Marine Shells of existing species in transported Gravel and Sand, resting upon a peat bog which contains embedded Trees", by Joshua Trimmer, Esq., F.G.S.

A paper was also read, entitled, "Description of some Fossil Crustacea and Radiata", by William John Broderip, Esq., F.G.S., F.R.S., &c.

A letter from Sir Philip de Malpas Grey Egerton, Bart., M.P., V.P.G.S., addressed to the President, "On the Discovery of Ichthyolites in the South-western Portion of the North Staffordshire Coalfield", was then read.

A paper was next read, "On the Bones of Birds from the Strata of Tilgate Forest in Sussex", by Gideon Mantell, Esq., F.G.S.

The next paper read was entitled, "Remarks on the Coffin-bone (distal phalangeal) of a Horse, from the Shingle Bed of the Newer Pliocene Strata of the Cliffs near Brighton", by Gideon Mantell, Esq., F.G.S., &c.

An extract was lastly read, of a letter from Dr. Daubeny.

67a. Charles Lyell wrote to Gideon Mantell on 21 June:

> I got your two papers into the last meeting but not without exerting my authority as Prest. In the first place, I made the Secrety. read only the titles, instead of long abstracts of the Papers read at the last meeting, & thus gained more than ten minutes. De la Beche, Sedgwick, Egerton & Broderip & Trimmer had papers, but I enlarged on your bird bones & told the story of the turtle's eggs in relation to them. [6]
>
> TL Mantell, f64

Notes, 1834-1835

1. It is not clear to which earlier paper Sedgwick is referring.
2. The background to this important paper is given in Rudwick 1985, chapter 5.
3. This locality has not been identified.
4. The Calvados case was described some years later in Austen 1845.
5. De la Beche's rejoinder is not referred to in the minutes of the meeting (Geological Society Archives, CM1/4).
6. Lyell had written to Mantell about some fossil turtle eggs from the Ascension Islands in April 1835 (Lyell 1881, 1, p447).

Session 1835-1836

68. 1835, November 18

A letter was first read from Dr. Pingel of Copenhagen to the President, containing a notice of some facts showing the gradual sinking of part of the west coast of Greenland.

Some notes by Capt. Fitzroy, R.N. read at a court martial at Portsmouth, Oct 19th, 1835, on Capt. Seymour and his officers for the loss of His Majesty's Frigate Challenger, wrecked on the coast of Chili, near the port of Conception, and communicated to the President by Capt. Beaufort, R.N., Hon.Mem.G.S. were then read.

A letter dated Valparaiso, 22nd of March 1835, from R. E. Alison, Esq. addressed to the President, on the earthquake of Chili of the 20th February 1835, was then read.
"Geological notes made during a survey of the east and west coasts of South America, in the years 1832, 1833, 1834, and 1835, with an account of a transverse section of the Cordilleras of the Andes between Valparaiso and Mendoza", by F. Darwin, Esq., [sic] of St. John's College, Cambridge, communicated by Prof. Sedgwick, were afterwards read. [1]

68a. Charles Bunbury wrote to Charles Lyell a few days later:

> Dr. Somerville walked with me to Somerset House, put down my name as candidate for the Geological Society [2] and got leave for me to attend the Meeting this evening. Accordingly, I went thither a little after eight o'clock and stayed till eleven, much interested with what I heard.
>
> Lyell 1906, 1, p78

The Meetings

68b. Charles Bunbury wrote to his father on 29 November:

> Dr Somerville proposed me for a member of the Geological Society, and got admission for me to one of their meetings, where I heard some interesting papers on South American geology, and on the effects of the earthquake of February last in Chili. Mr Greenough made a speech of some length, in his usual spirit of scepticism, attacking the Lyellian theory, with a good deal of humour, but not much argument; he seems to have become as much wedded to doubts, as other men to their theories.
>
> Bunbury 1891, p152

68c. Edward Turner wrote to Henry De la Beche on 28 November:

> We had at the last Geological sundry interesting details respecting the rise of land and earthquake last Feb. along the coast of Chili. It was all nuts of course for our President.
>
> NMW De la Beche

69. 1836, June 8

A paper was first read, entitled, "Notice respecting a piece of Wood partly petrified by Carbonate of Lime; with some remarks on Fossil Woods, which it has suggested", by Charles Stokes, Esq., F.G.S.

A paper was next read, entitled, "Further notice on certain peculiarities of Structure in the Cervical Region of the Ichthyosaurus", by Sir Philip Grey Egerton, Bart., M.P., V.P.G.S.

A communication was afterwards made, "On the coal-fields on the north-western coast of Cumberland, &c., &c.", by the Rev. Professor Sedgwick, M.A., F.R.S., F.G.S. and Williamson Peile, Esq., of Whitehaven, F.G.S.

69a. James Mitchell wrote to Samuel Woodward a few days later:

> ... at 8 o'clock to the Geological Society – a very full meeting being the last in the session. Lyell, Buckland, Sedgwick, Murchison, Fitton, Stokes, Parish, Russell, H Gurney, Davies Gilbert, Dr. Mitchell, Prestwich, Rose &c. Mr Stokes read a paper on Fossil Wood. Sir P. Egerton another on the cervical vertebra of

the Ichthyosaur & Professor Sedgwick extemporised on the Coal of Cumbria. The discussion was not over until 11 o'clock.

CMN Woodward, 1836

Notes, 1835-1836

1. The author was Charles Robert Darwin, formerly of Christ's College, Cambridge.
2. Charles Bunbury was elected a fellow on 16 December 1835, Certificate No 1087.

Session 1836-1837

70. 1836, November 2

A paper was read, entitled, "A general sketch of the geology of the western part of Asia Minor", by Hugh Edwin Strickland, Esq., F.G.S.

70a. George Greenough wrote to Henry De la Beche on 11 November:

In the discussion that arose on Strickland's paper Murchison paid some well-deserved Compliments to himself for having first brought the Author & Hamilton together, without which these grand discoveries might never have been made.

NMW De la Beche

71. 1836, November 30

A paper, "On certain elevated Hills of Gravel containing Marine Shells in the vicinity of Dublin", by John Scouler, M.D., F.L.S., Professor of Mineraalogy [sic] in the Royal Dublin Society, and communicated by Robert Hutton Esq., F.G.S. was first read.
A paper, "On the Geology of the Thracian Bosphorus", by Hugh Edwin Strickland, Esq., F.G.S. and William John Hamilton, Sec.G.S. was then read.

71a. James Mitchell wrote to Samuel Woodward on 5 December:

We had Professor Sedgwick at the Geological Society last Wednesday and had a good speech from him. I could easily see that he was totally unacquainted with the contents of the gravel which cover a great part of the surface of the Eastern counties of England, but no man however great can discover every thing. Still, knowledge fell very far short of what I expected and he clearly was in error on several points. He is not at all aware of the tenth part of the things that have been drifted in this part of the country from the north.

CMN Woodward, 1836, f118

72. 1836, December 14

A paper, "On Impressions in Sandstone resembling those of horses' hoofs", by Charles Babbage, Esq. and communicated by the President, was first read.

A memoir, "On the occurrence of silicified trunks of large trees in the new red sandstone formation or Poikilitic series, at Allesley, near Coventry", by the Rev. Wm. Buckland, D.D., Professor of Geology and Mineralogy in the University of Oxford was then read.

A paper entitled, "Further notice on a partially petrified piece of wood from an ancient Roman aqueduet at Eilsen, in the Principality of Lippe-Buckeberg", by Charles Stokes, Esq., F.G.S. was next read.

"Description of a Raised Beach in Barnstaple Bay, on the northwest coast of Devonshire", by the Rev. Professor Sedgwick, F.G.S. and Roderick Impey Murchison, Esq., F.G.S. was afterwards read.

72a. Roderick Murchison wrote to Adam Sedgwick on 14 December:

We had 4 things before the meeting. 1 impression of <blank> (a squib) 2. Buckland's silicified tree in the New Red near Coventry (much ado about nothing, for neither the exact age of the sandstone, nor any geology of the district were made out) & 3dly a few additional remarks of old Stokes on the process of silicification & <blank> of lime. These <blank> brought about a very lengthened discussion which called up 1 or 2 clever chemists, & were very interesting in their way, but all attention was carried away from our paper, & indeed seeing the evening so far advanced & not wishing to protract discussion I myself declined to say any thing

Session 1836-37

more, when to my surprize up started Buckland, & said "Mr President As you have enjoined us not to discuss the memoir of Messrs Sedgwick & M. I will only declare on this occasion that I disagree <blank> with the authors & do not believe one word of it." & having said this down he sat evidently in a great rage!! This extraordinary ebullition of bad temper evidently electrified the meeting & certainly I never saw (in all the years I have known the Society) such an inroad upon our habits of good & gentlemanly feeling. Then, rose however immediately one or more persons who declared that so good a memoir should not be swamped in this way & it was moved & carried by acclamation that the subject be resumed at the next meeting. Fortunately for us our fat friend Parson Williams was seated behind Buckland & he rose to state that not only he could testify from ocular inspection this summer that all we had stated was correct, but that he had observed balani adherent to the cliff above high water mark !! Greenough was foaming to let out, but the meeting was adjourned, the President just allowing me to say 10 words which I endeavoured to say in perfect good humour & therefore had the <blank> on the Doctor, saying that in this question there was one Professor of a great University versus another, but that luckily a third Revd gentleman present corroborated our statement. On rallying Buckland afterwards in the tea room I found that the outburst was produced by the allusion you made to the Diluvian theory in your description of the old mistakes concerning the <blank> beaches in Cornwall. On this I said that you abused yourself as much as any one, in having been in error, and that I thought he Buckland had long ago abjured the old diluvial <blank> in its extended sense. but the shoe pinched & on being pressed, he declared that great waves going over the island at all heights will account for all the phenomena & that he does not believe in a single raised beach!!! This is 1836!!! In vain I told him that De la Beche & some of his best adherents were quite of our opinion he was not to be stirred. So you see what a kettle of fish I have to cook next meeting (3 weeks hence) I would give something to see you present. ... The truth is that Buckland is in a most irritable condition on account of his <blank> & various criticisms on his book, so he let it all off upon us. Had you been here in the temper you described yourself to be in when you last wrote there must have been a "flare up", for Buckland's words were most offensive & <blank>.

CUL Sedgwick, transcript in Add 7652, IIID, 11

72b. James Mitchell wrote to Samuel Woodward on 15 December:

Last night we had 4 papers read at the Geological, the last being an account of a raised beach by Messrs Sedgwick & Murchison. The discussion on the three first lasted so long as not to allow time for the consideration of the last paper, & I moved that it should take place at our next meeting 4 January which was adopted. Dr Buckland distinctly declared his disbelief in raised beaches. He said he could talk an hour on the subject. So I hope we shall have a good and a long continued fight. Buckland v. Sedgwick & another.

CMN Woodward, 1836, f122

73. 1837, January 4

A paper entitled, "Some Observations on the Elevation of the Strata on the Coast of Chili", by Alexander Caldcleugh, Esq., F.G.S., &c. was first read.

A paper entitled, "Observations of proofs of recent elevation on the coast of Chili, made during the survey of His Majesty's ship Beagle, commanded by Capt. Fitzroy, R.N.", by Charles Darwin, Esq., F.G.S. was afterwards read.

73a. John Ruskin wrote to his father a few days later:

I was in the meeting room of the Geological Society in Somerset House on Wednesday evening last at half-past 8 o'clock precisely. The Geologicals dropped in one by one, and it greatly strengthened me in my high opinion of the science, to phrenologize upon the bumps of the observers of the bumps of the earth. Many an overhanging brow, many a lofty forehead, bore evidence to the eminence of mind which calculates the eminences of earth; many a compressed lip and dark and thoughtful eye bore witness to the fine work within the pericraniums of their owners. One finely made, gentlemanly-looking man was very busy among the fossils which lay on the table, and shook hands with most of the members as they came in. His forehead was low and not very wide, and his eyes were small, sharp, and rather ill-natured. He took the chair, however, and Mr. Charlesworth, coming in after the business of the meeting had commenced, stealing quietly into the room, and seating himself beside me, informed me that it was Mr. Lyell. I expected a finer countenance in the great geologist. Dr. Buckland was not there, which was some disappointment to me, and some disadvantage to him, inasmuch as a ground of dispute had started in the last meeting, about the elevation or non-elevation of a beach near Barnstaple bay, in which Dr. B. had taken the non-elevation, and Dr. Sedgwick the elevation, side of the question, and the decision of which had been referred to this meeting. Both the doctors being absent, two of the members rose – Mr. Greenau [Greenough] for Dr. Buckland, and Mr. Murchison for Dr. Sedgwick, Mr. Lyell being on Sedgwick's side, though, as chairman, he took no part in the debate, which soon became amusing and interesting, and very comfortable for frosty weather, as Mr. Murchison got warm, and Mr. Greenau witty. The warmth, however, got the better of the wit, and the question, unsupported by Dr. Buckland, was decided against him. The rest of the evening was occupied by a discussion of the same nature relative to the coast of Peru and Chili, and I was much interested and amused, as well as instructed by the conversation of the evening. They did not break up till nearly 11.

Cook and Wedderburn 1909, 1, p910

73b. Charles Lyell wrote to Adam Sedgwick in April:

It is rare even in one's own pursuits to meet with congenial souls & Darwin is a glorious addition to my society of geologists & is working hard & making way both in his book & in our discussions. I really never saw that bore Dr. Mitchell so successfully silenced or such a bucket of cold water so dexterously poured down his back as when Darwin answered some impertinent & irrelevant questions about S. America. We escaped fifteen minutes of a vulgar harangue in consequence. Whewell does famously in the chair. [1]

Clark and Hughes 1890, 1, p484; also in Wilson 1972, p441

74. 1837, January 18

A paper entitled, "An Account of a deposit containing land shells at Gore Cliff, Isle of Wight", by J. S. Bowerbank, Esq., F.G.S. was first read.

A letter addressed to Dr. Buckland by J. Wyatt, Esq. respecting a trap dyke in the Penrhyn Slate Quarries near Bangor, Carmarthenshire, was then read.

A notice of a successful attempt at boring for water at Mortlake in Surrey, by William Richardson, Esq., F.G.S. was next read.

The Meetings

A paper, "On the Strata usually termed Plastic Clay", by John Morris, Esq. and communicated by the President, was then read.

A memoir on the Geology of Suffolk, by the Rev. W.B. Clarke, F.G.S. was then commenced.

74a. James Mitchell wrote to Samuel Woodward on 19 January:

> It is now four years since I first of all at the Geological Society distinctly asserted that there was no such thing as the Plastic Clay. Last night a long paper was read by a friend of mine who maintained the same thing. I had satisfied him on the subject. I supported his views, Another member did the same. At last it was admitted ex Cathedra that such was the case as we maintained. 2
> CMN Woodward, 1837, f6

75. 1837, February 1

A paper, "On the occurrence of Keuper Sandstone in the upper region of the New Red Sandstone fomation or *Poikilitic system* in England and Wales", by Professor Buckland, D.D., V.P.G.S., was first read.

A paper, "On the geological structure and phenomena of the northern part of the Cotentin, and particularly in the immediate vicinity of Cherbourg", by the Rev. W.B. Clarke, F.G.S., was then read.

75a. Roderick Murchison wrote to Adam Sedgwick on 2 February:

> The part of Hamlet being omitted, the play was not perfomed, and all the scenic arrangements which I had laboured at were thrown away, though the room looked splendid. The morning's arrivals certainly surprised me!! Ten o'clock brought me your double letter; eleven o'clock by the same mail the maps, and a little note to Lyell, but in vain I looked through the parcel for the document to be read. I read and re-read your letter, and still I could not understand it. One thing I clearly perceived, and with great regret, that you were seriously out of sorts, and had been suffering; so after waiting till two, I journeyed down to the Society, still thinking that a third package with the paper might be sent to Somerset House – not so however. These things going on; the whole room decorated for the fight; Buckland arrived; Fitton present; and a large meeting expected; what was to be done? Fitton

and Lonsdale, considering what had been said and done <u>covertly</u> on the other side, and looking to the fact of the non-arrival of the despatch, counselled me to give up the thing, which I resolved to do, to the very great annoyance of the President, and of all the others who came to hear ... [3]

We had a good discussion on Buckland's Keuper, on which Greenough and myself agreed about the absurd term poikilitic, backed by old Paddy [Fitton], so the spots were damned. [4] We had a supper at Cole's – Buckland, Horner, Stokes, the Viscount, Sir Phil, and my friend Rosthorn of Wolfsberg, and a great friend of the Archduke John's, present.

Geikie 1875, 1, p254, and Clark and Hughes 1890, 1, p476

76. 1837, February 22

A paper on the Geology of Cutch, by Captain Grant, of the Bombay Engineers, and communicated by Charles Lyell, Esq., F.G.S. was read.

76a. James Mitchell wrote to Samuel Woodward on 6 March:

Our new Geological President Mr Whewell has entered on his office, and I hope great good will be done through his influence. He laid down some sound views on the 22nd ubtr [ubiter] that Geologists should adhere to matter of fact; that they should rigorously prove their assertions; and that the Geology of one country should not be made a model to which they should try to make the geology of other countries conform; but that the geology of every country should be searched out according as it might be found to be.

CMN Woodward, 1837, f21

77. 1837, March 8

The reading of a paper, "On the Geological structure and phenomena of Suffolk, and its physical relations with Norfolk and Essex", by the Rev. W. B. Clarke, F.G.S. began on the 18th of January, was concluded.

A paper, "On the raised beaches of Saunton Downend and Baggy Point", by the Rev. David Williams, F.G.S. was then read.

A communication by Mr. James de Carle Sowerby on his new genus of fossil shells, Tropaeum, was then read.

The Meetings

77a. Charles Bunbury wrote in his diary:

Went in the evening to the meeting of the Geological Society, where I met Sedgwick, Whewell, and Murchison, and was introduced to Mr Darwin the naturalist, who is lately returned from the surveying expedition under Captain Fitzroy. I had hoped to hear an account of some of his discoveries read this evening, but I was disappointed. Sedgwick made a very amusing speech, in his peculiar style of rough and ready eloquence mingled with humour, on the subject of raised beaches, which one would hardly have supposed to admit of much rhetorical ornament.

Greenough answered him with more humour than soundness of argument, and maintained the old Wernerian notion that the sea had sunk, instead of the land being raised. Sedgwick, in his reply, justly characterised this hypothesis as wild and irrational.

Bunbury 1891, p240

77b. Charles Bunbury wrote to Edward Bunbury on 13 March:

Many thanks for your agreeable letter about Mr. Darwin. I went to the Geological Society last Wednesday, in hopes of hearing some of his discoveries stated, but I was disappointed: the papers that were read were very dull, and it was not till after they were finished that there was some fun, in the shape of an animated debate between Sedgwick and Greenough; the former was in his glory, and very entertaining on the subject of raised beaches, which one would hardly have thought a very favourable topic for the exercise of wit or humour. Greenough still sticks to his notion of the sea having sunk instead of the land being raised, but I almost think he must cling to it more from caprice or habit than conviction.

Whewell introduced me to Mr Darwin, with whom I had some talk; he seems to be a universal collector, and among other things, to the surprise of all the big wigs, he discovered an entirely new quadruped (recent), a kind of tiger-cat, in the immediate neighbourhood of Rio, where I did not suppose there were any wild quadrupeds at all, except rats. [5]

Lyell 1906, 1, p95

77c. James Mitchell wrote to Samuel Woodward on 5 April:

Dr Buckland I fear will never come to the scratch on elevated beaches. He has thrice spoken very audaciously of what he was to do, but has done nothing, and I suspect he feels now that the facts are against him.

Session 1836-37

As to the elevations in Chili the supporters of that notion have reduced their assertions now to very moderate limits, & the truth seems to be nearly settled amongst all parties. We have had the subject brought on by Lyell so often that it became tiresome. They now contend for only small and local elevations produced by the earthquakes. The idea of a whole country 200 miles long & 100 inland being raised 100 or so feet is totally abandoned tacitly at all events.

CMN Woodward, 1837, f35

78. 1837, May 31

A paper, "On the Physical Structure of Devonshire, and on the subdivisions and geological relations of its old stratified deposits", by the Rev. Adam Sedgwick, F.G.S. & R.S., Woodwardian Professor in the University of Cambridge and Roderick Impey Murchison, Esq., V.P.G.S., F.R.S. was commenced.

79. 1837, June 14

The paper [6] by Prof. Sedgwick and Mr. Murchison, on Devonshire, began at the last meeting, was concluded.

A paper was then communicated, "On the upper formations of the New Red System in Gloucestershire, Worcestershire and Warwickshire, showing that the Red (Saliferous) marls with an included band of sandstone, represent the Keuper or Marnes irisées, and that the underlying sandstone of Ombersley, Bromsgrove and Warwick, is part of the 'Bunter Sanstein', or 'Gres bigarré' of foreign geologists", by Roderick Impey Murchison, F.R.S., V.P.G.S. and Hugh Edwin Strickland, Esq., F.G.S.

79a. Thomas Sopwith wrote in his diary:

At 6 Mr. Buddle and I, on the invitation of Doctor Buckland dined at the Geological Club. About 30 were present. the Chair was filled by Mr. Whewell the President of the Society. Mr. John Taylor was in the Vice chair and I had the pleasure of sitting next to Dr. Buckland and of enjoying a most agreable conversation with him.
The following were our respective positions

The Meetings

	J Taylor	
?		Mr. Buddle
?		Mr. Murchison
Lord Cole		Dr. Buckland
?		T. Sopwith
Sir R. Donkin		Mr. Hutton

Dr. Buckland introduced me to Mr Hutton who is one of the Secretaries of the Geological Society, he also introduced Mr Buddle and I to Lord Cole. We partook of an excellent dinner and I greatly enjoyed the intelligence and vivacity which prevailed. At 1/4 past 8 we adjourned to the Society's rooms in Somerset House and as I walked arm in arm with Dr. Buckland who had an umbrella and a blue bag I requested his permission to carry the latter and felt gratified by this and other opportunities of enjoying the delightful vivacity & intelligence of this eminent and highly respected gentleman. "The greatest honor" said the Doctor "which my bag ever had was when Lord Grenville insisted on carrying it, and the greatest disgrace it ever had was when I called on Sir Hy. Davy three or four times one day and always found him out. At last Sir H.D. asked his servant, has Dr. Buckland not called today?

"No Sir – there has been nobody here today but a man <u>with a bag</u> who has been here three or four times and I always told him you were out".

The Meeting of the Geological Society was highly interesting. Professor Sedgewick read part of a paper till 1/2 past 9 on a new Coal formation in North Devon the geological position of which has become a party question of considerable moment. From 1/2 past 9 until after 11 was occupied in warm discussion on this point in [which] great eloquence and ability was displayed. – The Speakers were all Geologists of the first rate eminence and were as follows:

Mr. Greenough, former President of the Socy. who decried the policy of making minute local distinctions in geology and contended that these secondary matters should be all traced to general & extensive formations. he spoke somewhat warmly and had evidently prepared for the occasion, the question in some measure trenched on the accuracy of his Geological Map and for a similar reason De Le Beche followed closely on the same side, the Geological colouring of the Ordnance Maps under his immediate superintendance being a point more tender than that of Greenough's, inasmuch as the one is in some degree exonerated by its remote date while the latter professes to give the most approved modern discoveries. Dr. Fitton the author of a most able paper on the South Eastern Chalk districts, Mr. Murchison and Professor Sedgewick severally addressed the Chair and the balance of the argument was in my opinion decidedly theirs.

NUL Sopwith

79b. Mrs Owen wrote in her diary:

R[ichard] to the Geological Society. It was his introduction as a Fellow, and after a very interesting evening with Buckland, Whewell, Sedgwick, Murchison, de la Beche, Stokes &c., they all adjourned to Lord Cole's to supper.

R S Owen 1894, 1, p113

79c. Adam Sedgwick wrote to Canon Wodehouse on 15 June:

We had a grand battle at the Geological Society last night, in which I bore the brunt on our side; but though well banged, I was not beaten.

Clark and Hughes 1890, 1, p483

Notes, 1836-1837

1. It is not certain to which meeting this note refers.
2. For an earlier discussion of the Plastic Clay, see the meeting of 17 June 1825.
3. A joint paper by Murchison and Sedgwick on the geology of Devonshire was expected at this meeting (Rudwick 1985, pp186-195). It was eventually read on 30 May and 14 June 1837.
4. 'Poikilitic' comes from the Greek word for variegated or spotted.
5. No carnivores are described among Darwin's Mammalia in R Owen 1840.
6. The background to this paper is given in Rudwick 1985, pp212-214.

Session 1837-1838

80. 1837, December 13

A paper, "On the geology of the southeast of Devonshire", by Robert Alfred Cloyne Austen, Esq., F.G.S. was read.

80a. Robert Austen wrote to Henry De la Beche on 15 December:

My paper "came off" last night, and as yours was touching the culm, so likewise shall be my answer. I imagined that you understood what my notion was respecting this debatable land. My paper only noticed that portion in my own neighbourhood, but in answer to some questions touching it, I stated as follows: "In the North of Devon, the old transition rocks pass upwards into the carbonaceous beds, by a change of mineral character and absence of organic remains, and that the section admits of no equivoque whatever. The same appearences are presented along the whole of that line, and that the deposit in this direction has no real boundary. That on the opposite side by Launceston and Tavistock the same beds rest unconformably on the old fossiliferous rocks, but that as probably those rocks were not very old the amount of overlap was not very great. That the same beds could be carried round the E. extremity of Dartmoor, and formed a band between the granite and the old rocks of South Devon. That in this part they are found upon the edges of the whole of this series from the slates below the Bickington Limestone to the great limestone of Newton and Torbay. The age therefore of this limestone must determine the real age of the so-called culm beds. This I stated I believed to be mountain limestone. You will kick at this. Is its position opposed to this? No. are its fossils then of the M.L.? Yes. I produced upon the table <illegible> and with references to Phillips and Sowerby 2 36 character[istic] species of fossil shells. A list which you shall have if you like. Lonsdale says that the rocks from which my fossils come must be younger than any he has examined for Murchison. I am not as you know one of those who would settle any such question by reference to organic remains, but when ten rocks contain not one single species in common, I think we should attend to it. My conclusion was: That it is incorrect to separate the Carbonif. strata from the Transition, that it is only the upper portion of a thick series – unconformable at places owing to local disturbance but that as in N. Devon, and in many other places it is continuous with the red rocks, the want of conformity, when presented, is to be considered only as the exception, not the rule, and that if the name grauwacke is retained for the older rock the proper name of the culm-measures is upper or carbonaceous grauwacke. So that you see, that I have both yourself and S & M [Sedgwick and Murchison] against me in certain points, and perhaps between "battlement and battering ram" my notions will be smashed – but think the thing well over, and I should like to hear that you adhered to the Mountain lime.

NMW De la Beche

Session 1837-38

81. 1838, January 3

A paper was read, "On the Geological relations of North Devon", by Thomas Weaver, Esq., F.G.S., F.R.S., &c. [3]

81a. Roderick Murchison wrote to John Phillips the following day:

> The paper by old Weaver was read last night, and the fight is over. He has sided completely with S[edgwick] and self. Austen, a remarkably clever young geologist, is also with us; Major Harding from the first with us. The case therefore stands thus: For the old constitution – Greenough, De la Beche, and Parson Williams. On our side are the two geologists of Great Britain who have given the longest attention to the old fossiliferous strata, and their opinions are supported by every man who has gone into the tract to judge for himself.
> Geikie 1875, 1, p252, and Rudwick 1985, p231

82. 1838, February 16

Annual General Meeting at which the Rev. Prof. William Whewell was re-elected President and read the Anniversary Address.

82a. Charles Lyell wrote to Leonard Horner on 24 February:

> Mary is going to send you a journal, but, as she did not attend the anniversary, I will send you a short account of the meeting. Not so full as usual, and most of the M.P.s absent on the Irish Poor Law question; nevertheless a grand display of talent. Whewell in the chair, Sedgwick, Buckland, Sir P. Egerton, Darwin, Owen (who is wonderfully pleased at receiving the Wollaston medal), Fitton, Greenough, Hallam, Milman, Murchison, Lord Burlington, Prof. Jones, Lubbock, Bayley, Clift, Hamilton, and on the whole the great horseshoe table tolerably well filled. A short time before the meeting, Whewell told me that I should have nothing to do, unless I would propose the President, which as ex-President fell naturally to me. So I began the speaking, and said it would be impossible for them to appreciate Whewell's services in the chair, unless I reminded them in what an eventful year of his career as author and scientific workmen he had rendered those services. I therefore enumerated his doings in the year, beginning with three volumes on the Inductive Sciences. I mentioned that on my return from Norway and Denmark, I mentioned to Lodge, fellow of Cambridge,

how good a companion Whewell's last work had been to me, but soon found myself at cross purposes, as he had to tell me of <u>two</u> other works published since my absence, viz. the 'Mechanical Euclid', which had already come to a second edition, and secondly, the 'Studies of the University of Cambridge'. On my return home, I found his paper (eighth series), 'Experiments and Observations on the Tides' in 'Philosophical Transactions', for which the Royal Society soon after gave him the royal medal. On my expressing to my friend Mr Jones (who sat opposite me) my wonder that Mr. Whewell, entering so much into literary and scientific society, could possibly, with all his Cambridge professional duties, find time even to pass through the press so much matter, supposing he did not write a word, what was my astonishment when Prof. Jones told me that his friend Whewell, then staying with him in town, was actually then passing through the press <u>four other works</u>, viz. two new editions in different foms of his 'Bridgewater Treatise', and thirdly, a long article in the 'Medical Gazette', on Physiology of Nerves of Sensation and Volition, relatively to the Bell and Mayo controversy and claims, and fourthly those four sermons preached at Cambridge in November last, which I had read with much pleasure, in which he has treated of Butler's and Paley's views of morals, moral philosophy, &c. There may be other writings, and certainly a controversial letter to the 'Edinburgh Review', but I asked, if these alone were considered, not as monuments of one year, but of a lifetime, would it not be thought sufficient for the zeal and industry of one man, and yet in this year Whewell had made an efficient President of the Geological Society? I would not dwell on that labour of love, the eloquent address they had heard the opening of that morning, but his sacrifices in attending our meetings, and the time given to details of management, of getting a new secretary and other internal rearrangements of the Society's official business, for doing this in so busy a year, called for their acknowledgements. This address was well received, and Whewell replied modestly, fearing that most of them would think when they heard of so many works, that he had done too much to do any well. In proposing Owen, he put very well his being a fellow townsman and schoolfellow of his own. In proposing the different Societies, he made a beautiful allusion to Terence, saying, 'I am a man; homo sum, humani nihil a me alienum puto', and parodied it well, 'We are geologists, and we regard nothing in physics and natural history as foreign to our purpose'. Sedgwick was uncommonly splendid in replying for Cambridge, and pointing out the connection between abstract science cultivated there, and all general reasoning on particular facts, geological and others; such

reasoning alone raised us above the dregs of matter &c. Whewell drank the 'Strangers,' and Prof. Jones last, who made a truly eloquent speech, and very extemporaneous, on the similarity of the prospects of the two new sciences, different as they are in their subjects, geology and political economy. After the anniversary evening, Lord Cole pressed me so hard to go and eat pterodactyl (alias woodcock) pie at his rooms, that I went, with Whewell, Buckland, Owen, Clift, Egerton, Broderip, Hamilton, Major Clerk, Lord Adair; and there we were till two o'clock, fines inflicted of bumpers of cognac on all who talked any 'ology.
Lyell 1881, 2, p37

82b. Richard Owen wrote to his sister on 28 February:

My first number of Darwin's "Fossils" (strange animals) is out, and most unexpectedly the Geological Society has awarded me the Wollaston Gold Medal for that and other services to geology. Is it not curious that Whewell should happen to be in the chair this year? He presented it to me in full conclave with a very handsome speech, to which I made the best acknowledgements I could. At the anniversary dinner, which I attended the same day, Whewell, when he proposed my health, alluded to me very feelingly as a fellow-townsman and old schoolfellow. After dinner I adjourned to Lord Cole's and finished in the usual manner a happy day, but poor Mr Stokes was sadly missed. He was too ill to come.
R S Owen 1894, 1, p121

83. 1838, March 7

A notice was first read, "On some remarkable dikes of calcareous grit at Ethie, in Ross-shire", by Hugh Edwin Strickland, Esq., F.G.S.

A paper, "On the connexion of certain volcanic phenomena, and on the formation of mountain-chains and volcanos, as the effects of continental elevations", by Charles Darwin, Esq., Sec.G.S. was then read.

83a. Charles Lyell wrote to Leonard Horner on 12 March:

... about the last meeting of the G.S. where Darwin read a paper on the connexion of volcanic phenomena & elevation of mountain chains in support of my heretical doctrines; he opened upon de la Bêche, Phillips & others, for Greenough was absent, his whole battery of the earthquakes and volcanos of the Andes & argued that spaces at least a thousand miles long were simultaneously subject to earthquakes & volcanic eruptions & that the elevation of the whole Pampas, Patagonia etc. all depended on a common cause & also that the greater the contortions of strata in a mountain chain the smaller must have been each separate and individual movement of that long series which was necessary to upheave the chain. Had they been more violent he contended that the subterranean fluid matter wd. have gushed out & overflowed & the strata would have been blown up and annihilated. He therefore introduced a cooling of one small underground injection & then the pumping in of other lava or porphyry or granite into the previously consolidated & first formed mass of igneous rock. When he had done his description of the reiterated strokes of his volcanic pump, De la Beche gave us a long oration about the impossibility of strata in the Alps &c., remaining flexible for such a time as they must have done, if they were to be tilted, convoluted, or overturned by gradual or small shoves. He never, however, explained his theory of original flexibility, and therefore I am as unable as ever to comprehend why flexibility is a quality so limited in time. Phillips then got up and pronounced a panegyric upon the 'Principles of Geology', and although he still differed, thought the actual cause doctrine had been so well put, that it had advanced the science and formed a date or era, and that for centuries the two opposite doctrines would divide geologists, some contending the greater pristine forces, others satisfied like Lyell and Darwin with the same intensity as nature now employs. Fitton quizzed Phillips a little for the warmth of his eulogy, saying that he and others who had Mr. Lyell always with them, were in the habit of admiring and quarreling with him every day, as one might do with a sister or cousin whom one would only kiss and embrace fervently after a long absence. This seemed to be Mr. Phillips' case, coming up occasionally from the provinces. Fitton then finished his drollery by charging me with not having done justice to Hutton, who he said was for gradual elevation.

I replied, that most of the critics had attacked me for overrating Hutton, and that Playfair understood him as I did. Whewell concluded by considering Hopkins' mathematical calculations, to which Darwin had often referred. He also said that we ought not to try and make out what Hutton would have taught and thought, if he had known the facts which we now know. I was much struck with the different tone in which my gradual causes were treated by all, even including de la Beche from that which they experienced in the same room 4 years ago when Buckland, de la Beche, Sedgwick, Whewell and some others treated them with as much ridicule as was consistent with politeness in my presence.

Session 1837-38

PS. Monday – I found that Darwin, who was with us yesterday evening, had felt very different in regard to Wed's discussion for not being able to measure the change of tone in the last 4 years he translated de la B's & Co's remarks into a vigorous defiance instead of a diminishing fire & an almost beating of a retreat. But I have restored him to an opinion of the growing progress of the true cause.
Wilson 1972, p455, and Lyell 1881, 2, p39

84. 1838, April 25

A paper was first read, entitled, "Notes on a small patch of Silurian rocks to the west of Abergele, on the north coast of Denbighshire", by J. E. Bowman, Esq. and communicated by R. I. Murchison, Esq., V.P.G.S.

A notice, "On the occurrence of Wealden strata at Linksfield, near Elgin; on the remains of fishes in the Old Red Sandstone of that neighbourhood; and on the raised beaches along the adjacent coast", by J. Malcolmson, Esq., F.G.S. was then read.

A paper, "On the origin of the limestone of Devonshire", by Robert Alfred Cloyne Austen, Esq., F.G.S. was afterwards read.

84a. Charles Darwin wrote to his sister Susan on 26 April:

– Last night Geological Soc. & a long discussion –
Burkhardt and Smith, 1985-2003, 2, p83

85. 1838 May 23

A memoir entitled, "A synopsis of the English series of stratified rocks inferior to the Old Red Sandstone – with an attempt to determine the successive natural groups and formations". By the Rev. Adam Sedgwick, Woodwardian Professor in the University of Cambridge, commenced on the 21st March, was concluded.

85a. Charles Darwin wrote to John Forbes Royle on 24 May:

You ought to have been at Geolog. Soc. last night. We had a grand battle between Sedgwick and Greenough, the former most eloquent, the latter most obstinate, but most good-humoured.
Burkhardt and Smith, 1985-2003, 2, p89

The Meetings

Notes, 1837-1838

1. The background to this paper is given in Rudwick 1985, pp224-230.
2. Phillips 1836 and Sowerby 1812-1846.
3. Background is given in Rudwick 1985, pp230-233.

Session 1838-1839

86. 1839, January 9

A notice was first read, "On the discovery of the Basilosaurus and the Batrachiosaurus", by Dr. Harlan.

A paper was afterwards read, entitled, "Observations on the teeth of the Zeuglodon, Basilosaurus of Dr. Harlan", by Richard Owen, Esq., F.G.S., Hunterian Professor in the Royal College of Surgeons, London.

A paper, "On the Geology of the Neighbourhood of Lisbon", by Daniel Sharpe, Esq., F.G.S. was commenced.

86a. Mrs Owen wrote in her diary:

> R[ichard] to the Geological Society, where he read the paper on Dr. Harlan's fossil and the Stonesfield jaw. Dr. Grant was obliged to admit, in spite of the teeth, that they were mammalia and not saurians.
>
> R S Owen 1894, 1, p152

87. 1839, March 13

A paper, "On the geology of the North Western part of Asia Minor, from the peninsular of Cyzicus, on the coast of the sea of Marmara, to Koola, with a description of the Katakekaumene", by William John Hamilton, Esq., Sec.G.S. was read.

87a. Thomas Sopwith wrote in his diary:

> At 6 I dined at the Geological Club which is a very pleasant Dinner party held on the evenings of Geological Meetings, at the Crown and Anchor. The following composed the party this evg.

Dr. Buckland

Mr. Haliburton	Lord Fitzallan
Mr. Broderick	Sir C. Lemon
Mr. Greenough	T. Sopwith
Capt. Pringle	Mr. Ferguson
Marquis of Northampton	Dr. Mantell
Col. Mudge	Mr. Barclay
Sir P.G. Egerton	Mr. Mantell
J.Taylor	

The following are a few brief notes respecting the several parties here named. Dr. Buckland occupied the head of the table as President of the Geological Society. Mr Haliburton is an American judge and is the author of Sam Slick's Sayings and doings. Mr Broderick [Broderip] is an able conchologist and possesses a very fine collection. Mr Greenough is well known as one of the leading geologists of the day. Capt Pringle is on the Ordnance Survey and I was introduced by Dr. Buckland to Col. Mudge who has so long been connected with the great ordnance Survey. Lord Northampton is President of the Royal Society. Sir Philip Egerton is a zealous geologist and Mr Taylor is the leading Engineer comected with Mineral Mining Dr. Mantells name is well known. Mr. Ferguson is a very agreable and talented gentleman – he married Lady Elgin. and Lord Fitzallan is a nephew of the Duke of Norfolk.

After dinner and wine had occupied two hours and a half, Tea and Coffee was brought in. On leaving the Dining room Dr. Buckland introduced me to Lord Northampton and I walked with them to the Geological Society – Sedgwick, De la Beche – Murchison Phillips and several other eminent geologists were present in addition to those I have already named at the Club. I was glad to meet my old friend Dr. Smith and many other valued friends. A very excellent paper was read by Mr. Hamilton on the geology of parts of Asia Minor and Murchison, Sedgwick, De la Beche and Phillips all spoke upon the subject. After the meeting I had a long conversation with De la Beche and went with Dr. Buckland to Lord Coles to supper.

NUL Sopwith

88. 1839, April 10

A paper was read, "On as much of the Transition or Grauwacke system as is exposed in the counties of Somerset, Devon, and Cornwall", by the Rev. David Willims, F.G.S. [1]

The Meetings

88a. Roderick Murchison wrote to Adam Sedgwick the following day:

The fight is over. It lasted till near midnight, and, all things considered, we have come off remarkably well. Parson Williams, who was present, had prepared an Ordnance map of Devon and Cornwall coloured on his own <u>mineralogical</u> plan ... Immediately after the memoir was read, De la Beche, who came up per mail for the nonce, rose, and holding in his hand our memoir, [2] commenced an exculpation of himself from the charge we bring against him in our conclusion. The two points to which he held were, first that <u>he did state</u> "[blank]" that we indicated the separation of the [blank] at Bristol & he read the passage from his work p. 43. 2ndly That in citing Mr Williams he alluded to what he believed to be true, namely that Mr Williams had spoken of a trough because he so stated it at Liverpool. [3] De la Beche dwelt a little on the harshness of our expressions "trusting" "insinuating" (which I told you in my former letter would be <u>the gravamen</u>). He spoke calmly, and sat down without going into the memoir of the evening. I immediately replied by first assuring the chair that I had no hesitation in expressing my regret that a word or two had been made use of in the hurry of composition which both of us were sorry for – and that it would be more in accordance with our feelings & our strong desire to preserve harmony among the cultivators of geology if we had said we "believed" that Mr D [De la Beche] was incapable of "stating" – disavowing the least personality, I immediately got D. <u>with me</u>, and having thus cleared the course I opened the discussion on Williams' paper & went "the whole hog" touching the Devonian case, as well as I could (you can imagine all I had to say). De la Beche then replied but did not attempt to shake one of our positions – did not place a veto on one of my assertions, & least of all on that which laid claim to the originality of the Culm trough: he bothered about a point or two near Chudleigh, as <u>difficulties</u> and ended by saying it was immaterial to him what the things were called. he spoke however in a very subdued tone though acknowledging that all unpleasant feelings were removed from his mind by my previous explanation.

Lyell then spoke & very adroitly put the case as one most agreeable to him, <u>now</u> that he perceived that Mr. D.[De la Beche] not only acknowledged that the view which we took at Bristol was <u>original</u>, but also that he (D.) was by no means indisposed to adopt our new views which got rid of all the anomalies & difficulties (about plants and fossils).

Paddy Fitton rose in <u>great solemnity</u>, and with deep pathos impressed upon the meeting the propriety of restraining the too pungent expression of controversial writing among geological friends, alluded to my having called him "my geological father" & only wished that I had submitted the paper in question to his parental revision before it was published – he acknowledged however, that the explanation had quite rectified the case & then he went on to expatiate on the value of our doings giving us superlative praise, & bringing out Lonsdale in the foreground.

Greenough made his oration as I expected – was very ingeniously sophistical – tried to throw all into chaos – saw nothing new in our views – adhered to his old belief – greywacke for ever! – & sustained old Williams by casting fossil evidence overboard.

Featherstonhaugh spoke well on the great subdivisions of the old rocks of N. America & said they were distinctly the same as ours. De la Beche asked him if the plants in the inferior "[blank] System" were <u>the same</u> as those of the overlying "bituminous coalfield" to which he replied that he had brought home many of the species, but could not speak decisively, though he believed that the species would be found to be <u>distinct</u>.

A South Wales coal owner who had been experimenting in Devon declared that he had in vain looked for the analogies between the Devon & S. Wales [blank] of which I had spoken at some length – In my reply I contended that as this gentleman draw his conclusions from a comparison of Devon with the <u>Glamorganshire field</u>, he was not likely to see any strong agreement, but that if he had followed his own wild beds into the west end of Pembrokeshire he would there have seen them put on such a greywacke aspect, that even such good geologists as Conybeare, Greenough, & De la Beche had there mistaken them for "Greywacke".

These & many other things being said & done, Buckland summed up at 1/2 past 11 ! & though he evidently wished to shield De la Beche, he ended by <u>approving</u> highly of "Devonian" – he now saw light – that light he referred to Lonsdale & henceforth said he there will be two great names in English geology – W. Smith and W. Lonsdale! he adhered entirely to the fossil evidence – did not give us the credit we deserved for our coal trough (which is the <u>key</u> to whole thing) nor did he do justice to my Siluriana (without which as you have justly said, no one could have started this new hare).

The room was a bumper – Warburton who sat it out, assured me afterwards he was quite prepared to understand the discussion by having read my work through in the Easter Recess & that merely sitting as he did & listening to my explanation of parson Williams' map, he was completely convinced that our position was sound & unassailable. I value his testimony more than that of any other person there present because I know it is unbiased & he further assured me that he looked upon the case <u>as settled</u>. as it was quite evident that Buckland had <u>completely given in</u>, De la Beche was ready to do so – & Greenough alone held out, standing like a knight-errant upon his 'antiquas vias'.

I had forgot to tell you that Lord Northampton also spoke to a point of conciliation – (in fact there was too much of this) for I sat next to De la Beche, <u>never lost my temper for an instant</u>, asked him to dine with me & all ended "a l'aimable", & would have done so without any of the surpassing efforts of these "good Samaritans".

Parson Williams spoke or rather read his speech near the end of the discussion. He contended that his views were original & derived from no one & he quoted these words from his one sheet of paper the original which he read at Dublin [4] stating that "the argillaceous schist reposes immediately upon the granite of Lundy Island, mantling round its SE angle on the one hand & dipping towards it from the granite of Dartmoor on the other" & hence it might be <u>inferred</u> that he indicated a trough; though he allowed that he had never made use of the expression, nor had ever done otherwise than consider the [blank] beds as part of the <u>Greywacke</u> albeit the upper part of that series. He quizzed our accommodating disposition in altering our views to suit the fossils & made various allusions in his usual style – all of which I considered unworthy of notice. The fact is that our paper <u>done the trick</u> & the recusants know it & feel it & soon or later must bow to it ...

I forgot to say that Buckland was particularly happy in assisting to demolish "Greywacke" by pulling old Greenough up, who with himself had declared a mass of rock in the Alps to be good <u>Greywacke</u>, which proved to be full of Tertiary shells! – that he had seen very good "greywacke" in oolites in Red Sandst. in Coal – in short in every thing & therefore he did think with Conybeare that it was 'Jupiter quodcunque vides', & agreed with us in the fitness of using it hereafter <u>entirely</u> as an adjective or expletive. Q.E.D. ...

It was right well that I was <u>not</u> absent in Paris, or things in your absence also might have gone <u>pro tempore</u> against us.

CUL Sedgwick, Add 7652 IIID, 24,
partly reprinted in Geikie 1875, 1, p265

Session 1838-39

88b. William Bilton wrote to John Phillips on 11 April:

We had a very interesting & marked personal discussion on the subject [of the Grauwacke of N. Devon] last night. The paper for the Evg. was by Revd D. Williams long, jumbled, confused, with occasional affectation of Classical facetiousness ill suited to the subject, but bearing evidence of laborious & detailed examination of the whole district, & accompanied by some very interesting fossils. The whole view founded on <u>Mineral</u>, in opposition to <u>Organic</u>, characteristics, & of course advocating De la Beche versus M. & S. [Murchison & Sedgwick] & asserting a priority of claim to the discovery of our celebrated "Trough". De la Beche thereupon made this a text to call for a preliminary explanation of the hard expressions & observations in the late paper in Jameson's journal, which he did, I thought, in a very temperate & unobjectionable manner. Sedgwick had taken care not to be present, but M. offered a proper explanation & expression of regret at some of the phrases, escaped "currento calamo" as he said. I think his explanation would have been fuller & more satisfactory had he not been irritated somewhat by some expressions of dissent from some present. However, as it was, it was voted nem. con. that the explanations were satisfactory & honorable on both sides &c. &c. and so I hope this business is ended. On the subject of the Geology of N. Devon however, he continued to assert most strongly his entire dissent from De la Beche's & Mr. W's views. & to be more than ever convinced that they had at last hit the right nail on the head, in ascribing the "Devonian System", as I am now to call my district, (till <u>further orders</u>) to a modification, as I understand it, of the Old Red Sandstone. This idea however he in great measure ascribed to Mr. Lonsdale – & the President & meeting responded in the most flattering manner to this new title Mr. L. has earned to the consideration of English geologists. Mr. Greenough stuck up for the old names, & old lights, & seemed greatly annoyed at the thought that we are to have a new "System" for every class of rocks that appear in a new locality to assume a slightly different aspect. He appeared to think it puzzling enough to English geologists to follow this daily varying nomenclature, but to be still more despairing to foreign Philosophers, who are all acquainted with these rocks under the title of Grauwacke, & have attached definite ideas to it. The discussion was prolonged to past 11 1/2 ! When our Revd. President amounced that tea & coffee were upstairs – ("<u>quite cold</u>" as he said). –

You would have been much interested by the discussion, I think the general impression with regard to the personal question was that De la Beche had not mentioned S. & M's previous labours as fully & honourably as he ought, but that the latter paper was unjustifiably severe, & indeed M. mentioned to me afterwards that now it was all over, he shd indite a line of explanation to the Editor. With respect to the Geol. question, I do not think it can possibly be considered to be decided, but that it preponderates in favour of S. & M.

OUM Phillips, JP, 1839/22

89. 1839, April 24

A paper was first read, "On the Climate of the newer pliocene tertiary period", by James Smith, Esq., F.G.S.

A paper was then read, entitled, "Remarks on some fossil and recent shells, collected by Capt. Bayfield, R.N. in Canada", by Charles Lyell, Esq., V.P.G.S.

A paper was then read, "On the classification of the older rocks of Devonshire and Cornwall", by the Rev. Professor Sedgwick, F.G.S. and Roderick Impey Murchison, Esq., F.G.S.

A paper was afterwards read, "On the structure of South Devon", by Robert A. C. Austen, Esq., F.G.S.

89a. William Bilton wrote to John Phillips on 30 April:

I hear that I lost a very interesting discussion last Wednesday – when Sedgwick expressed himself very strongly & eloquently in favour of the new views of our N. Devon "Grauwacke" – De la Beche was <illegible>. You will, I think, find our rocks there a tough morsel whenever you are called upon to crack them, & a still tougher job to reconcile all to your decision whatever it may be. But every one appears to consider the last new light as much more vraisemblable than the former.

OUM Phillips, JP, 1839/21

Notes, 1838-1839

1. Background given in Rudwick 1985, pp289-294.
2. Sedgwick and Murchison 1839.
3. At a meeting of the British Association for the Advancement of Science held in September 1837.
4. At a meeting of the British Association for the Advancement of Science held in July and August 1835.

Session 1839-1840

90. 1839, December 4

A paper was first read, entitled, "A Description of the Soft Parts and of the shape of the Hind Fin of the Ichthyosaurus, as when recent", by Richard Owen, Esq., F.R.S., F.G.S.

A paper was afterwards read, "On as much of the Great graywacke system as is comprised in the group of West Somerset, Devon, and Cornwall", by the Rev. D. Williams, F.G.S.

90a. Robert Austen wrote to John Phillips on 8 December:

> The subject of Devon Geology came on again at G.S. on Wednesday last, but what the subject wants is to be treated Zoologically which was not attempted in the least, but which I shd. be much pleased to hear we might soon expect from you.
> OUM Phillips, JP, 1839/54

90b. Roderick Murchison wrote to Adam Sedgwick on 8 December:

> Parson Williams gave us another diatribe on Devon last meeting & I was compelled to speak. The blundering Welshman has now got into a more extraordinary blunder than ever. He makes the whole of Devon to overlie the central trough, because the sections between the Eastern end of Dartmoor & Chudleigh appear to throw the beds into this position. I think I settled the Parson's hash to the satisfaction of every real geologist present: for I simply asked him if he still considered the [Culm] measures to lie in a <u>trough</u>, to which having responded yea, I then shewed that his ascending section from the N. of Devon to the South was a "reductio ad absurdum" inasmuch as it was impossible that (the limestone on the south side of the trough being granted to be equal to that of the North) the [Culm] measures could be overlaid by the slaty [blank] series. But enough of this dull dog.
> CUL Sedgwick, Add 7652, IIID, 27

91. 1840, February 5

The President first read from the chair an extract of a despatch from Consul Chatfield, dated San Salvador, Oct. 10, 1839, and forwarded to the Society by Mr. Backhouse, by direction of Viscount Palmerston.

The Meetings

A paper was next read, "On Orthoceras, Ammonites, and other cognate genera; and on the position they occupy in the animal kingdom", by Robert Alfred Cloyne Austen, Esq., F.G.S.

The memoir to accompany the Second Edition of the Geological Map of England and Wales, by George Bellas Greenough, Esq., V.P.G.S. was then read.

A paper was afterwards read, "On the Detrital Deposits of part of Norfolk, between Lynn and Wells", by Joshua Trimmer, Esq., F.G.S.

91a. Roderick Murchison wrote to Adam Sedgwick on 10 February:

Before I dress to go to see the Queen in her bridal attire, [1] I must tell you that I have had a sharp set to with Greenough & Buckland. At our last meeting Greenough hung up his new map in the Society's rooms & gave a short sketch of its construction of which he read 2 parts. The one referred to his principle of colouring the other to what he justly called the greatest change yet effected in England Geology the conversion of the greywacke of Devon & Cornwall into <u>Coal</u> & <u>Old Red</u>. In stating this change he never <u>once mentioned our names</u> although he cited Harding, Phillips & De la Beche, & he absolutely had the wilfull dishonesty of taking to himself the views which we alone propounded & which he opposed vehemently up to Saturday night!! Wonders will never cease. I said nothing at the time, for Buckland the President stated <u>from the Chair</u> that no observations were to be made on Mr Greenough's description of his map, but the following day I wrote an urgent private letter to Greenough & begged him for his own sake not to allow this document to go forth without after the words "This great change" the interpolation of the words "first propounded by Prof. Sedgwick & Mr Murchison". [2]
CUL Sedgwick, Add 7652, transcript in IIID, 30

92. 1840, May 27

The Memoir, "On the classification and Distribution of the Older Rocks of the North of Germany", &c., by Prof. Sedgwick and Mr. Murchison, commenced at the previous meeting, was concluded.

Session 1839-40

92a. Adam Sedgwick wrote to Roderick Murchison on 25 July:

... There I finished off the second part of our paper which was read in due form at the next meeting & went off well. Nobody made any fight.

GSL Murchison S11/173

93. 1840, June 10

Eleven communications were read.

1. A notice, "Of a mass of trap in the mountain limestone on the western extremity of Bleadon Hill, Somersetshire, and on the line of the Bristol and Exeter Railway", by the Rev. D. Williams, F.G.S.

2. A memoir descriptive of a "Series of Coloured Sections of the Cuttings on the Birmingham and Gloucester Railway", by Hugh Edwin Strickland, Esq., F.G.S.

3. A letter addressed to Mr. Murchison by Capt. Lloyd, dated London, May 11th, 1840.

4. "On the mineral veins of the Sierra Almagrera, in the province of Almeria, in the South of Spain", by J. Lambert, Esq., F.G.S.

5. A notice, "On the Sierra de Grador, and its lead mines", by Josias Lambert, Esq., F.G.S.

6. "On the polished and striated surfaces of the rocks which form the beds of Glaciers in the Alps", by Professor Agassiz.

7. "On a bed of lignite near Messina", by Dr. R. Calvert.

8. A letter from Richard Greaves, Esq., addressed to Dr. Buckland, and dated June the 6th, 1840, "On the discovery of bones of birds, fishes, and mammalia, in the limestone cliff at Eel Point in Caldy Island, and about eighty feet above the sea".

9. A note from Mr. Hamilton, Sec.G.S., addressed to Dr. Buckland, "On the irregular occurrence of rounded fragments of rock crystal, throughout the Hastings sands, in the neighbourhood of Tunbridge Wells".

10. A letter, dated May 6th, 1840, from M. Roemer, of Hildesheim, to Dr. Fitton, "On the chalk and the subjacent formations to the Purbeck stone inclusive in the north of Germany".

11. A letter from H. B. Mackeson, Esq. to Dr. Fitton, dated Hythe, June 7th, 1840.

93a. Thomas Sopwith wrote in his diary:

At 6 o'Clock I dined at the Geological Club on the invitation of Dr. Buckland. This dinner takes place at the Crown & Anchor Tavern on the Evenings of the Meetings of the Geological Society, at 6 precisely. About 8 o'Clock Coffee and tea are handed round and at 1/2 past 8 the party adjourns to the Society's rooms in Somerset House. The following were the company present on this occasion.

 Rev. DR. BUCKLAND President G.S.
T. SOPWITH F.G.S. FEATHERSTONHAUGH
CAPT. IBBETSON Do. SIR T. MITCHELL F.G.S.
FORBES Do. CAPT. BASIL HALL Do.
 COL. MUDGE Do.
HAMILTON Do. Earl of Enniskillen Do.
SIR C. LEMON Do. MAJOR CLARKE Do.
CAPT. PRINGLE, Do. R. INGHAM ESQ. M.P. Do.
 JAMES HALL Esq. Do.
 JOHN TAYLOR Esq. Treasurer G.S.

While we were at dinner an attempt was made to assassinate her Majesty by a youth named Edw. Oxford who fired two pistols at the Carriage containing the Queen and Prince Albert. The news spread rapidly and naturally created a deep sensation ... [3]

T Sopwith's diary, NUL Sopwith

93b. John Ruskin wrote in his diary:

Geological Society. Notice by Agassiz of the polish of the rocks beneath, and on the sides of glaciers owing to the motion of the ice. It is found, Basil Hall said, high on the flanks of the hills above, where it would seem that no ice could ever come, and in the same degree. Agassiz's notice unsatisfactory. Then of lead mines in Spain, in Sierra Morena, found in nests and detached beds, and rolled pieces in gravel (chiefly galena), worked with great ignorance and wasting: one year produced thirty-five thousand tons – average twenty-five thousand even now.

Evans and Whitehouse 1956, 1, p82

Notes, 1839-1840

1. Queen Victoria was married to Prince Albert of Saxe Coburg and Gotha at the Chapel Royal, St James Palace at 12.00 on Tuesday, 10 February 1840. Murchison was presumably one of the 'immense multitude' assembled in St James Park and all the surrounding streets, some standing on chairs and some even climbing trees for a better view (*The Times*, 11 Feb 1840).
2. The work of Sedgwick and Murchison is referred to in a footnote in the published memoir, Greenough 1840.
3. This, the first attempt on the Queen's life, happened when she and Prince Albert were driving up Constitution Hill in a low carriage. Edward Oxford, the culprit, was later declared insane. (Charlot 1991, pp220-221).

Session 1840-1841

94. 1840, November 4

A paper was read, "On Glaciers, and the evidence of their having once existed in Scotland, Ireland, and England", by Professor Agassiz of Neuchatel.

The reading of the first part of a Memoir, "On the Evidences of Glaciers in Scotland and the North of England", by the Rev. Prof. Buckland, D.D., Pres. G.S. was commenced.

94a. Samuel P. Woodward [1] wrote:

> Mr Murchison called upon the mathematicians & physical geographers present to speak of the <blank> objections to Dr. Buckland's glacial hypothesis, himself shd attend only to the facts of the case. Of the scratches & polish on the surface of crtn rocks there is no doubt, & are glaciers the cause is the question. Could they be done by ice alone? If we apply it to any as the necessary cause, the day will come when we shall apply it to all. Highgate Hill will be regarded as the seat of a glacier, & Hyde Park & Belgrave Sqre will be the scene of its influence. Dr B. has in his paper <u>assumed</u> that all these heaps of diluvium are moraines – but I would rather examine the subject under the old name Diluvium and with our old ideas of diluvial action than by using the <u>term</u> moraines assume the question proved. On Schichallion there are <blank> rocks. If S has been covered with glaciers there ought to be some <blank>. If the height be great the result should be proportionate. There ought to be a coordinate relation in the

phenomena. But in the Highland mtns not 1/3 the elevation of the Alps, we have moraines 2 & 3 times the magnitude of any known in Switzd. Formerly, when we found terraces of fragmented rocks disposed around a mountain, we attributed it to the successive periods of elevation in that mntn. The Parallel Roads of Glen roy were compared to sea beaches. Now all are attributed to the action of Ice. & not only these but Edinburgh & Stirling, & other places equally out of the reach of such action, did glaciers ever exist in the higher chains, are to be covered with a mass of ice. These grooved & striated surfaces and heaps of boulders are also to be found in Scandinavia, on the E. of the gulf of Bothnia, all proceeding from N and NW. have these crossed the gulf on ice? In Russia too we shall find them where there are no mntns. And if we look to the remains of marine shells found in beds elevated, differing in no respect from those in our present seas except that they are called Pleistocene (by Smith and Lyell) we have proof of a lower elevation at the very time, the period following upon the more tropical epochs, when these glaciers shd be introduced. On these accts I am still contented to retain our old ideas, that when a mntn was elevated, or a body of water passed over a series of elevations, the diluvium would descend with the Strike & be disposed in mounds & terraces according to the direction of currents, &c.

Prof. Agassiz. Mr M. has objected to the glacial theory in the only way in wh it cd be objected to – he allows that the whole is granted as soon as you grant a little bit. For here as in other cases we argue from what is proved, to what is to be proved. In Switzd the action of glaciers is yearly seen by thousands of foreigners & of these facts there can be no doubts. Extent of glaciers. In the Glacier de l'Aar, grooves &c. are to be found in the valley, seven leagues (22 m) from the end of the present glaciers. Did we find these surfaces only on the hard rock we might suppose they were merely uncovd by the action of the glaciers. but on the soft Limestone rocks these grooves are only to be seen on the surfaces from wh the glacier has just retreated. Many glaciers traverse such rocks only (equivts of our Lias) & there the grooves are annually renewed in winter & removed by the atmospheric action in Summer. I have been many hundred feet under the glacier of Mont Rose, & found the quartzose sand forming a bed beneath & acting like emery upon the rocks. A moraine may be distinguished by certain characters from any other accumulation of fragmented rocks. From the sides of the glaciers moving faster than the middle there is a continual tendency to throw the fragments into lines at the sides (lateral moraines), & when two glaciers descending from difft gorges unite a medial moraine is fomed. The lateral are exposed to constant friction with the rocks with wh they are brought in contact & their terminations are passed over by the whole mass of the glacier so that they become rounded & striated, whilst the medial moraines remaining on the surface continue angular. When the glacier retreats in the summer, the medial moraine composed of angular fragments is spread out over the surface of the lateral & the terminal moraines, composed of rounded fragments. & it is by these characters that we have proved the existence of moraines in Scotland Ireland, and N. England. There are moraines in the Alps 200 feet wide, composed of boulders several feet in diameter.

Mr. Lyell spoke of the size of moraines & the way in which they might under certain circumstances attain any magnitude. A glacier has been known to retire 1/2 a mile in a single summer, 16 moraines have been in succession left, & in severe winters all these might be driven successively into one by the downward motion of a glacier.

Mr Greenough. Spoke of the arguments derivable from analogy &c, & objected to the mode in wch the Geol Socy was in the habit of acc'ing [accounting] for phenom [phenomena]. Instances of accumulations of travelled rocks – N. Germany – from a careful comparison some of these must have crossed the Baltic. In the valleys of Switz'd some deposits must have crossed Lake Geneva, & ascended very high mountains. ("Does Prof. Agassiz suppose that the Lake of Geneva was occupied by a glacier 3,000 feet thick?" Agassiz "At least!") Change of climate necessary to acct for these phenomena – objection from the Tropical nature of remains in recent deposits – Climax of absurdity in Geological Opinions. In one period, the Crag, we have three opposite conditions blended: corals – tropical; peat – temperate; shells – pronounced by Dr. Beck, arctic!

Mr Lyell. "Mr G. confuses 4 distinct epochs under the name of Crag. The first comparatively tropical (Coralline Crag), the others Temperate (Red & Norwich Crag), & the period of the Peat bogs (Lacustrine deposits) more recent than any".

Mr Gray. – "The corals of the Crag appear to me as arctic as the shells. I know no reason for making them tropical".

Mr Greenough. On the size of the blocks on mtns – agency of floating ice, on mtns as the physical boundaries of different kinds of diluvium.

Dr. Mitchell. Enquired if Dr. Buckland confined the glaciers to the Highlands or whether he made them descend to the Lowlands.

Dr. Buckland. Expressed himself ready to answer any questions on the subject under discussion, or any involved in his paper, but considered the present question irrelevant.

Dr. Mitchell considered his question relevant to the subject. Dr. Buckland rose to reply, but Mr Whewell rose. (cheers, & 'Mr Whewell!'). At this late hour it is impossible to go into the question of the physical changes necessary to allow of the existence of glaciers in this country. I shall, therefore, confine my remarks to the subject as discussed this evening, & it does appear to me that the way in wch Mr Lyell has treated it is not the most fair & legitimate. He says: 'if we do not allow the action of glaciers, how shall we acct for these appearances?' This is not the way in which we shd be called upon to receive a theory. Now, it is not within our reach at present to refer each set of phenomena in geology to its adequate cause, but that is no reason why we should receive any theory that is offered to acct for it. This glacial theory is brought forward to explain what has hitherto, to a great extent, been found inexplicable – the nature & position of diluvial detritus over considerable areas & in widely different climates. So far it is founded on strict comparison & analogy it is to be received, but we must not overrate its influence; & it appears to me <u>incomplete</u> in 3 important particulars: – <u>First</u> in accounting for such an extent of diluvium over such wide areas, in countries of such opposite physical structure, surface, climate & <u>Secondly</u> Marine remains of glacial period, shewing the continents to be submerged. (Mr Darwin has described an Island capped with snow in the equivalent latitude of Yorkshire, & by supposing an equal extent of water in our Polar regions, we might induce a degree of cold sufficient for that, but the existence of these glacial phenomena are found over too wide an extent to allow of that.) (Mr Lyell here interrupted – "I have attempted to account for that in my paper &c. Dr. Buckland "So have I in a paper – wh is not yet written!" Mr Whewell "Our attention to-night is limited to Dr. B's paper.) <u>Thirdly</u> Physical conditions under wh glaciers now exist.

We find them universally stretching out from lofty mountain chains wh take their rise in <u>warm</u> climates, so as to allow of the downward motion & the retiring in summer. Mr Lyell speaks of the prodigiously <u>rapid</u> retreat of a glacier which amounted to 1/2 a mile in a single summer. but where shall we obtain mountains as <u>fulcra</u> for glaciers stretching many leagues into the plains producing such results as are ascribed to their action in Scotland. &c. &c.

Dr. Buckland. Resigned the chair to Mr Greenough, and argued the a priori credit to be attached to his "narrative" from the circumstances of his having been a 'sturdy' opponent of Profr.

Agassiz when he first broached the glacial theory, & having set out from Neufchatel with the determination of confounding & ridiculing the profr. & he went – & saw all these things, & returned converted – & he considered the testimony of four such competent observers as himself & Agassiz & Renouard & <blank> [2] who next to Saussure had spent more time in the Alps than any o' Geologist sufficient to prove to all the truth of their obsns & the correctness of their inferences – he referred to Prof. Agassiz's book, [3] & condemned the tone in wh Mr Murchison had spoken of the "beautiful" terms employed by the Prof. to designate the glacial phenomena. That highly expressive phrase "roches moutonnées" wh he had done so well to revive, & that other "beautiful designation" the glaciers remaniere – "<u>remaniere!</u>" – "<u>remainiere!</u>" continued the Dr. most impressively amidst the cheers of the delighted assembly, who were by this time elevated by the hopes of soon getting some tea (it was 1/4 to 12pm) & excited by the critical acumen & antiquarian allusions & philological lore poured fourth by the learned Dr. wh. after a lengthened & fearful exposition of the doctrines & discipline of the glacial theory concluded – not as we expected with lowering his voice to a well bred whisper "Now to – &c. – but with a look & tone of triumph he pronounced upon his opponents who dared to question the orthodoxy of the scratches & grooves, & polished surfaces of the glacial mtns (when they should come to be d---d the pains of <u>eternal itch</u> without the privilege of scratching!

BGS Archives, GSM1/588,
reprinted in Woodward 1907, pp138-142

95. 1840 November 18

The reading of the first part of a Memoir, "On the Evidences of Glaciers in Scotland and the North of England", by the Rev. Prof Buckland, D.D., Pres. G.S. commenced on the 4th of November, was resumed and concluded.

A paper, "On the Geological Evidence of the former existence of Glaciers in Forfarshire", by Charles Lyell, jun., Esq, F.R.S., F.G.S. was commenced.

95a. Samuel P. Woodward wrote:

Mr Smith of Jordan Hill. Pointed out the differences betn the Upper & lower beds of marine shells along the coast of Scotland. "one 40 feet above the level of the sea – composed of shells identical with the recent – the other 50 feet high, wh must have been deposited in 5 or 6 fathom water making 80 feet of elevation. But one in 20 of the shells in these beds has not been discovered in the present seas – & they have all an arctic character – The homogeneous character of the Till – its distribution from the W. towds the centre of Scotland – & from the low ground to the mountains.

Mr Whewell. Proceeded to examine Dr. B's concluding address at the last meeting – the slight value of <u>authority</u> in physical questions – & the absurdity of asserting its sufficiency to prove an hypothesis – The Glacial theory regarded as a generalization from facts – and as a mathematical question wh may be examined logically without any practical acquaintance with its facts – Examination of facts – & of principles – deduction of laws from established facts – Observations made upon Glaciers – Mr. Agassiz book – distinct causes necessary to produce gravel & moraines – Physical changes necessary for the existence of glaciers in Scotland. Diluvium – either a decrease of central heat which has since returned – a supposition at variance with all the known laws of physics, or a different distribution of land & water in the northern hemisphere, whilst a large portion of the existing continents – over which glacial action is predicated must still occupy its present place & present similar physical appearances. Granting the change of climate where would be the Alps from which to suspend the glaciers of Scotland. They cannot be supposed to have formed upon & descended from such isolated peaks as Schichallion or Ben Nevis.

Mr De La Beche. Changes of condition necessary for the existence of glaciers in Scotland – Recency of elevatory movements – proofs of such movements – raised beaches – raised bars of havens – other Diluvial phenomena.

Mr Lyell. Explained the distribution of superficial debris in a portion of Scotland – 3 distinct covers – 1st <u>universal</u> composed of fragments of the subjacent rock with a slight admixture of foreign matter. 2. <u>Till</u> Unstratified drift clay with boulders – covered by <u>3</u> Stratified gravel – The 1st supposed to have been distributed by sheets of ice spreading all over the country. The <u>2nd</u> by glaciers & the <u>3rd "Remainié"</u> by melting of glaciers &c. The confinement of each kind of gravel is to its own valley.

Mr Phillips. Examined the question of the Shapfell granite boulders carried over Stainmore across a valley 12 or 14 miles wide – to Darlington &c.

Mr Agassiz. Argued the origin of gravel from glacial action & not from marine currents – from the fact of the numerous lakes of

Scotland in which there was no gravel. had marine currents formed the Till it would have filled all these hollows. On the glacial hypothesis they would be filled with ice & thus preserved – Recommended the same <u>caution</u> to his opponents in making objections wh had been so strongly urged upon himself in generalizing – The distribution of gravel in the Alps & proofs of more extended glacial action fomerly.

Dr. Daubeny. On the wide extent over which these grooved surfaces are found in America &c. The difficulties attending the degree of cold necessary.

Mr Greenough. argued against the Recent elevatory movements – the decreasing level of the Baltic he attributed to the clearing the forests – & consly smaller supply of water – & the widening of the entrance which promoted its escape.

Mr Murchison argued the universality of the cause wh produced the till &c of Scotland, its operation over Russia &c The agency of drift & floating ice.

Dr. Buckland – Did not explain all diluvial phenomena by the operation of glaciers – allowed the existence of raised bars & beaches – of currents – of floating & drift ice – but contended that glaciers alone would acct for many phenomena observable in Scotland &c The possibility of a glacier descending from Shapfell & crossing the valley of the Eden & over Stainmore & then repeated debacles spreading the detritus still further.

BGS Archives, GSM1/588.
An emended version is in Woodward 1907, pp143-144

95b. Louis Agassiz wrote to Sir Phillip Egerton on 24 November:

Our meeting on Wednesday passed off very well; none of my facts were disturbed, though Whewell and Murchison attempted an opposition; but as their objections were far-fetched, they did not produce much effect. I was, however, delighted to have some appearance of serious opposition, because it gave me a chance to insist upon the exactness of my observations, and upon the want of solidity in the objections brought against them. Dr. Buckland was truly eloquent. He has now full possession of the subject; is, indeed, complete master of it.

E C Agassiz 1885, 1, p304

The Meetings

96. 1840, December 2

Mr Lyell's memoir, "On the Geological Evidence of the former existence of Glaciers in Forfarshire", commenced on the 18th November, was concluded.

The second part of Dr. Buckland's Memoir, "On the Evidence of Glaciers in Scotland and the North of England", was then read.

96a. Mary Lyell wrote to her sister-in-law, Marianne on 2 December:

> They had a capital meeting at the G.S. on Wednesday, a great fight and I hear (not from himself) that Charles spoke extremely well. There was a sort of renewal of the discussion at Mr. Greenough's where we dined next day and met the Murchisons, Dr. Buckland, Profr. Phillips, Mr. Agassiz, Mr Stokes & some others. It was a pleasant lively party.
>
> Wilson 1972, p501

97. 1841, January 6

A paper was first read, "On the Illustration of Geological Phaenomena by means of Models", by Thomas Sopwith, Esq., F.G.S.

A paper was next read, "On the Geology of the island of Madeira", by James Smith, Esq. of Jordan Hill, F.G.S.

A letter, dated Madras, July 1840, addressed to John Taylor, Esq., Treas.G.S., by Mr Frederick Burr, "On the geology of Aden, on the coast of Arabia", was afterwards read.

97a. Thomas Sopwith wrote in his diary:

> I went at 6 o'Clock to the Geological Club where I met several of the most eminent geologists & spent a delightful evening here (Crown & Anchor) & at the Society. The following are some of the parties who occupied the President's end of the table.
>
> DR. BUCKLAND P.G.S.
>
> | MR ASBURNHAM. | T SOPWITH. |
> |----------------|----------------|
> | MR MURCHISON. | MR STOKES. |
> | MR LYELL. | MR R. TAYLOR. |
> | MR HAMILTON. | MR J. HALL. |

Mr John Taylor occupied the Vice Chair as usual. At 1/2 past 8 we adjourned to the Geological Society where my paper on Geological models was first read, the series of models having been previously laid on the table. [4] It was followed by a description of the geological structure of the Island of Madeira by Mr Smith of Jordanhill and a paper by Mr Frederick Burr on a volcanic town in Arabia (Aden).

On the President inviting observations on those papers Mr Greenough rose and said that he had a series of models made sometime ago from Mr. Farey's designs and which he thought had never recd. from the Geol. Society the attention they deserved – he said they were less instructive than those now on the table but that he would present them to the Society. [5] Dr. Buckland commented upon my models in a very flattering manner – he alluded to the model of Dean Forest and said that he considered the facile construction of such models as forming a new era in geological science – he noticed also the subject of mining records and his remarks on the conservation of mineral treasures were received with marked approbation. After the meeting several gentlemen examined the models and Mr Tennant expressed his conviction that sets of them would be purchased by students of geology & others. After taking tea I returned to Charing Cross with Dr. Buckland & thence to Berners St.

NUL Sopwith

98. 1841, January 20

A paper was first read, "On the Teeth of Species of the Genus Labyrinthodon (Mastodonsaurus Salamandroides, and Phytosaurus (?) of Jager) from the German Keuper and the Sandstone of Warwick and Leamington", by Richard Owen, Esq., F.G.S., F.R.S.

A paper was next read, entitled, "Observations relative to the Elevation of Land on the shores of Waterford Haven during the Human Period, and on the Geological Struture of the District", by Thomas Austin, Esq.

A paper by C. Lyell, Esq., F.G.S. was afterwards read, "On the Freshwater Fossil Fishes of Mundesley, as determined by M. Agassiz".

98a. Thomas Sopwith wrote in his diary:

I wrote to Mr Botfield and at 6 o'Clock dined at the Geological club. There was a most agreable party and Dr. Buckland desired

The Meetings

me to sit next to Capt. Basil Hall and "have some crack with him" In former pages of my journal I have legibly inscribed the names of parties who were present as a means of recording so agreable a subject of Reminiscence as the society of the eminent geologists who usually attend the Club. Following this plan I insert the names of the gentlemen present this evening.

DR. BUCKLAND. P.G.S.
BASIL HALL.   L. HORNER.
T. SOPWITH.   G.B. GREENOUGH.
C. LYELL.   - BARCLAY.
R.I. MURCHISON.   J. HALL.
MAJ CLARK.   - BRODERICK.
COL. MUDGE.   R. INGHAM M.P.
            - STOKES

I had a pleasant conversation with Capt. Basil Hall and Mr. Lyell. – the entertaining vivacity of our worthy president and the agreable manners and intelligence of the eminent leaders in Geological science always renders the dinner party of this Club a source of great enjoyment. I was introduced to Mr Horner whom before I had known only by name. At 1/2 past 8 we went to the Society where Mr Owen read a most elaborate and interesting paper on the Sandstones of Warwickshire as identified by their fossil remains & he particularly illustrated the structure of the Labyrynthodon – An animated discussion followed the perusal of this and other papers in which several of the most eminent Geologists took a part and the acuteness, research and humour of their several addresses afforded a high intellectual treat. Before leaving Somerset House Dr. Buckland opened out a packet he had just received from Agassiz and I got the first copy thus sent of "Etudes sur les Glaciers" by that distinguished naturalist ... At the meeting of the Geological Society it was interesting to observe the following distinguished geologists [m]illing together.

Dr. BUCKLAND was in the chair – on his left sat OWEN, SEDGWICK, LYELL, MURCHISON, GREENOUGH and DE LA BECHE.

In the course of the discussions some one asked De la Beche what he meant by very great antiquity, this having reference to the supposed age of the world – De la Beche replied "If I am to be hard pressed on that point I should say that I consider these remains to be of very great antiquity as regards historical periods and of very little antiquity as regards geological periods" I had the honor to be introduced to Mr J.S. Bowerbank whose extensive researches in fossil botany are well known & whose splendid collection is thrown open to the inspection of his friends on Monday Evenings. – At 12 o'Clock I accompanied Dr. Buckland to the Ship Tavern and returned to Berners Street.

NUL Sopwith

98b. Robert Austen wrote to Henry De la Beche on 27 January:

My newspaper gives an account of your last meeting at Somerset House, and of Labyrinthodons and Keuper &c. "which gave rise to animated discussions and a fine display of intellectual gladiatorship the combatants being ... De la Beche ..." [6]

NMW De la Beche

99. 1841, March 10

A paper, "On the Geological Structure of the Northern End and Central Regions of Russia in Europe", by Roderick Impey Murchison Esq, P.G.S and M E de Verneuil, V.P.G.S. of France, was commenced.

99a. Charles Bunbury wrote in his diary:

Went to a meeting of the Geological Society, where was read a long paper on the geological structure of part of Russia, by Murchison and a French gentleman who had accompanied him. Afterwards a lively and amusing discussion on various subjects (some of them not immediately connected with the paper), in which Fitton, Lyell, Greenough, Murchison, Lord Northampton, and others took part. Lord Northampton is a remarkably neat and fluent speaker; Murchison not much less so. Murchison obtained in Russia the most satisfactory proofs of the identity of the old red sandstone with the "Devonian" rocks; he found extensive tracts of real red sand-stone, similar to that of Herefordshire, &c., containing the same shells which are found in the limestones and slates of Devonshire, <u>together with</u> the fishes characteristic of the old red sandstone of Scotland. After the meeting, Edward introduced me to Mr Featherstonhaugh, who is lately returned from the United States.

Bunbury 1891, pp299-300

100. 1841, March 24

The reading of the paper on Russia, by Mr Murchison and M. E. de Verneuil, was resumed and concluded.

100a. Andrew Ramsay wrote to his brother William on 25 March:

> At six I dined with the Geological Club at the Crown and Anchor, Strand. It has a most shabby outside, but is one of those old-fashioned splendid inns inside, which, I suppose, are not to be found out of London. [7] It was here that Fox and the great Whigs of that great day used to meet and enjoy themselves. Lyell and Featherstonhaugh were there, and Captain Pringle; Murchison in the chair. There were about twenty-five gentlemen present. I was introduced to Dr. Buckland and some others. Murchison introduced me also to Mr Taylor, the croupier and treasurer of the Society and asked him to take me beside him. I heard him say to Buckland: 'You remember young Ramsay, who made the model of Arran? I shall introduce him to you.' 'Oh yes,' quoth the Doctor. So I was introduced and the Doctor gave me two of his digits to shake. There were a lot of big-wigs there whose names I do not know – members of Parliament and others. Mr Taylor, whom I sat next, knows, or knew, Dr. Thomson of Glasgow, Dr. Ure, Charles Mackintosh, C. Tennant, and others, who were old friends of my father's, and we had a great deal of conversation together. After dinner we went to Somerset House to hear Murchison on Russia. The Marquis of Northampton was there. The discusson broke up about eleven, when we all went upstair to tea.
>
> Geikie 1895, p30

100b. Andrew Ramsay wrote, many years later:

> I think I must have dined five or six times with Mr M. [Murchison] during my thirteen days' stay in London; once at the Geological Club, at the Crown and Anchor by Temple Bar, where I first met some of the great geologists whom I had not previously seen in Glasgow at the B.A. meeting. Mr M. introduced me specially to old John Taylor, a famous man in the mining world, and much respected and beloved by all the geologists, and indeed by every one, He was treasurer to the Club. I sat between him and Major Clerke – an old warrior, with a cork leg, a man of perfectly polished manner, witty, and with a vast fund of anecdotes, some of which were of the complexion called blue. At that Club meeting

Session 1840-41

I recollect Sedgwick and Buckland, Phillips, Greenough, Fitton, Lyell, Sopwith, and Owen, and there were others that I forget, Forbes was than a young man just of the eve of starting to join Graves in the Aegean. The dinner made a great impression on me. Mr M., as President of the Society, was in the chair, but I do not recollect anything that took place except the mirth created at our end of the table by Major Clerke and old John Taylor's deep voice and pleasant laugh.

Geikie 1875, 1, p313

101. 1841, May 19

A paper, "On the Agency of Land Snails in corroding and making deep Excavations in compact Limestone Rocks", by the Rev. Professor Buckland, D.D., F.G.S. was first read.

A paper, "On Moss Agates and other Siliceous Bodies", by John Scott Bowerbank, Esq., F.G.S. was then read.

101a. Thomas Sopwith wrote in his diary:

I then returned to Berners Street and at 1/2 past 5 called on Mr Buddle who accompanied me to the Geological Club where we dined and afterwards attended the meeting of the Society. The following was the dinner party at the Club.

PROF. WHEWELL.
? J. TREVELYAN.   SIR J. McNIEL.
W. BUCKLAND.   CAPT. PRINGLE.
J. BUDDLE Esq.   MR. BUNBURY.
R.C. LEMON.   C. LYELL Esq.
    J. HALL Esq.
    T. SOPWITH.
    J. TAYLOR Esq.

A paper was read by Dr. Buckland on the holes bored by Snails in the under side of limestone rocks and another by Mr Bowerbank on the fomation of what are commonly called Moss agates. I presented a set of twelve 4 inch models to the Society.

NUL Sopwith

The Meetings

Notes, 1840-1841

1. Samuel P Woodward (1821-1865) was the Geological Society's Sub-curator from 1839 to 1845, and he may have taken these notes in an official capacity.
2. Woodward 1907, suggests the name De Charpentier to fill this blank.
3. Agassiz 1840.
4. These models were described in Turner and Dearman 1979.
5. See Dearman and Turner 1983.
6. Austen's newspaper has not been identified.
7. For an account of the 'Crown and Anchor' see Walford [*ca* 1875], 3, p75.

Session 1841-1842

102. 1841, November 3

A memoir, entitled, "Supplement to a 'Synopsis of the English Series of Stratified Rocks inferior to the Old Red Sandstone', with Additional Remarks on the Relations of the Carboniferous Series and Old Red Sandstone of the British Isles", by the Rev. Adam Sedgwick, F.G.S., Woodwardian Professor in the University of Cambridge was begun.

102a. Edward Bunbury wrote to Charles Lyell on 13 December:

The greatest novelty in the geological world since my return has been Sedgwick's paper, a "Supplement to an introduction" as he called it, but which supplement seemed to prove that there was nothing for the Introduction to lead to. Everyone was in hopes that we were now at length to have some definite account of the Cambrian system, but as the paper proceeded & one tract of country after another was described & we heard of <u>Caradoc sandstone</u> fossils in the heart of Snowdonia, & first Cumberland & then North Wales seemed to be given up as indistinguishable from the Lower Silurian system, every one was disposed to cry out "The Cambrian system where is it?" And Echo answered where? – for from beginning to end it was not to be found. In the next edition of your Elements your chapter on that subject may be like Bishop Horrebow's on the snakes of Iceland [1] – "There is no Cambrian system".

EUL Lyell 1/462, printed in Secord 1986, p129

102b. Charles Moxon wrote in an editorial in *The Geologist*:

On the occasion of Professor Sedgwick submitting his elaborate paper on the stratified rocks of the English series, inferior to the old red sandstone, in which he described the *Cumbrian* rocks of the neighbourhood of Kendal and Kirby Lonsdale, he admitted, amongst other statements in his recapitulation of the constituents of the district, that "a second band existed (among the Cumbrian rocks), of calcareous slates, with lower Silurian fossils"; and an interesting and highly valuable discussion ensued, on the comparative merits of the terms *Cumbrian, Cambrian,* and *Silurian*. If we recollect aright, Mr Greenough contended that a *Cumbrian rock with Silurian fossils, was an anomaly*, and judged from the author's paper, that the Cambrian strata, and the so called Cumbrian rocks, were quite or nearly identical; he could not, therefore assent to the application of another term to those strata, which Geologists already understood by the appellation of "Cambrian rocks". The "pro's" and "con's" were not, however, equally sustained, and we were much pleased with the learned Professor's brief acknowledgement, after long addresses from Messrs. Greenough, Fitton, Murchison, and others, that his communication was only to be considered the outline of one much more elaborate and explicit in its details, and "for what it concerned him, they *might call the rocks what they pleased*". We contend, that with such an opinion expressed by the learned Professor himself, the Society should have hesitated to record the title of "Cumbrian rocks", in their published abstract of the proceedings of the evening (3rd of November 1841); or had they considered it indelicate to alter the phraseology of the author, it was but justice that some remark should have been appended to the effect stated, which might caution Geologists against the reception of the title.

C Moxon 1842, p130

103. 1841, December 1

A paper was first read entitled, "Report of the Destruction by Earthquake of the Town of Praya de Victoria, on the 15th of June, 1841", by Mr. Consul Hunt, communicated by direction of the Right Hon. the Foreign Secretary of State.

A paper, entitled, "Some Geological Remarks made in a Journey from Delhi, through the Himalaya Mountains, to the frontier of little Thibet, during 1837", by the Rev. Robert Everest, F.G.S. was then read.

The Meetings

A paper was afterwards read, containing a "Description of the Remains of Six Species of Marine Turtles (Chelones) from the London Clay of Sheppey and Harwich", by Richard Owen, Esq., F.R.S., F.G.S. Hunterian Professor in the Royal College of Surgeons.

103a. Leonard Horner wrote to Charles Lyell on 3 December:

The evening began with an account of a great earthquake that took place at Terceira, one of the Azores, last June, which threw down the whole town of Praya, consisting of five hundred houses. Some facts that were mentioned are interesting, particularly a great rent of a mile long from the shore inland, and the rising up in the sea of a shoal, which shortly afterwards was washed away. It was stated that several such shoals exist, raised within a short period, and that the navigation is thereby rendered very dangerous. The paper was sent to us by Lord Aberdeen, Secretary of Foreign Affairs. Next we had an account by the Rev Mr Everest (who was present) of a journey from Delhi to a place considerably within the range of the Himalayas. He states that as you approach the central range, the same rocks assume a metamorphic character, and he describes some remarkable rocks of granite intersected by granite veins. But the most interesting part of the paper was the announcement of vast numbers of monkeys living at an elevation of 8,000 feet above the sea. I sat next him, and he told me that he lived in that spot for a year, that in the month of February, while the country far and wide was covered with deep snow, he had seen groups of the monkeys sitting on the pine trees picking the seeds out of the cones and feeding upon them. He said they were surrounded with them. Owen was much struck with this announcement. Everest also stated that he saw the skin of a leopard that had just been shot at an elevation of 11,000 feet, and that they are frequently met with, as they follow the wild goats to those heights. He told me that he had seen the Bengal tiger amidst the snow at 8000 feet elevation, that they do not go higher he believes only because the mountains are too precipitous for their heavy bodies to climb, whereas the lighter and more agile leopard finds less difficulty. He says that the species of monkey is identical with that living in the plains.

We had then a paper from Owen on fossil *marine* turtles, found in the London Clay of Sheppy and Harwich. Hitherto it had been supposed that the Chelonian remains found in that deposit, belonged exclusively to the Emys, but on examining specimens in Bowerbank's collection, and others sent to him by Sedgwick, Sir P. Egerton, and Dr. Dickson [Dixon] of Worthing, he has made out six distinct species of marine turtles. He told us that there are only six living species known, and that never more than two have been found together in one region, whereas here, in this confined spot, six have been found. There is, however, this remarkable anomaly, that whereas all the living species attain a considerable size, none of those found in the London Clay exceed ten inches in length, hence he supposes that they lived in brackish water in an estuary. He gave us a most lucid description of the specimens on the table.

Lyell 1890, 2, pp39-41

104. 1842, February 18

Annual General Meeting at which R. I. Murchison was re-elected President and read the Anniversary Address.

104a. J. Beete Jukes wrote to Adam Sedgwick on 21 February:

We had the Duke of Richmond, the Russian Ambassador, Lord Lansdowne &c at the anniversary dinner on Friday and Murchison was in fine feather accordingly. There was much mention of "His Imperial Majesty", – and other dulcet diversions.

CUL Sedgwick Add 7652, 11/128

104b. Leonard Horner wrote to Charles Lyell on 24 February:

Last Friday we had our Anniversary at the Geological Society, there was a full attendance – the Wollaston medal was awarded to Von Buch, but Bunsen was unwell and could not attend to receive it. Murchison's address was excellent, very comprehensive in his view of what has been doing in the last year, and with a great deal of valuable matter. Greenough said that it had never been surpassed by former addresses. We had a good party at the dinner, about ninety, and some excellent speaking. Murchison had Baron Brunow, the Russian Ambassador, on his right, the Duke of Richmond on his left, and farther on the right Lord Lansdowne and Lord Sandon, on the left Lord Enniskillen and Sir John Johnstone. I was well placed between Hallam and Symonds.

Lyell 1890, 2, p42

104c. Roderick Murchison wrote to Adam Sedgwick on 26 February:

The anniversary went off gloriously, though I say so, the morning discourse was well received, and in truth I put a deal of

The Meetings

powder and shot into it, foreign and domestic, and took so much pains as to stop my original work on Russia ... [I write] as well as a man can whose first soirée begins to-night with probably 200 or 300 people coming!! The morning room <u>was full</u>, and I read for two hours without losing a man. I entered at length into the Silurian & 'Palaeozoic' questions & gave Phillips <u>my mind</u> for suppressing the title of my work in his new book. 2 & also for suppressing in his table of <u>equivalents</u> to my word "Silurian", though he introduced a still newer term "Eifel of S. Devon" as an <u>ordinary</u> term though Sedgwick & Murchison are the first who ever used it & long after the <u>Silurian System</u> was established! ... I defended the temporary division set up between your lower slaty rocks and my superior groups on the ground of positive observation of infraposition, and if in the end (as I now firmly believe) no suite of organic remains will be found, even in the lowest depths, which differs on the whole from the Silurian types, why then we prove the curious law that in the earliest inhabited seas of our planet the same forms were long continued.

I took care to show that any other plan than that which we adopted would have led to fatal errors, such as 'Système Hercynien' and other hypotheses, and that now all must come right, to whatever extent (and the extent can probably never be identified) the base of the Lower Silurian zoological type may be extended ...

Our dinner went off '<u>con amore</u>', and every one says it was the best (Adam Sedgwick only wanted) which we ever had. I did my best to make it of a public character, and had my two knights of the Garter, one on either side of the President, and the representative of my Emperor Nicholas. Brunnow spoke admirably, and I never heard Lord Lansdowne speak so well as for the toast of 'The Universities of this Land' ...

CUL Sedgwick, transcript in IIID, 36,
partly reprinted in Geikie 1875, 1, p365

105. 1842, February 23

A memoir was read, entitled, "Report on the Missourium now exhibiting at the Egyptian Hall, with an inquiry into the claims of the Tetracaulodon to generic distinction", by Richard Owen, Esq., F.G.S., &c.

105a. Leonard Horner wrote to Charles Lyell on 24 February:

Last night we had an admirable paper by Owen. A description of the fossil skeleton now [on] exhibition by Herr Koch at the

Egyptian Hall, the man you saw at New York; I will try to give you an outline of the paper. [3] This great Missourian quadruped, as Owen termed it, has been made a monster both in name and in putting together by Koch – he has lengthened the back bone by intervertebral substances, and by additional vertebrae by a wrong position of the scapulae, he has raised up a ridge on the back, and he has added a lower jaw which did not belong to the individual, and the penetrating skill of Owen discovered that he had unwittingly suspended a *female* under jaw to a male. When Owen detected this, he admitted that the lower jaw of the individual found in the pit, and which he represents as having been bogged in a hole, was wanting. Then he has placed the tusks so that they extend horizontally, whereas their true position is with their curvature upwards – Owen states that the roots of the tusks and the sockets are quite cylindrical, so that when the ligatures or soft animal substance which held them fast was destroyed, they might be easily turned round in any direction, and so it is very possible that what the man says may be true, that he found them extended horizontally. Owen considers it a male Mastodon Giganteum, and he went on to shew that that genus, and the Tetracaulodon of Godman, are one and the same. He says that hitherto, naturalists have been led into errors, in considering individuals as belonging to distinct genera and species by the state of the tusks. In the male and female, there are rudiments of the same tusks, but they are never developed in the female, and he points out the analogy in this respect with the Dugong and Narwal. ... He considers the Tetracaulodon to be a Mastodon in an immature state. There is one short straight tusk in the lower jaw of the Mastodon, the use of which is very obscure. After he had finished his paper, he said, he received Dr. Hayes' of Philadelphia (I think), paper on the Tetracaulodon, but after going over it carefully he saw no ground to alter the conclusion he had come to before, viz., that the Mastodon Giganteum and Tetracaulodon belong to the same genus. The paper was eulogised by Buckland. Charlesworth, who stated he had recently been examining specimens in museums at New York, Philadelphia, and Baltimore, spoke, and Owen told us afterwards that he had spoken well. After the paper we had a very masterly verbal elucidation of the case by Owen, referring to an admirable drawing made under his direction by our sub-curator, Woodward, about seven feet long. [4]

Lyell 1890, 2, pp43-44

The Meetings

106. 1842, May 18

A memoir, "On the Geological Structure of the Ural Mountains", by Roderick Impey Murchison, F.R.S., Pres. G.S., M. E. de Verneuil and Count A. von Keyserling, was read.

106a. Thomas Sopwith wrote in his diary:

At 6 o'Clock I dined at the Geological Club

        R.I. MURCHISON, Esq., P.G.S.

Baron Von Buch.	Marqs. of Lorne.
Count le Keyserling.	Mr. Hallam.
Mr. Featherstonhaugh.	Dr. Buckland.
Mr. Gilbert.	Thos. Sopwith.
Marqs. Northampton.	Sir Chas. Lemon.
Profs Whewell.	Mr. James Hall.
Mr. Greenough.	Sir P.G. Egerton.
Mr. Dawson.	

        Major Clarke Vice Prest.

To those who by living in the country have few opportunities of seeing or meeting with the distinguished literary and scientific persons who abound in the metropolis, it is extremely interesting to spend a few hours in such a party as usually assembles at the Geological Club. Thus on the preceding page I have inserted the names of the gentlemen present this evening and their position at the table. They comprise The Presidt. of the Society – two distinguished foreigners, One of the Maine Boundary Commissrs – The son of the celebrated Davies Gilbert formerly President of the Royal Society and next to him sat the nobleman who now so ably fills that loftiest throne of Science in this kingdom. The Master of Trinity – Mr Greenough whose name is well known in connection with English Geology – Mr Dawson an experienced surveyor and engineer who took an active part in the publication of an account of the Landslip near Axmouth. Major Clarke a man of science & a veteran soldier who lost a leg at Waterloo – Lord Lorne, eldest son of the Duke of Argyle – The author of the Constitution history of England – Professor Buckland – Sir Charles Lemon Prest. of the Cornish Royal Institution – Mr Hall, son of Sir James Hall and Sir P.G. Egerton a zealous geologist & ichthyologist. At 1/2 past 8 I went to Exeter Hall and heard an excellent lecture on Chemistry

Session 1841-42

by Dr. Reid after which I returned to the Geological Socy. and heard an interesting discussion.

NUL Sopwith

107. 1842, June 15

A paper was first read, "On the packing of Ice in the river St. Lawrence; on a Landslip in the modern deposits of its valley; and on the existence of Marine Shells in those deposits as well as upon the mountains of Montreal", by W. E. Logan, Esq., F.G.S.

A communication was afterwards made by Dr. Grant, F.G.S., "On the Structure and History of the Mastodontoid Animals of North America".

107a. Gideon Mantell wrote in his diary:

Attended the meeting of the Geological Society; an angry discussion between Owen and Dr. Grant on the Mastodon and Tetraculodon remains now exhibiting in the Egyptian Hall, Piccadilly by a Mr Kosch [Koch]. [5] Gossiped with Dr. Buckland, Grant, Lord Enniskillen, Sir P.G. Egerton, Mr Greenough, Murchison, Pentland, Featherstonhaugh etc. –

SAS Mantell, quoted in Curwen 1940, p159

Notes, 1841-1842

1. Chapter 42 of Horrebow's *Natural History of Iceland* consists of the single sentence, 'No snakes of any kind are to be met with throughout the whole island'. Horrebow 1758, p91.
2. Phillips 1841.
3. An account of Albert Koch and his Missourium is given in Stadler 1972, xxiv-xxviii.
4. A large drawing of this skeleton is preserved in the Owen Collection at the Natural History Museum, London.
5. On the relations between Grant and Owen and on this episode in particular see Desmond 1989, pp320-321.

The Meetings

Session 1842-1843

108. 1842 November 30

"On the Bala Limestone", by Daniel Sharpe, F.G.S.

"Notice on the discovery of the Remains of Insects in the Lias of Gloucestershire, with some remarks on the Lower Members of this Formation", by the Rev. P. B. Brodie, F.G.S.

"On certain impressions on the surface of the Lias bone-bed in Gloucestershire", by H. E. Strickland, M.A., F.G.S.

108a. The Rev. P B Brodie wrote to Adam Sedgwick on 6 December:

> My paper was read on the 30th, and thinking you will like to hear the result I now hasten to inform you of it. It appears that the general opinion (so Strickland tells me) was, that there was not <u>sufficient</u> evidence in support of a freshwater formation – (tho' by the way I did not exactly say freshw, but rather estuary) that the Cypris <u>might</u> belong to a <u>marine</u> Genus, and that the Cyclas might be a sea-shell. Strickland urged this against the conclusion I had drawn ... Buckland agreed with Strickland – Lyell said that a dragon fly's wing had been found 100 miles from land; ... He allowed too that the fossils appeared to belong to those of freshwater. I was not present myself but this is all I can gather from a friend who was there, & from the note Strickland afterwards wrote me.
>   CUL Sedgwick, II 168

109. 1843, January 20

"On the Silurian Rocks of the South of Westmoreland and North of Lancashire", by Daniel Sharpe, Esq., F.G.S.
"On the Stratified Rocks of Berwickshire and their imbedded Organic Remains", by Mr. William Stevenson, of Dunse, communicated by the President.

"Description of some Fossil Fruits from the Chalk-formation of the South-east of England", by Gideon Algernon Mantell, Ll.D., F.R.S., &c. [incorrectly listed in *Proceedings of the Geological Society* under next meeting].

"Notice on the fossilized remains of the soft parts of Mollusca". By Gideon Algernon Mantell, Ll.D., F.R.S., &c. [incorrectly listed in *Proceedings of the Geological Society* under next meeting].

109a. Gideon Mantell wrote in his diary:

Attended with my dear boy, and Mr Bensted the meeting of the Geological Society. Read my paper on "Molluskite" and on "Fossil fruits from the Chalk formation of S.E. of England". Returned home by 1/2 past 12.

SAS Mantell

109b. John Ruskin wrote in his diary:

Yesterday with Richard [1] to Geological: dull paper, but a little amusing disputation by de la Becke [Beche] and Sharpe, and Richard enjoyed it.

Evans and Whitehouse 1956, 1, p239

110. 1843, February 1

A paper was read, "On the Tertiary Strata of the Island of Martha's Vineyard in Massachusetts", by Charles Lyell, Esq., V.P.G.S., &c.

Letter from J. Hamilton Cooper, Esq., to Charles Lyell, Esq., V.P.G.S., "On some Fossil bones found in digging the New Brunswick Canal in Georgia".

"On the Geological position of the Mastodon giganteum and associated fossil remains at Bigbone Lick, Kentucky, and other localities in the United States and Canada", by Charles Lyell, Esq., V.P.G.S.

110a. Gideon Mantell wrote in his diary:

Attended the Council of the Geological Society. Dined at the Athenaeum. Went to the evening meeting of the Geological Society; Lyell on the big-bone-lick. Mr. Conybeare, whom I had not seen for many years, was present. [2]

SAS Mantell

110b. John Ruskin wrote in his diary:

Went into Geological in evening. Lyell's paper given in other book, but too much talking and verbiage. Conybeare made a fool of himself: the most extraordinary delivery I think that ever disgraced our human faculty of speech.

Evans and Whitehouse 1956, 1, p242

The Meetings

111. 1843, February 17

Annual General Meeting at which Roderick Murchison read the Anniversary Address and Henry Warburton was elected President.

111a. Gideon Mantell wrote in his diary:

> Drove to Somerset House, and attended for about 20 minutes the reading by Mr Murchison of the President's address, being the Anniversary of the Geological Society: too unwell to attend the dinner.
>
> SAS Mantell, quoted in Curwen 1940, p166

111b. Edward Forbes wrote to William Thompson the following day:

> Yesterday the Geological Society's dinner came off. Lots of butter, of which I got a share, and as [Murchison] was the plasterer, it of course fell thick. I know the value of all such too well ... A short summary of the geological and zoo-geological results of the Aegean expedition rather astonished the audience, who had no very distinct idea before how much had been done. Warburton is our new president. He is rather austere, but just, and I rather want a strict man at present to keep my ribs in order.
>
> Wilson and Geikie 1861, p334

111c. Adam Sedgwick wrote to Dean Ingle on 19 February:

> On Friday I went to the anniversary of the Geological Society, and the excitement of the day, for the time, did me much good, and I spoke as well as I have ever done.
>
> Clark and Hughes 1890, 2, p55

Notes, 1842-1843

1. Richard Whiteman Fall, a young friend of Ruskin's.
2. William Daniel Conybeare had been an active geologist and palaeontologist in the 1820s, but did little geology after his move to Sully in 1831.

Sessions 1842-43, 1843-44, 1844-45

Session 1843-1844

112. 1844, January 17

"On certain Crustaceans found at Atherfield by Dr. Fitton", by T. Bell, Esq., F.R.S., Professor of Zoology in King's College, London.

"On the Occurrence of Phosphorite in Estremadura", by Charles Daubeny, M.D., F.R.S., Professor of Chemistry in the University of Oxford and Captain Widdrington, R.N., F.R.S.

"Notes on the Cretaceous Strata of New Jersey, and other parts of the United States bordering on the Atlantic", by C. Lyell, Esq., M.A., F.R.S.

112a. John Ruskin wrote in his diary:

> In at the Geological Society ... several valuable references got. Met Buckland, Danberry [Daubeny], Twiss &c. at Geological – Buckland has never time to speak to me – but valuable paper on the phosphate of lime of Spain, which I hope I shall remember something of.
>
> Evans and Whitehouse 1956, 1, p260

Session 1844-1845

113. 1845, January 8

"On the geology of the eastern frontier of the Colony of the Cape of Good Hope", by Andrew Geddes Bain, Esq.

"Description of the fossil skulls of three species of an extinct genus of Reptilia (Dicynodon), discovered by A.G. Bain, Esq., in the sandstone rocks, Algoa Bay", by Richard Owen, Esq., Hunterian Professor of Anatomy in the Royal College of Surgeons, F.G.S.

113a. Andrew Ramsay wrote in his diary:

> Playfair & I dined together. Geol Soc night. Paper on the <blank> by Owen. He, Forbes & I supped with Playfair after. Owen's genius throws light on every thing.
>
> IC Ramsay, and Geikie 1895, p62

114. 1845, February 5

"On certain raised beaches, and the shells found in them, occurring in the coast of Essex, near Walton", by J. Brown, Esq., F.G.S.

"On the geology of the vicinity of the Wollondilly River in Argyle County in the Colony of Sydney, New South Wales", by the Rev. W. B. Clarke, M.A., F.G.S.

"On the Atherfield section of the Lower Greensand, in the Isle of Wight", by W. H. Fitton, Esq., M.D., F.R.S.

114a. Gideon Mantell wrote in his diary:

> Attended meeting of the Geological Society – paper by Fitton on the 'Lower Green Sand' – his last. A very dull affair altogether.
> SAS Mantell, quoted in Curwen 1940, p191

114b. Andrew Ramsay wrote in his diary:

> Geological night. Fitton on Greensand; a tremendous row and a regular blow up after between Fitton & Forbes.
> IC Ramsay, and in Geikie 1895, p64

115. 1845, February 21

Annual General Meeting at which Henry Warburton read the Anniversary Address and Leonard Horner was elected President.

115a. Andrew Ramsay wrote in his diary:

> Geol. Soc. Anniversary. Phillips rec'd the Wollaston medal. Left soon after. Went to the dinner. Sir H [Henry De la Beche], Phillips, Sanders, Ibbetson, Sopwith, McLauchlan & self all at one end of the table.
> IC Ramsay

115b. Charles Bunbury wrote in his diary:

> Anniversary meeting of the Geological Society; – Mr Horner elected President; Wollaston medal awarded to Professor John Phillips (who is nephew of the famous William Smith); and the Wollaston Fund donation to a Mr Bain, an engineer, who has discovered the remains of an extraordinary genus of saurians on the eastern frontier of the Cape Colony.

Dinner of the G.S. at the Crown and Anchor; many distinguished men present.

Bunbury 1890-1891, 1, p37

115c. Edward Forbes wrote to William Thompson:

Look at the last <u>Literary Gazette</u> for a song of mine. [1] Buckland amusingly enough quoted it in full at the geological anniversary dinner yesterday, not knowing the author. De la Beche afterwards, in returning thanks for the Survey, wickedly proclaimed that it came from our staff, and urged it as a proof that any sort of article could be produced in the Museum of Economic Geology.

Wilson and Geikie 1861, p387

116. 1845, February 26

"On the Miocene Tertiaty strata of Maryland, Virginia, and North and South Carolina", by Charles Lyell, Esq., M.A., F.G.S., &c.

"On the White Limestone formations of Georgia and South Carolina", by Charles Lyell, Esq., F.G.S.

116a. Charles Bunbury wrote in his diary:

Meeting of the Geological Society. Two good papers by Lyell on the Eocene and Miocene tertiary deposits of the coasts of the United States, followed by an interesting discussion. The geological formations of the United States are on a grand scale; the tertiary deposits extend without interruption down the coast from Maryland to Florida, and, as Mr. Featherstonhaugh afterwards stated, round the great promontory of East Florida and along the coast of the Gulf of Mexico, even to New Orleans, a length altogether, of not less than 2,500 miles, with a breadth in some parts of 150 miles.

The principal constituent of the Eocene deposit is a white limestone, which has often been supposed to belong to the Cretaceous period, and which contains flints often very similar to those of the chalk; but its fossils are decidedly tertiary. Sir Henry de la Beche compared this white limestone with that which occurs very extensively in Jamaica and other W. Indian islands, a considerable part of the latter he considers to be of the same period, though it occurs often under very different circumstances, the white limestone of the U.S. being undisturbed and nearly horizontal in position, and forming low plains while that of the

The Meetings

W. Indies is often very much tilted up, and rises in some places to the height of 4,000 feet above the sea. Occasionally, he said, the Eocene limestone of Jamaica is covered by another white limestone lithologically indistinguishable from it, but of very recent formation, full of the same corals which at present compose the reefs in the neighbouring seas. Mr. Featherstonhaugh spoke of the extension of these tertiary beds to the S. and W. of the parts visited by Lyell, and mentioned that in East Florida, the white limestone which is found beneath the sand that covers the whole surface of the country, is, when first penetrated, as soft as soap, and may be cut by the spade into any shape, but by exposure to the air, becomes as hard as statuary marble.

Bunbury 1890-1891, 1, pp39-40

117. 1845, March 12

"On the comparative classification of the fossiliferous strata of North Wales, with the corresponding deposits of Cumberland, Westmoreland, and Lancashire", by the Rev. Adam Sedgwick, M.A., F.R.S., Woodwardian Professor of Geology in the University of Cambridge.

117a. Andrew Ramsay wrote in his diary:

Reeks came home with me, & we had tea & ham together. Then the Geol Soc, scrimmage between Sedgwick and Greenough. Playfair & I had a long talk about my Welsh affairs.

IC Ramsay, and Geikie 1895, p64

117b. Charles Bunbury wrote in his diary:

Meeting of the Geological Society – a paper by Sedgwick – comparison of the lower fossiliferous rocks of North Wales and the Cambrian district. The paper did not interest me particularly, but it was followed by a very entertaining fight between Greenough and Sedgwick; the former in his most caustic style, attacked the paper as vague and unsatisfactory. Sedgwick's reply was in his best manner, full of rough humour and fun and strong good sense, and pretty severe too; but though there was plenty of hard hitting on both sides, there was perfect good humour.

Bunbury 1890-1891, 1, pp45-46

118. 1845, April 2

"On a supposed aerolite, said to have fallen near Lymington, Herts", by R. A. C. Austen Esq., F.G.S.

"On the junction of the Transition and Primary rocks of Canada and Labrador", by Capt. Bayfield, R.N., F.G.S.

118a. Charles Bunbury wrote in his diary:

Meeting of the Geological Society. The proceedings began with a short paper by Mr. Austen, giving an account of a supposed meteoric stone which had been found in a ploughed field near Lymington, after a thunderstorm; it was however extremely different from any aerolite hitherto recorded, being a mere piece of slaty micaceous sandstone, without any of the characteristic peculiarities that have been observed in every well-ascertained aerolite; and the evidence as to its origin seemed extremely weak. Warburton and Buckland attacked with great force the notion of its meteoric origin, and the general opinion of the Society seemed to be with them; Buckland mentioned that he had met with two different persons who had actually seen the fall of meteoric stones, and in both cases the phenomena described were the same – a strong light moving with great rapidity, and becoming brighter as it approached to the moment of the fall, attended with a whizzing noise, but no explosion or sound like thunder.

The principal business of the evening was an important paper by Captain Bayfield, on the junction of the granitic and transition (Silurian) rocks in British North America. He traced this junction in a satisfactory manner along the whole chain of the great lakes, and the whole course of the St. Lawrence, from the western extremity of Lake Superior to Labrador and Newfoundland, a distance of 2,000 miles. There seems to be, as Lyell and Murchison noticed in their remarks on his paper, a most striking analogy between the geology of this vast tract of country, and that of Scandinavia and the northern parts of Russia, nay, many of the same fossil species which characterize particular beds of the Silurian system in England and Wales, are found to be equally characteristic of them on the shores of the great North American lakes.

Bunbury 1890-1891, 1, pp51-52

118b. Andrew Ramsay wrote in his diary:

Went to the Geol Soc, where old Warburton frightened me out of my wits by calling on me to speak.

IC Ramsay, and Geikie 1895, p64

The Meetings

119. 1845, April 16

"On the supposed evidences of the former existence of glaciers in North Wales". By Angus Friend Mackintosh, Esq., F.G.S.

119a. Andrew Ramsay wrote in his diary:

> Jolly night at the Geological. Buckland's glaciers smashed.
>
> IC Ramsay, and Geikie 1895, p64

119b. Charles Bunbury wrote in his diary:

> Meeting of the Geological Society. A paper by Mr. Mackintosh, in opposition to the Glacial Theory as applied to North Wales, followed by a very good debate, in which Buckland, Sedgwick, Lyell, De la Beche, and Murchison figured to advantage. After the discussion, Mr. Morris showed me some plates of fossil plants of the coal measures of New South Wales, which he has prepared for the illustration of Count Strelezki's book.
>
> Bunbury 1890-1891, 1, p53

120. 1845, May 14

"On the coal beds of Lower Normandy", by R. A. C. Austen, Esq., F.G.S.

"Notes of a microscopical examination of the chalk and flint of the southeast of England", by G.A. Mantell, Ll.D., F.G.S.

"On some specimens of pterodactyle, recently found in the Lower Chalk of Kent", by J. S. Bowerbank, Esq., F.G.S.

120a. Gideon Mantell wrote to Benjamin Silliman:

> The only important thing in science I have attempted is a 'Memoir on the Microscopic Examination of the Chalk and Flint of the S.E. of England'; which was illustrated by drawings and six microscopes with fossil and recent subjects; it drew a large auditory to the meeting of the Geological Society. I dwelt on the silicification of organic bodies and availed myself of Mr. Dana's judicious remarks on pseudo-morphism in your last two journals. [2] The affairs of the Geological Society are so stupidly managed, that no proper notice is given of the meetings; and probably the only account of this paper, which cost much labor, will be an abstract,

written by someone who knows but little of the subject, some twelve months hence.

Spokes 1927, p172

Notes, 1844-1845

1. Forbes's poem is published in Wilson and Geikie 1861, p387.
2. Dana 1845.

Session 1845-1846

121. 1845, November 5

The following communications were read:

"Observations on a slab of New Red Sandstone from the Quarries at Weston, near Runcorn, Cheshire, containing the Impressions of Footsteps and other markings", by J. Black, Esq., M.D., F.G.S.

"On the circumstances and phaenomena presented by the Granite of Lundy Island, and of Hestercombe in the Quantock Hills, compared with those that characterise the Granites of Devon and Cornwall", by the Rev. D. Williams, F.G.S.

"On the Geology of the neighbourhood of Tremadoc, Caernarvonshire", by J. E. Davis, Esq., F.G.S.

121a. Gideon Mantell wrote in his diary:

> Attended the meeting of the Geological Society. A very thin attendance and a poor affair.
> SAS Mantell

122. 1845, November 19

The following communications were read:

"On the Age of the newest Lava Current of Auvergne, with remarks on some Tertiary Fossils of that Country", by Charles Lyell, Esq., M.A., F.R.S., F.G.S., &c.

"Geological Position of the Bitumen used in Asphalte Pavements", by S. P. Pratt, Esq., F.R.S., F.G.S., &c.

The Meetings

"On the Occurrence of Coal in Formosa", by – Cooper, Esq.

122a. Gideon Mantell wrote in his diary:

Attended the meeting of the Geological Society. Met Lord Northampton, Mr Greenough, Prof Sedgwick etc.

SAS Mantell

122b. Leonard Horner wrote to Roderick Murchison on 21 November:

We had a good meeting – a paper by Lyell on the calcareous bed with the mammalian remains under the newest lava stream in Auvergne – Tarbaret, near Nechers. The observations were made three years ago, & he wrote the paper on his voyage out.

GSL Murchison, H29/12

122c. Leonard Horner wrote to Charles Lyell on 30 November:

Your paper on Auvergne was read on the 19th and discussed by Hamilton, Sedgwick, Forbes and Mantell. Your letter of the 1st came in time for our last meeting [*ie* the meeting of 5th November], I read the geological part at the club, to the great amusement of all present in what you say of Koch's Leviathan, and at the meeting I read what you say about the perfect skeleton of the Mastodon. Owen was not present, but Mantell got up and told us of the letter he had received from Silliman, describing a very remarkable fossil animal recently discovered by M. Koch, quite gravely, upon which Hamilton and some of the Clubists said in a loud whisper "Pray read the rest of Lyell's letter", so I got up and said that Mr. Lyell had alluded to the remarkable fossil beast of which Dr. Mantell had spoken, but as his communication was not exactly of a kind to be read before a grave Society, I should dissolve this meeting and consider ourselves a social party, and amuse them with Mr. Lyell's account of Mr. Koch's discovery. [1] I then read what you say, and much to the entertainment of those present, Mantell joining heartily in the laugh. I called on Owen, and gave him the extract of the geological part of your letter, and it has produced a communication from him to you on the Mastodon, which shall go by the same ship as this.

Lyell 1890, 2, p86

123. 1845, December 3

"On fossil Ferns from Maryland", by C. J. F. Bunbury, Esq., F.G.S.

"On the bones of Iguanodon recently found in the Wealden Strata of the Isle of Wight", by G. A. Mantell, Ll.D., F.G.S.

123a. Charles Bunbury wrote in his diary:

Meeting of the Geological Society: my paper on Fossil Ferns from Maryland was read, and was very well received. Sir H. de la Beche and Buckland, who were the principal speakers in the discussion that followed, expressed great approbation of my paper, and gave me much encouragement. I was also much complimented afterwards by several others, and (what gave me especial pleasure), by Owen among others. But nothing gave me so much delight as my dear wife's joy and sympathy when she heard of my success. The discussion between De la Beche and Buckland turned on various points relative to the coal formation in general, and particularly on the <u>rolled pebbles</u> of coal, which in some localities (especially in South Wales), are found forming entire beds between the regular seams of coal.

Buckland conceived these to have been pieces of wood rolled into the form of pebbles (as we often see on modern beaches, at Cromer for instance), <u>before</u> they were carbonized; while De la Beche maintained that they were actually rolled fragments of pre-existing beds of coal. Both agreed that they proved that the coal beds <u>above</u> which they occur, had been submerged and covered, either by the sea or by inundations before the foundation of the next solid seam of coal. Buckland remarked that something like a parallel to what we may suppose to have occurred during the carboniferous era, is now going on in Morecambe Bay (in Lancashire), where the sea has been gaining upon extensive peat mosses, sometimes covering extensive tracts of them.

Afterwards, Dr. Mantell read an interesting paper on the Wealden strata at Brook Point in the Isle of Wight, and the fossil remains found in them. Immense quantities of fossil trunks and branches of trees, often of great size, lie on the beach and imbedded in the cliffs, heaped together, and laid across one another without any order; their bark is carbonized, their wood is of the carboniferous structure, agreeing with that of the Araucarias, mineralized by carbonate of lime, and much incrusted and penetrated by pyrites. Among these are found occasionally cones, numerous fresh water shells, of a species which Mantell calls <u>Unio Valdenses</u>, and innumerable bones of huge reptiles, especially of the Iguanodon. Dr. Mantell justly observed that this remarkable accumulation of organic remains presented a most striking analogy to those great natural drafts of drifted wood,

The Meetings

which are so frequent in the Mississippi and the great South American rivers, and which carry down with them the bodies of numerous quadrupeds and reptiles. He suggested also that the abundance of pyrites encrusting the remains, might owe its origin to the development of sulphurated hydrogen from the decaying animal matter.

Some of the bones of Iguanodon procured from this locality and exhibited on the table were of astonishing size, exceeding any that had been seen before.

Another great curiosity, collected by Dr. Mantell at Brook Point, was a specimen of that singular fossil plant, the Clathraria Lyellia, exhibited its internal structure, which had hitherto been unknown. It has been examined by Robert Brown, who pronounces it to be unlike any plant previously known, either in the recent or fossil state, but with some general and vague analogy to the Cycadeae – certainly not endogenous.

Bunbury, 1890-1891, 1, pp84-86

123b. Gideon Mantell wrote in his diary:

Meeting of the Geological Society; read a paper on the Wealden strata of the Isle of Wight. A full attendance; but my paper was put off till ten o'clock, owing to a long desultory discussion between Dr Buckland and Sir Henry De la Beche upon rolled blocks of coal! sad twaddling indeed. Obliged to omit half my paper and read the remainder very hurriedly. Broke my large thigh-bone of the Iguanodon in the carriage. Reginald accompanied me.

SAS Mantell, quoted in Curwen 1940, p199

123c. Gideon Mantell wrote to Benjamin Silliman on 20 December:

A fortnight since I sent a paper on some discoveries I made in the Wealden of the Isle of Wight, with a splendid collection of specimens, to the Geological Society. A trifling paper on some two species of fossil fern leaves from the American coal, sent over by Mr Lyell, written by another son-in-law of the President, was allowed to take precedence; and a discussion followed by Buckland and others, of the most rambling and absurd description, and this was allowed to go on till past ten o'clock. I was then called on to read my paper consisting of about 30 pages of this kind [foolscap] and I was directed to begin at the 15th page, and to read it short. The consequence was, I was obliged to slur it over, in the most unsatisfactory manner, for we break up at half past ten. I would have declined reading it at all, as some of my friends wished, but there were present many persons who came purposely to hear it, so that I could not disappoint them.

Spokes 1927, p180

123d. Charles Bunbury wrote to Charles Lyell on 31 December:

My paper on your Frostley ferns was read before the Society on the 3rd, and was very well received – indeed I received a good many compliments on it.

Bunbury 1890-1891, 1, p97

124. 1845, December 17

"On the supposed fossil bones of birds from the Wealden", by Richard Owen, Esq., F.G.S., Hunterian Professor of Anatomy at the Royal College of Surgeons.

124a. Gideon Mantell wrote in his diary:

Geological Society: Professor Owen read a paper to shew that the bird's bone I had described upon his authority as a tarsimetatarsal bone of a wader, was the lower extremity of the humerus: a statement I had always made, but Owen would insist the two portions of the bone did not belong to the same; but that one was the head of the humerus, and the other the lower extremity of a tarsal. Now he concludes that it is the humerus of a pterodactyles and not a bird, and that all the other bones of the Wealden 'birds' are pterodactylian: as rash a conclusion as a former one. It is deeply to be deplored that this eminent and highly gifted man can never act with candour or liberality. In his paper he did not make the most distant allusion to the fact that I had always asserted both portions belonged to the same bone, and that it was only by his positive determination that the lower end was tarsal that I gave in. Dr Buckland as a <u>matter of course</u> got up and entirely agreed in all Professor Owen stated. I then rose, and stating the real facts of the question, condemned the present sweeping conclusions as being as rash as his previous one: for though it is <u>probable</u> the bones may be Pterodactyles, there is no proof they may not belong to birds: the specimens are all too imperfect to admit of positive inferences as to the original; and the question must be considered an open one, till more certain data are obtained.

SAS Mantell, quoted in Curwen 1940, p200

The Meetings

124b. Charles Bunbury wrote in his diary:

Meeting of the Geological Society; four papers read, but short ones, and of no particular interest. The first was Owen, on some bones from the Wealden formation, which he had formerly referred to wading birds, but having since cleared them more thoroughly from the matrix, and examined them more minutely, he has come to the conclusion that they are more probably bones of a Pterodactylus than of a bird. Dr. Mantell (who was the discoverer of the said bones), made some observations.

The second paper of the evening was on an interesting subject, but too brief to be satisfactory; it was an abstract communicated by Murchison of Professor Goppert's researches on Amber, which according to Goppert, is the resin of an extinct species of Fir, nearly allied to the Spruce Fir. The extensive deposits of it which are known to exist on the south of the Baltic, are said by the author to have been drifted from forests now covered by that sea, and their geological age is believed to be that of the Molasse.

Among the substances enclosed and preserved in amber, Goppert has ascertained a great many species of plant – not less than 48, if I remember right – principally dicotyledonous, but some cryptogamous, and among the number some mosses, a tribe of plants extremely rare in a fossil state. The plants preserved in amber are mostly of existing genera, but all of extinct species, and have more analogy on the whole to the recent Flora of North America than of Europe. Insects as is well known are found in great number and variety in the amber of the Baltic.

After this was read an extract of a letter, describing a late earthquake in Cutch, by which a pretty extensive submergence of land had been occasioned. Sir H. de la Beche made some remarks on the small change of level which would be sufficient, on some parts of our own coast, to cause extensive submergence. Lastly, there was a short communication from Buckland, on some round bodies which are found on the shores of Lough Neagh, and are called by the country people "petrified potatoes". He exhibited some of them, and explained his idea of their origin, that they were masses of clay or marl, rolled into a round shape by the action of the water, and which in that process had picked up small pieces of stone of various kinds, which were now partly imbedded in them, and partly adhering to their surface; and that they had afterwards become indurated. The explanation seemed very probably, but De la Beche dissented from it, considering them as concretions, analagous to Septaria. Mr. Bowerbank mentioned a curious fact, that among the fossils of the London Clay at Sheppey, are found real tubers of some plant in a fossil state, much resembling those of Oxalis crenata, and showing, when slices of them are examined under the microscope, their cellular tissue in good preservation.

Bunbury 1890-1891, 1, pp93-94

125. 1846, January 7

"On the fossil remains of birds in the Wealden strata", by G. A. Mantell, Ll.D., F.G.S.

"On the Palaeozoic rocks of Cumberland", by the Rev. Adam Sedgwick, F.G.S., Woodwardian Professor in the University of Cambridge.

125a. Gideon Mantell wrote in his diary:

Attended Geological Society: a short notice of mine was read on Prof. Owen's notice of supposed Birds' bones of the Wealden. Prof. Owen commented on it, but not in a fair spirit; I replied that my opinion remained the same, 'that the bones hitherto found in the Wealden were too imperfect to admit of any certain inferences as to whether they belonged to Birds or Pterodactyles'.

SAS Mantell, quoted in Curwen 1940, p201

125b. Andrew Ramsay wrote in his diary:

Geological Society at night. Rambling paper by Sedgwick.

IC Ramsay

126. 1846, January 21

Continuation of the memoir on the Palaeozoic rocks of Cumberland, by the Rev. Adam Sedgwick, F.G.S., Woodwardian Professor in the University of Cambridge.

"On the so-called 'Jackstones' of Merthyr Tydvil", by Joseph Dickinson, Esq., F.G.S.

"On the coal plants of Nova Scotia", by J. W. Dawson, Esq., and C. J. F. Bunbury, Esq., F.G.S.

126a. Gideon Mantell wrote in his diary:

Went afterwards to the meeting of the Geological Society. Met Mr Murchison who has recently returned from Russia.

SAS Mantell

The Meetings

126b. Charles Bunbury wrote in his diary:

Meeting of the Geological Society. First was read the conclusion of Sedgwick's paper on the Geology of Westmoreland, the first part of which I had missed, having been absent from one meeting of the Society on account of influenza. This concluding portion was rather unintelligible and consequently uninteresting to me, depending on local details, and on an intimate knowledge of the characters and subdivisions of the Silurian System.

Nor could I follow, nor take much interest in the discussion that ensued, principally between Mr Daniel Sharp [Sharpe] and Professor Sedgwick and which turned mainly on the question whether certain beds belonged to the upper or lower Silurian group.

Afterwards was read a paper by Mr. Dawson, on the stigmaria and other fossils from Nova Scotia, to which I had added some botanical notes, but there was no discussion of it. Sir Henry de la Beche, whom I had expected to oppose the root theory of the stigmaria, was absent, and it happened there was no one present who had paid any attention to botany, except Mr Morris, and he was too diffident to speak. Dr Mantell only spoke, and expressed with great positiveness his conviction that stigmaria was sufficiently proven to be the root of sigillaria.

After the reading of the papers I had some talk with Mr Pratt, a distinguished geologist, who promises to show me a collection of fossil plants that he has procured from coal mines near Oviedo.

Lyell 1906, 1, p219

126c. Andrew Ramsay wrote in his diary:

Came up to hear Sedgewick's [Sedgwick's] paper on Wales, Cumberland &c. Made a speech about S. Wales. The old man horribly wrong-headed. Capt. James & I afterwards had a farewell wag & a cigar.

IC Ramsay, and Geikie 1895, p77

126d. Andrew Ramsay wrote to William Aveline on 31 January:

Sedgwick is at work attempting to show that we are all wrong, and that all North Wales I think, and all South Wales – Cardigan and Caermarthenshire – is Upper Silurian. He vows that Aberystwyth is Ludlow. I flared up the other night after his paper at the Geological when he said that that was the case, and thus we must not leave him the shadow of a leg to stand on. He is not content with the Cambrian, and so, gulping it down, he wheels about ten times, and turns it all in Upper Silurian.

Geikie 1895, p77

126e. John Salter wrote to Adam Sedgwick on 24 December:

I saw & spoke to you on Wednesday night, but you had so many Geological grandees about you afterwards that I quite forgot to ask you for the mss. I find I do not really want it, & so do not trouble yourself to send.

What a pity De la Beche was not at hand to give us the result (if he would) of his examination. I think Ramsay was hardly in possession of the facts of the case – they seem to think the Llandeilo must be the bottom & so that the System of S. Wales is only the bottom beds rolled over & over. How unconsciously Ramsay gave us a most capital argument on our side – for <u>deep down</u> he said in the Llandeilo flags was what ? – a development of slaty fossiliferous rocks? – no – but a quartzose sandbank full of Pentamerus oblongus & Turbinolophus. I need not tell you this is just the very top bed in all the Llandovery & Pembroke sections. nay it is the very Woolhope Limestone that Murchison said was all that intervened between the Wenlock shale & the true Caradoc. he has traced it over all Europe in the same position – & yet they tell us the Caradoc is a mere gravel-bank, & the Llandeilo a mere set of mud beds of no definite extent – but Murchison forgot we were pleading that the very Woolhope Limestone (the conglomerate of Malverns & May hill & the equivalent of the Methyafal [?] conglomerates certainly) with the Wenlock shales & limestones was just the representative of the flags, & here without intending it comes the accurate Ordnance man & tells us this <u>top bed is deep down</u> in the series. there could hardly be a stronger proof of the correctness of the position you have taken.

Poor Sharpe, you must not hit him any more – it is cowardly to strike a boy when you have knocked him over – & sure enough he made but a poor play. now pray shake hands with him, for I am going to rummage his Coniston over some evening for your plates, he has a few good things.

CUL Sedgwick IE, 138b

127. 1846, February 4

"On the Tertiary formations of the Isle of Man", by the Rev. J. Cumming.

The Meetings

"On Sternbergia", by J. S. Dawson, Esq., F.G.S.

127a. Andrew Ramsay wrote in his diary:

Geological Society at night. Paper by Cumming, Confused. At home by 12.

IC Ramsay

127b. Charles Bunbury wrote in his diary:

Meeting of the Geological Society: a long paper by Mr. Cumming on the teriary strata of the Isle of Man. These deposits, which were described with great minuteness, appear to be chiefly Post-Pleiocene, or what used to be called diluvial, gravel, boulders, and drift of various kinds.

Bunbury 1890-1891, 1, p113

128. 1846, February 20

Annual General Meeting at which Leonard Horner read the Anniversary Address and was re-elected President.

128a. Charles Bunbury wrote in his diary:

Anniversary meeting of the Geological Society, Mr. Horner presiding. Wollaston medal and proceeds of Wollaston Fund awarded to Mr. Lonsdale. An admirable address from the President. Dinner at the "Crown and Anchor", and much toastifying and speechifying as usual. I was fortunate in sitting next to Sir John Moore, whom I like particularly. Sir Roderick Murchison was there, adorned with the star of his Russian Order. Conybeare appeared for the first time as Dean of Llandaff. The affair was fatiguing, like all public dinners, but went off very well.

Lyell 1906, 1, p226

128b. Andrew Ramsay wrote in his diary:

Anniversary of the Geol Society. Heard some of it. Went to the dinner after; sat beside Sir H [De la Beche] and Henry, Ansted, Strickland, Sopwith, Austin [Austen], and others of our party. Good fun. Got slightly screwy. Murchison awfully grand.

IC Ramsay, and Geikie 1895, p78

129. 1846, February 25

The following papers were communicated:

"On a Calcareous Bed in the Thames", by George Rennie, Esq., F.G.S.

"On the Tertiary or Supracretaceous Formations of the Isle of Wight", by Joseph Prestwich, jun., Esq., F.G.S.

129a. Andrew Ramsay wrote in his diary:

> Went at night to hear paper on the Tertiaries of the Isle of Wight at the Geological. Excellent. The Dean [Buckland] made an ass of himself & Sir H [De la Beche] spoke admirably.
> IC Ramsay, and Geikie 1895, p78

129b. Charles Bunbury wrote in his diary:

> Meeting of the Geological Society. At the General Meeting was read a long paper by Mr. Prestwich, on the tertiary fomations of the Isle of Wight, which was considered valuable by those most conversant with that particular branch of geology.
> Bunbury 1890-1891, 1, p120

130. 1846, March 11

The following papers were communicated:

"Geological Report on a portion of the Beloochistan Hills", by Capt. N. Vicary, communicated by Sir R. I. Murchison, F.G.S.

"On Markings in the Hastings Sand Beds near Hastings", by the Rev. E. Tagart, F.G.S.

130a. Andrew Ramsay wrote in his diary:

> In the evening went to Geol. Soc. Paper on Scinde. Murchison in the chair. Excellent evg. Cigar divan after.
> IC Ramsay

130b. Gideon Mantell wrote in his diary:

> Geological Society. Took part in a discussion on some supposed imprints of feet on the Hastings sand.
> SAS Mantell

130c. Charles Bunbury wrote in his diary:

Meeting of the Geological Society. – Sir Roderick Murchison presided, in the absence of Mr. Horner. Darwin and Forbes were at the council, and I had some talk with them. I asked Forbes why he considered the Flora of the south-eastern or cretaceous districts of England to be more ancient than the prevailing or Germanic Flora, as he had stated in his lecture? He said that he was himself very doubtful on that point, and that it was the part of his theory on which he had least made up his mind. At the evening meeting was read a paper by Captain Vicary, on the geology of that part of Beloochistan which was traversed by Sir Charles Napier's army in the expedition against the robber tribes of the hills. The principal rock appears to be a limestone particularly characterized by the abundance of nummulites; this is overlaid in many places by a ferruginous gravel, in which are found great quantities of fossil wood and bones of large quadrupeds; these bones being penetrated by oxide of iron like those found in the Sewalik Hills. – Murchison stated that from 15 to 20 of the fossil shells and echinida sent home by Captain Vicary had been ascertained to be identical with species formerly collected in Cutch, and described in the Society's transactions.

He read part of a very characteristic letter from Sir Charles Napier, giving a most spirited and striking account of the aspect of the country. The Dean of Westminster (Buckland) and Sir H. de la Beche, expressed their approbation of the paper. Mr. Hamilton and Mr. Forbes spoke of the similarity between the geology of this tract and that of Asia Minor; and Forbes made some interesting observations on the vast formation of nummulite limestone (scaglia), which appears to range from the south of Spain through Italy, Greece, Asia Minor, Syria and Persia, even to the Indus, and which he suspects to be equivalent in point of time, not merely to the cretaceous system, but to the whole of the secondary series of our countries.

The next paper read was a short notice, by Dr. Taggart, of some supposed casts of foot-prints of birds, lately found at Hastings. This gave rise to a very entertaining discussion, Murchison and Buckland bandying jokes with each other, with great good humour.

Mantell gave his opinion that it was somewhat doubtful whether the objects in question were foot-marks at all, but that if they were so, they were more probably the tracks of reptiles than of birds; perhaps indeed they might be those of the Iguanodon.

Bunbury 1890-1891, 1, p124-126

130d. John Salter wrote to Adam Sedgwick on 12 March:

I suppose you know we had a paper on Scinde by Sir C. Napier last night. "Nummulitic Limestone & osseous gravel over a volcanic country bordering Cutch" – & R.I.M. [Murchison] read a letter or two from the gallant geologist in which he said we had a whole camel's burden for the Geol. Soc. & that it was pretty well for soldiers who cared infinitely more about the muscles of Bos than the shells of Mytilus.

CUL Sedgwick, 3, 138g

131. 1846, March 25

The following papers were communicated:

"On the Geology of the Falkland Islands", by C. Darwin, Esq., F.G.S.

"Notice on the Coal-Fields of Alabama", by Charles Lyell, Esq., F.G.S.

131a. Andrew Ramsay wrote in his diary:

Geological Society night. Had a luxurious hot bath & a cigar in it before going.

IC Ramsay

131b. Charles Bunbury wrote in his diary:

In the evening was at the meeting of the Geological Society, when a very good paper by Charles Darwin, on the Geology of the Falkland Islands was read, also Lyell's notice on the Coalfield of Alabama; and there was a good discussion.

Bunbury 1890-1891, 1, p128

132. 1846, April 118

The following papers were communicated:

"On the Superficial Detritus of Sweden, and on the Probable Causes which have affected the Surface of the Rocks in the Central and Southern portions of that Kingdom", by Sir R. I. Murchison, F.G.S.

The Meetings

132a. Gideon Mantell wrote in his diary:

Geological Society: a very interesting paper on the Drift of northern Europe by Sir R. Murchison.

SAS Mantell

132b. Andrew Ramsay wrote in his diary:

At the Geological Sir Roderick read a prime paper on boulders drift &c. Met Walton there & had a chat with him.

IC Ramsay

132c. Charles Bunbury wrote in his diary:

Meeting of the Geological Society. A long and important paper by Sir Roderick Murchison, on the distribution of drift and erratic blocks in Scandinavia. Sedgwick, De la Beche, and Buckland took part in the ensuing discussion, which was rather entertaining.

Bunbury 1890-1891, 1, p132

133. 1846, April 22

The following papers were communicated:

"On the Subdivisions of the genus Terebratula", by John Morris, Esq., F.G.S.

"Description of the Dukinfield Sigillaria", by E. W. Binney, Esq.

"On Erect Fossil Trees in Cape Breton Coal-Field", by Richard Brown, Esq.

133a. Charles Bunbury wrote in his diary:

Meeting of the Geological Society, Mr. Morris read an interesting paper on the structure of Terebratulae, pointing out the concurrence of certain structural characters, by which that extensive and important genus can be divided into natural groups. Edward Forbes spoke highly of the value of this paper. Then came two short papers, one by Mr. Binney, on a specimen discovered in the Duckinfield colliery, and now in the Manchester museum, which is supposed to prove that Stigmaria is really the root of a tree. The other by a Mr. Brown of Sydney, Cape Breton, on some upright fossil trees, in the carboniferous strata of that country, which appear to adopt the same vein of the nature of Stigmaria. A very good discussion ensued on this question, in which the Dean of Westminster, myself, Sir Henry de la Beche, and Dr. Mantell took the chief part. Buckland declared himself satisfied with the evidence of the <u>root</u> theory, and Mantell was quite vehement on the same side, not allowing that there was even the least room for doubt.

To De la Beche and myself, on the contrary, the evidence did not appear conclusive or unquestionable.

De la Beche mentioned several instances observed by himself in the Welsh coal fields, in which deceptive juxta-positions occurred that might lead to the belief of connexions between Stigmaria and the erect stems in the strata above them. He also suggested that essentially different things might be confounded under the name of Stigmaria. The Dean mentioned the rhizome of the Nymphaea, as exhibiting an articulated insertion of the fibres analogous to what occurs in Stigmaria, and seemed to think that this latter was of the same nature; if so, it would be a rhizoma, or subterranean stem, not properly a root; but in recent vegetable kingdom, as far as I am aware, such <u>rhizomata</u> belong only to herbaceous plants.

Bunbury 1890-1891, 1, pp133-134

133b. Charles Bunbury wrote to Mary Lyell on 22 April:

We had a very good discussion last Wednesday at the Society, on Stigmaria, in which I took a part. Some more evidence as to its <u>radical</u> nature was brought before us, both from Manchester and Nova Scotia, but not quite satisfactory yet. Sir Henry de la Beche is still incredulous, and I am doubtful.

Bunbury 1890-1893, 1, p141

133c. John Salter wrote to Adam Sedgwick:

Last night we had a paper at the Geol. Soc. by Morris on two neat divisions of the Terebratula one with a hole cutting off the end of the beak, & the other with the aperture beneath the curved beak. Phillips indicated it long ago – but Morris has found out a structure of the shell itself peculiar to each. I ventured to make a few remarks on the gradual development of the means of attachment as we ascend from the lowest to the highest rocks. The habitants of the ancient turbulent seas having scarcely any means of attachment, & the modern ones most fully developed.

Undated, CUL Sedgwick 3, 138f

The Meetings

135. 1846, June 17

The following papers were communicated:

"On the Silurian and Associated Rocks in Dalecarlia", by Sir R. I. Murchison, F.G.S. (conclusion).

"Description of a Fossil Chiton from the Silurian Rocks", by J. W. Salter, Esq., F.G.S.

"Notice of the occurrence of the *Elephas primigenius* at Gozo near Malta", by James Smith, Esq. of Jordan Hill, F.G.S.

135a. Gideon Mantell wrote in his diary:

Attended meeting of the Geological Society. Mr Lyell was there, having just returned from America.

SAS Mantell

135b. Edward Forbes wrote to Andrew Ramsay on 20 June:

Last Wednesday at the Geolog. C. Murchy [Murchison] had his grand sling at Sedgwick, who was absent (I believe on purpose). Old Buckland attacked Murchy who replied rather fiercely that he had lately observed symptoms of the Dean having forgotten his geology. This caused some amusement to all but Bucky. Sir Henry [De la Beche], Lyell (who had just come back) & Sharpe supported Murchy, & did it well. Salter made a speech too recanting part of the fossil data in Sedgwick's paper. His speaking was unfortunate as I fear it may set Sedgwick against him. Salter is a most valuable man but wants ballast & training. He read a very good little paper on a fossil chiton after.

IC Ramsay, f9

Notes, 1845-1846

1. Koch's fossil was a sea serpent from Alabama which he named Hydrarchos. It was later reinterpreted as the fossil whale *Zeuglodon* (Stadler 1972, xxix-xxxi).
2. Sedgwick wrote apologetically that 'neither engagements here nor my health will permit me to be at your grand meeting'. This letter is not particularly long, and may not be the one referred to. (GSL Murchison, M/S11/235).
3. Willy nilly.

Session 1846-1847

136. 1846, November 4

The following papers were communicated:

"Notice of the existence of Purbeck Strata with remains of insects, at Swindon, Wilts", by the Rev. P. B. Brodie, F.G.S.

"Additional Remarks on the Deposit of Oeningen", by Richard Owen, Esq., F.G.S., Hunterian Professor of Anatomy in the Royal College of Surgeons.

"On the Geology of the Island of Lâfu", by the Rev. W. B. Clarke, F.G.S.

136a. Gideon Mantell wrote in his diary:

> Last evening went to the Geological Society. A very thin and chilly meeting.
>
> SAS Mantell

136b. Richard Owen wrote to Adam Sedgwick:

> The Geolog. Session began well last night Oeningen (your old ground) & its fossils; Darwin's coral islands, and a good paper by your former pupil Mr Peter Brodie.
>
> CUL Sedgwick 3, 150

137. 1846, November 18

The following papers were communicated:

"On the Laws of Development of Existing Vegetation, and the application of these laws to certain Geological Problems", by John Walton, Esq.

"Remarks on the Geology of the Islands of Samos and Euboea", by Lieut. T. Spratt, R.N., F.G.S.

"On the Fossils collected by Lieut. Spratt, R.N., in the islands of Samos and Euboea", by Edward Forbes, Esq., F.G.S., Professor of Botany in King's College London.

The Meetings

137a. Edward Forbes wrote to Andrew Ramsay the following day:

> Last night was occupied with Spratt's Euboean paper – very good in its way, & leading to a good discussion led by Lyell (who is as friendly as ever).
>
> IC Ramsay, f17

138. 1846, December 2

The following papers were communicated:

"On the Coal Plants of Nova Scotia", by C. J. F. Bunbury, Esq., F.G.S.

"On Slaty Cleavage", by Daniel Sharpe, Esq., F.G.S.

138a. Charles Bunbury wrote in his diary:

> Meeting of the Geological Society. My paper on the Coal-plants of Cape Breton was read, and was well received, and what particularly pleased me was the favourable opinion of it that Dr. Hooker expressed. But the discussion on it was cut very short, in order to make room for Daniel Sharpe's paper on "Slaty Cleavage" which after all had to be very much clipped, itself, that it might be finished this evening. Sharpe's paper, however, seemed, as far as I could understand it, to be a curious and important one.
>
> Bunbury 1890-1891, 1, p196

138b. Edward Forbes wrote to Andrew Ramsay on 3 December:

> Sharpe came on last night with his cleavage. The paper was too long & complicated for me to follow without sleeping so I lost much of the drift of it. His main point is to shew that pressure has been a main agent in the production of cleavage & he brought forward some very ingenious observations & inductions drawn from the manner & directions in which fossils are squeezed (of which he certainly had many very extraordinary & beautiful specimen illustrations). There was great ingenuity shewn in the paper on this point (which he made the prominent feature of it), & it elicited cautious but favourable comments from most men present especially Darwin.[1] From a conversation this morning with Sir Henry [De la Beche] it appears to have made an impression on him, though last night they were scrimmaging. In

this dispute, neither party was very clear & both rather sharp. Sir Henry appeared to lose his self command & the clue of his argument – mainly owing to his making the latter too lengthy. However they parted good friends & I believe with mutual concessions. Except in the discussion Sharpe did not attack the Survey – & then it was not the Survey but the inferences drawn by Sir Henry (in debate) from Hunt's experiments.

IC Ramsay, f18

139. 1846, December 16

The following communication was read:

"On the Classification of the Fossiliferous Slates of North Wales, Cumberland, Westmoreland and Lancashire", (being a supplement to a paper read to the Society, March 12, 1845), by the Rev. A. Sedgwick, M.A., F.R.S., Vice-pres.G.S., Woodwardian Professor of Geology in the University of Cambridge.

139a. Leonard Horner wrote to Charles Bunbury on 20 December:

You asked me to give you some account of the proceedings at the Geological Society last Wednesday. Sedgwick came to town with a very bad cold, so he took the field with some disadvantage. He brought a very long paper, with numerous sections, part of which only he read, delivering the rest [of what] he had to say orally, and gave us an hour and a quarter of reading and speaking.

He had some descriptions of parts of North Wales he visited last summer, but the chief points in his communication was to stand up for the restoration of the lowest sedimentary rocks into a distinct system, with the old name of Cambrian, and not to have them merged into the Lower Silurian beds. His main arguments are, distinct lithological characters, position and great development, and throwing zoological evidence into subordinate importance. He was answered most ably by Murchison, who clearly established the superiority of zoological evidence as a basis of classification above all other, and as Sedgwick had claimed certain rocks as Cambrian, which Murchison had classed as Lower Silurian, and as he even went so far as almost to deny the application of the term Silurian to any other than the upper part of the series, Forbes shewed that in a deposit near Bala, in the very heart of Sedgwick's Cambrian Rocks, numerous specimens of fossils had been found, that are common both to the Upper and

The Meetings

Lower Silurian beds in other places. If we had come to a division among those geologists present who understand the subject, I suspect that the learned Professor would have gone forth alone, notwithstanding his eloquence and his long established authority.

Lyell 1890, 2, pp109-110

140. 1847, January 6

The following papers were communicated:

"On the Classification of the lowest Fossiliferous Rocks of North and South Wales", by Sir R. I. Murchison, F.G.S.

"On the Island called the Calf of Man", by the Rev. J. Cumming, F.G.S.

"Notes on some portion of the Geology of the neighbourhood of Bombay", by G. Clarke, Esq.

"On the Fossil Remains of Frogs in the Deposits of Bombay, described by Mr. Clarke", by Richard Owen, Esq., F.G.S., Hunterian Professor of Anatomy in the Royal College of Surgeons.

"On the Geology of the neighbourhood of Bombay", by Mr. Conybeare, communicated by W. J. Hamilton, Esq., Sec.G.S.

140a. Andrew Ramsay wrote in his diary:

Went to the Geological Society where I saw lots of people to shake hands with. Paper (only the preamble) read by Murchison. Introduced Captain Otter to the Chair. Had a long talk with Murchison after the meeting while at Coffee about Siluria & Cambria. He is in a state of needless alarm. Sedgewick [Sedgwick] uses him scurvily in attempting sans rhyme or reason to cut away the lower half of his system.

IC Ramsay

141. 1847, January 20

The following papers were communicated:

"On a new Clinometer", by R. B. Grantham, Esq., F.G.S.

"On the slow Transmission of Heat through Clay", by Mr. Nasmyth, communicated by the President.

"On the Wave of Translation, in Connection with the Northern Drift", by the Rev. William Whewell, D.D., F.G.S., Master of Trinity College, Cambridge.

141a. Andrew Ramsay wrote in his diary:

Dined with Sir Henry [De la Beche] at the Geological Club. Oldham also there as Forbes' guest. A very pleasant party, consisting in part of Horner, Lyell, Hallam, Forbes, Old John Taylor, Smith of Jordanhill, Pratt, Hopkins of Cambridge, Sharpe, Captain Ibbetson &c. I sat opposite Hopkins & had much discussion with him about ups & downs, lakes of fire inside the crust &c &c. Went after to the Society with Lyell, and took George Williams & Sanders there. They were much pleased. Reintroduced Williams to Smyth, Aveline, Sir H & Baily. Went home from there at 12.

Papers, about a clinometer, Naismith on the nonconducting power of clay, Whewell on waves of translation, & Prestwich on the London Clay. I always wish to speak but my heart always fails me when it comes to the point.

IC Ramsay

141b. Leonard Horner wrote to Sir Roderick Murchison:

We had a capital Club & evening, but did not overtake to paper of Prestwich, as the discussion on Nasmyth's & Whewell's papers lasted till eleven.

GSL Murchison, M/H29/14

142. 1847, February 3

The following papers were communicated:

"On the London Clay", by Joseph Prestwich, Jun., Esq., F.G.S.

"On recent depressions of Land", by James Smith, Esq., of Jordan Hill, F.G.S. (commenced).

142a. Andrew Ramsay wrote in his diary:

Paper at the Geological by Prestwich. Excellent. On the London Clay & Hampshire affair. Many havering & some good speeches made. Among others Bowerbank on the spur of the moment (after Forbes had declared how much information was scattered) proposed to get up a publishing tertiary society, and this when we went down stairs to tea, expanded into a proposition that a Society should be formed on the model of the Ray Soc. for the purpose of publishing descriptions & illustrations of all the British fossils, beginning at the top. Bowerbank got lots of names down at once, & thus they take out of our hands what all the world looked for us to do. So much for the Palaeontological department & its six years work!

IC Ramsay

142b. Leonard Horner wrote to Charles Bunbury a few days later:

We had an excellent meeting last Wednesday. It was entirely taken up with a valuable paper by Prestwich, the result of twelve years' observation, making out very clearly that the so-called London clay of Bracklesham near Portsea and of Barton in Hordwell Cliff, is not equivalent to the London Clay in the London Basin, but of posterior date, and that the Calcaire Grossier of the Paris Basin, supposed to be synchronomous with the London Basin, is the equivalent of the Hampshire Beds. This view involves a very different state of the sea bottom over that area at two different periods. The paper was much lauded by all who spoke, and the observations it gave rise to, lasted till elevn o'clock.

Misdated 27 February 1847, [2] in Lyell 1890, 2, p113

142c. Forbes's biographers recorded:

At a meeting of the Geological Society a discussion ensued upon a paper by Mr Prestwich on the <u>Tertiaries of the London and Hampshire Basins</u>. Forbes, in the course of his speech, remarked with regret how much infomation on this subject lay scattered in different books and periodicals. Mr. Bowerbank followed, and on the spur of the moment, suggested the establishment of a Tertiary Publishing Society. The idea immediately found favour, and afterwards at tea downstairs, it was expanded into a proposition to found a society for publishing plates of fossils, not from the Tertiary deposits only, but from all the British formations. This was the origin of the Palaeontographical Society. [3]

Wilson and Geikie 1861, p412

143. 1847, February 19

Annual General Meeting at which Leonard Horner read the Anniversary Address and Sir Henry De la Beche was elected President.

143a. Andrew Ramsay wrote in his diary:

Anniversary Meeting of the Geological Society. Horner prosy. Sat with Forbes & Darwin. At night Anniversary dinner of the Society. Sir Henry [De la Beche] being new President in the chair. On his right sat the American Minister [4] on his left Lord Morpeth. We made a pleasant party at our part of the table. Jukes, R. Chambers, Forbes, Reeks, Percy, Playfair, Ibbetson &c &c. Sir H did remarkably well, speaking loudly clearly & concisely & keeping down much of the ordinary adulation.

IC Ramsay

143b. Gideon Mantell wrote in his diary:

Anniversary of the Geol. Society. Went to the meeting but stayed only a few minutes; being very ill, from a night passed in great suffering.

SAS Mantell

143c. Charles Lyell wrote to his father on 21 February:

Horner, to whom as President of the Geological Society I have dedicated my book, got great credit, as he deserved, for his two years' service to the Geological Society. Sir H. De la Beche, the new President, was supported by Lord Morpeth, who spoke with his usual eloquence, and after him Bancroft made a very good speech, ending with saying he had obtained leave to give my health. So I was called up very early, and told them my last news from De Verneuil and Agassiz, both foreign members of the Geological Society, and who having both visited the United States since I returned from America last spring, had given us as flattering an account of their reception, and the number of congenial enthusiastic minds they had been in contact with, as I could have done. I amused them by narrating what De Verneuil had said to me, when I asked him if he was not struck with the reigning idea which cheered one in travelling in that country: progress, progress. 'Yes', he said, 'your information is quite antiquated; it is six months old. You have only seen the railroad penetrating westward 300

The Meetings

miles, through forests and morasses, but I have seen the electric telegraph extending beyond the termination of the railway; the wires attached to the trunks of trees from which the boughs had just been lopped off, and the news carried with the speed of lightning to villages and towns which have never yet seen a locomotive engine'. The Bishop of Norwich [Edward Stanley] spoke well, though some might have been less pleased than we geologists to hear him wish that 'they who differ but in a little in theological matters, would only live in as great harmony with each other as he saw scientific men do, who differed so widely in their theoretical opinions on many points, which they could discuss, as we did, without quarrelling, and cherishing, as became Christians, the unity of spirit and the bond of peace'. Poor man! he has enough of it in his diocese, although he has not, I believe, been of late personally embroiled in the ecclesiatical disputes that divide many of his clergy. 5

Lyell 1881, 2, p120

144. 1847, March 10

The following papers were communicated:

"On the Gypsiferous Strata of Nova Scotia", by Richard Brown, Esq., communicated by Charles Lyell, Esq., F.G.S.

"On the Soft Parts of Orthoceras", by J. G. Anthony, Esq., communicated by Charles Lyell, Esq., F.G.S.

"On the Structure of Trinucleus", by J. W. Salter, Esq., F.G.S.

144a. Gideon Mantell wrote in his diary:

Attended the meeting of the Geological Society: a thin attendance: Mr Lyell in the Chair: a very uninteresting affair. Left soon after ten.

SAS Mantell, quoted in Curwen 1940, p214

144b. Andrew Ramsay wrote in his diary:

Then loitered to the Geological Society where I heard sundry small papers read. Lyell was in the Chair. Never saw the Geol. Soc. as Joyce remarked look so like a family party before, the attendance was so small.

IC Ramsay

145. 1847, April 14

"On the Structure and Probable Age of the Coal-field of the James River, near Richmond, Virginia", by Charles Lyell Esq, V.P.G.S.

"Descriptions of Fossil Plants from the Coal-field near Richmond, Virginia", by C. J. E. Bunbury, Esq., F.L.S.

145a. Charles Bunbury wrote in his diary:

I hear a very satisfactory account of my paper on the Richmond Fossil Plants, which was read on the 14th, together with Lyell's geological account of that coal field. I hear that the discussion was excellent, and that my paper was highly approved of by those most competent to judge it.

Bunbury 1890-1891, 1, p226

146. 1847 April 28

The following paper was communicated:

"On the Geology of Scinde", by Capt. N. Vicary, with an introduction by Sir R. I. Murchison, F.G.S.

146a. Charles Bunbury wrote in his diary:

I went to the Council of the Geological Society, where a rather active debate took place, on some propositions of Daniel Sharpe; and in the evening to the general meeting of the Society. A paper by Captain Vicary, on the Geology of Scinde, was read. It was dry enough in itself, being little more than a collection of rough notes, but it gave occasion to a very interesting lecture from Dr. Falconer, on the geology and physical geography of the northern and northwestern boundaries of India. He pointed out the striking agreement in geological structure between the Hala and Sulimaun mountains, which run northwards from near the mouth of the Indus to within sight of Caubul, and the Siwalik mountains, which form the outer or advanced range of the Himalayas. He noticed also the prodigious development of the nummulitic limestone and of the bone beds or very late tertiary deposits, in which the remains of large extinct mammalia were found in such extraordinary abundance and variety by himself and Major Cautley. These bone beds have been traced at intervals along the Hala range and other mountain chains connected with it, for

The Meetings

nearly a thousand miles from south to north, and along the Siwalik hills for 1700 miles from north-west to south-east. He then remarked the great contrast presented by the actual condition of these mountain-chains, which appear from geological evidence to have been formerly so very similar; the Siwalik hills being covered with luxuriant forests, while the mountains of corresponding geological structure on the West of the Indus are utterly bare and barren, like skeletons of mountains, without a tree or shrub, or a green spot, and almost without a drop of water. He gave us a striking picture of the utter desolation of those mountain tracts, and of the wild and fierce character of their human inhabitants. Finally he noticed the great salt range cut through by the Indus at Kalabaugh, which he considers of secondary age; and he mentioned the existence of Palaeozoic rocks in the mountains east of Caubul. Murchison observed that the remarkable conformity of geological structure between the Sewalik [Siwalik] Hills and the mountains west of the Indus, while their directions are so entirely different, is adverse to Elie de Beaumont's theory of the parallelism of contemporaneous mountain chains. [6]

Bunbury 1890-1891, 1, pp230-232

147. 1847, May 12

The following papers were communicated:

"On Fossil Chimaeroid Fishes", by Sir P. G. Egerton, Bart., M.P., F.G.S.

"On Kent's Cavern, Torquay", by E. Vivian, Esq., communicated by R. A. C. Austen, Esq., F.G.S.

147a. Gideon Mantell wrote in his diary:

Attended Council of the Geological Society and the evening meeting. A large attendance.

SAS Mantell

147b. Charles Bunbury wrote in his diary:

I dined at Richard Napier's, and went late to the Geological Society, where, however, I heard a very good discussion, on the subject of the human remains in Kent's Cavern at Torquay. The question was, whether the human bones and works of art found in that cave were contemporaneous with the remains of extinct quadrupeds, with which they occur apparently mixed. Austin maintained that they might be contemporaneous, and Sedgwick appeared somewhat inclined to the same opinion; but Buckland, Lyell and Mantell took the opposite view, and seemed to have the general opinion of the meeting on their side. [7]

Bunbury 1890-1891, 1, p237

Notes, 1846-1847

1. Darwin's interest in slaty cleavage is shown by his letter to Sharpe of 1 November 1846, Burkhardt and Smith 1985-2003, 3, pp360-361.
2. This letter must be misdated; perhaps it should be 7th February.
3. See Anon 1896, for a brief account of the founding and early history of the Society.
4. George Bancroft, Esq.
5. Edward Stanley was a vigorous reformer who strictly enforcd the Plurality and Non-residence Act, seriously disrupting the tranquility of his diocese (Stanley 1879).
6. For an account of Elie de Beaumont's theories on mountain building *see* Greene 1982, 6.
7. The background to Vivian's paper, which was never published, is given in Van Riper 1993. Vivian himself commented on the rejection of his paper in MacEnery 1859, p60.

Session 1847-1848

148. 1847, November 17

The following papers were communicated:

"On the Geology of the Coasts of Australia", by J. B. Jukes, Esq., F.G.S.

"Remarks to accompany a Geological Map of Western Australia", by Messrs. J. W. and F. T. Gregory, communicated by the President.

148a. Gideon Mantell wrote in his diary:

Attended the Council and Meeting of the Geological Society: Sir Thomas Mitchell (from Australia) was present.

SAS Mantell

The Meetings

148b. Edward Forbes wrote to Andrew Ramsay:

I don't think I mentioned but Jukes's paper on Australia was read at the Geological Society on Wednesday last. It came on too suddenly but was fairly used, especially by Greenough who made a handsome speech about Jukes. Sir Thomas Mitchill [Mitchell] was there which was fortunate though he threw but little light on the subject.

IC Ramsay, f54

149. 1847, December 1

The following papers were communicated:

"Report on the Fossil Remains of Mollusca from the Palaeozoic Formations of the United States, contained in the Collection of Charles Lyell, Esq.", by Daniel Sharpe, Esq., F.G.S.

149a. Edward Forbes wrote to Andrew Ramsay on 16 November:

At the last Geolog. Soc. meet we had a most interesting paper by Sharpe on the relations of the American & English Silurian fossils. I had occasion to pitch into De Verneuil & the French pretty strongly in return for a side slap at me in the last Bulletin, where there is a long & very interesting paper by De Vernl on the same subject with Sharpe [1] ... Salter put in a squeak contradicting everybody & everything, but ?without assigning a reason why, so sat down unattended to.

IC Ramsay, f40

150. 1848, January 5

The following paper was communicated:

"On the Silurian Rocks in the Valley of the Tweed", by James Nicol, Esq., F.G.S.

150a. Andrew Ramsay wrote in his diary:

Dined at the Geological Club, Clunn's Hotel, Covent Garden, for the first time since becoming a member. Selwyn accompanied Sir Henry [De la Beche]. Sir H. was in the chair & all the rest were Horner & Prevost, so we were but 5 in all. The dinner was splendid and the wine not bad. At the Geological after we had a paper by Nichol [Nicol] the new Secretary, which he read in a monotonous, drawling, school boy voice like some of the old scholars I remember at the Parish School at Saltcoats 24 years ago. The paper was good enough on the Silurian and part of the O.R. [Old Red Sandstone] of the south of Scotland. Lyell, Salter, Greenough, and I spoke. I rose a little afraid, but got on famously before I had said a dozen words & as I was told after gave great satisfaction to Greenough & some others, who liked the Survey style of treating such subjects. ... I took good care in my speech to clinch two things; first stating that on analogous subjects some papers would be read by the Survey; & 2nd, giving Selwyn a bit of laudation to the cheering of his heart.

IC Ramsay, and Geikie 1895, p122

150b. Andrew Ramsay wrote to William Aveline on 6 January:

I saw Sir H. [De la Beche] in the chair last night for the first time. I flared up and made a Silurian and Old Red speech about a paper on Scotch Silurians by Nichol [Nicol] the Vice-Secretary.

BGS Archives, GSM1/420

151. 1848, January 19

The following paper was communicated:

"On the Agates of Oberstein", by W. J. Hamilton, Esq., Sec.G.S.

151a. Andrew Ramsay wrote in his diary:

Dined at the Geol. Club. Oldham and Jukes there. Pleasant party. Slow evening at the Society. I fell asleep! Bad!!!

I was proposed today as a Member of Council at the Geol. Soc. Got home from the Society by one in the morning. It is always too late there.

IC Ramsay

151b. Edward Forbes wrote to R I Murchison on 31 January:

The Society is going on pretty well, & the debates have been now & then well supported. We want you however sadly. Sedgwick is an invalid & never appears: Dr. Fitton is almost a stranger: the Dean [Buckland] grows wilder in his orations every day – so you see how we are. The Club has been hardly attended & wants a

The Meetings

revival. Many schemes for its reformation are broached – not always those most likely to reform it.

GSL Murchison, M/F11/1

152. 1848, February 2

The following papers were communicated:

"On the Fossil Remains of Birds from New Zealand", by G. A. Mantell, LL.D., F.G.S.

"On the Organic Remains in the Skiddaw Slates", by the Rev. Adam Sedgwick, F.G.S., Woodwardian Professor in the University of Cambridge.

152a. Gideon Mantell wrote in his diary:

Read a paper on the Fossil birds' bones from New Zealand, collected by Walter, before the Geological Society. A full attendance. Mr Darwin was present, and expressed himself much gratified. The Dean of Westminster [William Buckland] unfortunately indulged more than usual in buffoonery, and completely marred the discussion, which consequently was utterly unworthy the subject.

SAS Mantell, quoted in Curwen 1940, p219

152b. Andrew Ramsay wrote in his diary:

Dined at the Geological Club with Mallet for my guest ... Bristow was there, & we had a capital party. There was at the Society first a paper by Mantell on the Dinornis & then one by Sedgwick on Cumberland. I spoke on the latter, & was almost surprised at my own fluency. It was late then. Darwin left immediately after I was done, I ran out to shake hands with him on the stair. He said he highly approved of what I said, was delighted to hear me say so, & asked my address. Sedgewick [Sedgwick] made but little reply, for he did not seem well. I had a chat with him after, most amicably, tho' I had relieved my mind by repaying him for the slight he once put on me in the Society, by saying in a speech he did not believe a word of what I had uttered.

IC Ramsay

153. 1848, February 18

Annual General Meeting at which Sir Henry De la Beche read the Anniversary Address and was re-elected President.

153a. Andrew Ramsay wrote in his diary:

>Anniversary of Geol. Soc. Did not get down from my lecture till after the medal had been given to and acknowledged by Dr Buckland. [2] Staid [Stayed] at Sir H [De la Beche]'s address which passed off very well. I sat mostly next Darwin. I was elected a member of the Geol. council.
>
>Anniversary dinner after. Sir Henry did most admirably in the chair, turning off all his speeches. Sedgwick made the best speech of the evening. I was called on to return thanks for the Survey. Playfair for the Museum. I got on well all save one short hesitation caused by my being so intent on my first paragraph, that I quite forgot the second. We broke up abt eleven, and in the long room Smyth, Reeks, Bristow, & I had some supper in the "dilly" [Piccadilly Hotel]. Got home at half-past three.
>
> IC Ramsay, and Geikie 1895, p123

154. 1848, March 22

The following papers were communicated:

"On the internal Structure of Halonia", by J. S. Dawes, Esq., F.G.S.

"Observations on the Cystidea and the Crinoidea generally", by Major Thomas Austin, F.G.S.

"On Fossil Bones from the Crag, Suffolk", by John Wiggins, Esq., F.G.S.

154a. Andrew Ramsay wrote in his diary:

>Geological Society night. Dined at the Club. Sir H. [De la Beche] gone, & Moore in the chair. I sat next Prestwich & Austin [Austen] & opposite Forbes & Lord Selkirk. All pleasant men. The last seems most agreeable & unaffected.
>
>Good night at the Soc. Buckland made a most witty speech. It was abt Crinoids, & he began by saying that the debate seemed to him to have "more of a gastronomic than a palaeontological character, for all that had been said bore upon the relation of the plates to the mouth and the mouth to the plates". Forbes spoke

The Meetings

well, & to the purpose. So did Charlesworth & Carpenter. I was glad of this, for Emmerson, the American, was there. Got home late. Had George Williams & Sanders there.

IC Ramsay, and Geikie 1895, p124

155. 1848, April 5

The following papers were communicated:

"Sketch of the Structure of part of North Wales", by J. B. Jukes, Esq., F.G.S., and Alfred Selwyn, Esq.

"Sketch of the Structure of part of North and South Wales and Shropshire", by Prof. A. C. Ramsay, F.G.S. and W. T. Aveline, Esq., F.G.S.

155a. Andrew Ramsay wrote in his diary:

Jukes & I read papers tonight at the Geological on N. Wales and South Wales. Sir H. [De la Beche] was in great alarm beforehand. Jukes read first. Sedgwick was present and most agreable & conciliatory. He made a most complimentary speech after. Lyell ditto. Buckland was all in favour, but in attempting to quote Scripture made a great mull of it, & broke down greatly to the amusement of all, especially the Bishop of Oxford [Samuel Wilberforce]. I lectured rather much (they told me) the natural effect of a 3 months first course of lectures.

IC Ramsay, and Geikie 1895, p124

156. 1848, June 14

The following papers were communicated:

"On Organic Remains recently found in the Wealden", by G. A. Mantell, LL.D., F.G.S.

"On the Strata from Christ Church Harbour to Poole Harbour", by Joseph Prestwich, jun., Esq., F.G.S.

"On the Geological Structure of Western Australia", by Dr. Sommer, communicated by the President.

"On Ingleborough Cave", by J. W. Farrer, Esq., F.G.S.

"Notes on Corals from the Greensand at Atherfield", by William Lonsdale, Esq., F.G.S.

156a. Gideon Mantell wrote in his diary:

Geological Society. Read my paper on the Wealden, and exhibited my jaw of the Iguanodon. A very full meeting. Dr. Buckland, Faraday, Lyell, Sir H. De la Beche, etc. present: Capt. Lambart Brickenden, who sent me the fossil was there, and we met for the first time. [3] The affair passed off capitally; every one was in good humour, and I had every reason to be gratified with the cordial manner in which this fortunate confirmation of my early researches was received.

SAS Mantell, quoted in Curwen 1940, p223

Notes, 1847-1848

1. Verneuil 1847. The side slap is not obvious, but may be the footnote on p686 on life at depths in the sea.
2. Ramsay was in the middle of his first course of lectures as Professor of Geology at University College London (Geikie 1895, pp117-120).
3. The fossil in question was the lower jaw of an iguanodon with three teeth in place.

Session 1848-1849

157. 1848, December 13

The following paper was communicated:

"Notes on the Alps and Appenines, more particularly on the Cretaceous and Supracretaceous Groups", by Sir R. I. Murchison, F.G.S. (commenced).

157a. Gideon Mantell wrote in his diary:

In the evening attended meeting of the Geological Society, and the Council in the afternoon. An interesting paper by Prof. Rod. Murchison on the Alps and Appenines. A full meeting. Prof. Henry Rodgers [Henry Darwin Rogers] explained his theory of elevation, flexures, faults etc. – Returned soon after midnight.

SAS Mantell

The Meetings

158. 1849, January 3

The following communications were read:

"On the Hampshire Freshwater Tertiaries", by J. C. Moore, Esq., Sec.G.S.

"Additional Observations on the Ridgway Cutting", by C. H. Weston, Esq., F.G.S.

"On the Silicified Soft Parts of a Zoophyte", by J. S. Bowerbank, Esq., F.G.S.

158a. Andrew Ramsay wrote in his diary:

Club dinner after. Small but pleasant party. I sat between Sir Charles Lyell & Forbes. So so night at the Society after. I spoke a few words on the Ridgeway cutting. Sir Roderick Murchison was there – the first time I have seen him for nearly two years. He has given up his wig on the Continent & looks much better in consequence!

IC Ramsay, and Geikie 1895, p143

159. 1849, January 17

The following papers were communicated:

"Notes on the Alps and Appennines, more particularly on the Cretaceous and Supracretaceous Groups", by Sir R. I. Murchison, F.G.S. (concluded).

159a. Gideon Mantell wrote in his diary:

Attended evening meeting of the Geological Society: Sir R. Murchison on the Alps etc. A very full attendance. Mr Brunel [Isambard Kingdom Brunel] the C.E. [Civil Engineer] was admitted a fellow.

SAS Mantell

160. 1849, February 16

Annual General Meeting at which Sir Henry De la Beche read the Anniversary Address and Sir Charles Lyell was elected President.

Session 1848-49

160a. Gideon Mantell wrote in his diary:

Anniversary of the Geological Society: unable to attend the meeting. To the dinner at Willis's rooms, St James Street.[1] A very good company: the Archbishop of Canterbury, the Dean of Westminster [William Buckland], Sir Robert Peel, Sir R. Murchison, Prof. Sedgwick addressed the company; Lyell the President in the Chair. I returned thanks for the Vice-Presidents. Got home soon after eleven.

SAS Mantell

160b. Andrew Ramsay wrote in his diary:

Sir H.'s speechifying day. The Geological Anniversary. Prestwich was presented with the Wollaston medal. In rising to present it Sir H. [De la Beche] upset two large oil lamps that stood on the table before him & made a prodigious smash. All the house laughed & poor P. was a trifle discomposed. He has a glorious head. Sir H.'s speech was said to be excellent. I was obliged to run off to lecture. Went down from College to the dinner at the Thatched House Tavern.[2] I sat betwixt Playfair & Capt James. Reeks, Bristow, Smyth, M'Coy, Tyler, Austin [Austen], Forbes, & I were all in a lump. Lyell made a poor speaker in the chair & purposely harried the Survey, leaving the impression, in spite of the affected praise, that the men of the Survey were unable to generalise, & that he & such as he were the men for that. This he did deliberately to show that a man like himself, who knows nothing of practical work, would yet be a very proper Director for the Survey. It was inconceivably shabby. He always looks awkward when we meet. Constrained and conscious.

Sedgwick made a magnificent speech. The Archbishop a goodish one, Van der Weyer a good one, Sir H a good one, Buckland a fair, Sir Robert Peel a splendid one, Murchison an indifferent one, from trying too much.

IC Ramsay, and Geikie 1895, p144

160c. Gideon Mantell wrote to Benjamin Silliman on 20 February:

The anniversary dinner of the Geological Society was held on Friday; the Archbishop of Canterbury, Sir Robert Peel, the Russian Ambassador, were there; and my friend, Sir Charles Lyell, the new President, took the chair. Murchison, De la Beche, Buckland,

The Meetings

Sedgwick, and almost all our great men, were present. The Archbishop made an admirable speech in defence of scientific pursuits and geological in particular; and Sir Robert a senatorial declamation in like spirit. Lyell spoke good sense, but was so long in his pauses, and so hesitating, that I was frightened out of my wits lest he should break down. Dr. Buckland made an academical oration, like one got by heart by a young collegiate; and Sedgwick poured forth a flood of eloquence, which in spite of the discordant tones in which it was uttered (for his voice is most harsh), carried everything before it. The Belgian Ambassador, in capital English, with just sufficient foreign accent to add to its interest, gave a luminous address in praise of science, and in just encomiums on his own country for having remained unmoved in the midst of the revolutionary tempest which had swept over the Continent. Murchison made a courtly speech, highly complimentary to the nobles present; and your humble servant, who had to respond as one of the Vice-Presidents, gave a flourish of trumpets, which concluded the entertainment. Sir H. De la Beche has been a capital President; his address, I hear, was excellent ...

Spokes 1927, p214

160d. Sir Charles Lyell wrote to George Ticknor:

I have been very busy with my inauguration dinner as President of the Geological Society, and suceeded in getting the Archbishop of Canterbury (Dr. Sumner, author of 'Records of Creation', a geologico-theological work), Sir Robert Peel, Van de Weyer, and a great many M.P.'s and notabilities to come, so that the speaking is allowed to be the most brilliant we ever had at any anniversary. Sedgwick spoke very eloquently, and Peel; and the Archbishop made a straightforward and manly speech.

Misdated 7 Feb 1849, Lyell 1881, 2, p154

161. 1849, March 21

The following communications were read:

"Description of the Erect Sigillaria with Conical Tap-roots, from the Sydney Coal, Cape Breton", by R. Brown, Esq., communicated by the President.

"Notice of Recent Researches in Asia Minor", by M. P. de Tchihatcheff, communicated by Sir R. I. Murchison, V.P.G.S.

161a. Andrew Ramsay wrote in his diary:

... to the Geological. Interesting night there. Lots of evidence of local growth of coal in Nova Scotia, & a prize debate in which Bunbury showed well that Sigillaria was not a true fern.

IC Ramsay

162. 1849, May 30

The following communication was read:

"On the Superficial Detritus of the Alps as compared with that of Northern Europe", by Sir R. I. Murchison, V.P.G.S.

162a. Gideon Mantell wrote in his diary:

Last evening went to the Geological Society to receive Prince Albert, who attended and was admitted a Fellow. Sir Roderick Murchison read a paper on the glaciers, and the erratic boulders of the Alps: maintaining that the phenomena were solely attributable to the agency of ice-floes when the country was submerged. Professor James Forbes, of Edinburgh, who had supported the glacial theory, rose and defended his own opinions, which he stated were in no respect weakened by the facts and arguments of Sir Roderick. Sir R. made an able reply. The Prince gossiped a while with several of the Fellows. I shewed him a beautiful tooth of ptychodus imbedded in a flint, belonging to Mr Wetherell of Highgate. The meeting passed off very well. The Prince and his three attendants left before eleven.

SAS Mantell, quoted in Curwen 1940, p236

Notes, 1848-1849

1. Willis's Rooms were in King Street, St James, and were also known as Almack's (Walford *ca* 1875, 4, pp196-197).
2. The Thatched House Tavern in St James Street was used by many learned societies for their dinners, including the Linnean, Royal Geographical and Astronomical (Walford *ca* 1875, 4, pp154-156). Clearly Mantell and Ramsay cannot both be correct as to the location of the dinner, and there is no evidence in the Society's archive.

The Meetings

Session 1849-1850

163. 1849, December 19

The following communication was read:

"On Craters of Denudation and the Structure of Volcanic Cones", by Sir Charles Lyell, Pres.G.S.

163a. Andrew Ramsay wrote in his diary:

Lyell's paper after. He got so long winded that at 10 I was obliged to leave ere it was over.

IC Ramsay

164. 1850, January 9

The following communications were read:

"Observations on Dudley Trilobites", by T. W. Fletcher, Esq., F.G.S.

"Remarks on the Inferior Oolite near Cheltenham", by the Rev. P. B. Brodie, F.G.S.

Letter from G. F. Ruxton Esq., to Prof. Daubeny, M.D., F.G.S. on Volcanic Rocks in Northern Mexico.

Letter from Prof. Eugene Sismonda to Sir R. I. Murchison, V.P.G.S., "On the discovery of a nearly perfect Skeleton of *Mastodon angustidens* near Asti in Piedmont".

164a. Andrew Ramsay wrote in his diary:

A large party at the Club. Over 20. I took Dr. Falconer, Forbes took Captn Graves & Professor Munch. The papers but so so. Salter made the whole Society laugh by unwittingly pointing at a certain spine in a most awkward position as the distinguishing type of the male trilobite, & to mend matters when he heard us all laugh (Lyell in the chair among the number) he said "not being a caudal appendage of course it presented no similarity –" & here he stopped & dashed out his chalked diagram.
I spoke on Brodie's paper on the absurdity of calling the Cotswold valleys signs of disturbance & dislocation, and pointed out the true way in which they were formed by an old Atlantic

when the Cotswolds formed a coastline. The President said in his speech, he hoped I would make my interesting observations the subject of a special paper.

At ten after Sharpey [Sharpe] took me to task on the easy way I took it for granted that such an old fashioned notion ought to be extinct as that of a fault or a disturbance for any valley. He never saw one that wasn't. "I wish too I could get all the world to think as I do, as you Survey folk seem to do". "I would be very sorry to see it", quoth I. Home shortly after 12.

IC Ramsay

165. 1850, January 23

The following communication was read:

"On the Structure of the Deposits between the London Clay and the Chalk. Part 1. On the Basement bed of the London Clay", by Joseph Prestwich, jun., Esq., F.G.S.

165a. Andrew Ramsay wrote in his diary:

Dined at home, & went to the Geological Society. Good paper by Prestwich on the division between the London & Plastic clays. Sir H. [De la Beche] made a great mull of his speech. I spoke & felt I did so easily & was applauded.

IC Ramsay

166. 1850, February 6

The following communication was read:

"On the Pseudo-Volcanic Rocks of the Papal States and adjacent parts of Italy", by Sir R. I. Murchison, V.P.G.S.

166a. Andrew Ramsay wrote in his diary:

Murchison read a paper at the Geol Soc on the Pseudo Volc phenomena round Rome. Sir H. [De la Beche] made his usual rigmarole speech. I spoke also.

IC Ramsay

167. 1850, February 15

Annual General Meeting of the Geological Society at which Sir Charles Lyell read the Anniversary Address and was re-elected President.

The Meetings

167a. Gideon Mantell wrote in his diary:

> Anniversary of the Geological Society: sent my specimens from the Royal [1] to lay on the table. Arrived too late for the meeting. Dined with the Society in the evening: my son accompanied me. Met my old friend Mr Martin of Pulborough. A pretty good attendance: but the absence of Dr. Buckland (and the distressing cause), [2] Prof. Sedgwick, Dr. Fitton, and other old familiar faces, was to me a source of deep regret.
>
> SAS Mantell, quoted in Curwen 1940, p250

167b. Andrew Ramsay wrote in his diary:

> Geol. Soc. Anniversary. Did not hear Lyells speech. Was lecturing. Ann. Dinn. at the Thatched House. I observe that Forbes & I creep higher & higher at table each year. We were close by the corner this time. Jukes, Van Voorst, Forbes, Austen & I made a merry group.
>
> IC Ramsay

168. 1850, February 27

The following communications were read:

"On the Strata and Organic Remains exposed in the Cutting of the Branch Railway from the Great Western Line near Chippenham through Trowbridge, to Westbury in Wiltshire", by R. N. Mantell, Esq., communicated by G. A. Mantell, LL.D., F.G.S.

"On the Dinornis and other Birds, and the Fossils and Rock-specimens from New Zealand", by G. A. Mantell, LL.D., F.G.S.

168a. Andrew Ramsay wrote in his diary:

> With Sir H. [De la Beche] to the Geological Club. Reeks said to him, "by the way what do you intend to do about young Tyler". He hummed & hawed & did not know what to say, so I recommended him to withdraw him or he might get his man blackballed. [3] So he withdrew him after dinner, & two other men were elected both of whom I blackballed, on the ground that neither of them were geologists. I sat next Sir Philipp Egerton, & said Morris ought to be a member which he cordially agreed in. A hot & fierce discussion

Session 1849-50

followed the Geol paper, between Owen & Mantell. It was terrible to listen to the cold cutting irony of both. [4] Morris, Van Voorst & I went to have some supper after ...

IC Ramsay

168b. Gideon Mantell wrote in his diary:

Attended the Council of the Geological Society; took my New Zealand, and Reginald's Oxford Clay fossils to Somerset House. In the evening Reginald's Notes on the Wilts Somerset and Weymouth Railway was read; and afterwards I read mine on Walter's collections. Prof. Owen, who came loaded with Moa bones, commented in his usual deprecating manner on my remarks, and vowed that the pair of perfect feet were imperfect, and that the bird had hind toes; and declared that he had a perfect foot etc. which he had described the night before at the Zoological Society! Poor envious man! Professor Forbes made some interesting remarks corroborative of Walter's geological discoveries: having received specimens from New Zealand but a few days ago. I replied to the attack of Prof. Owen, and in relation to the supposed hind toe reminded the Society of the egregious blunder made by Prof. O. on the very same subject: having mistaken the end of a humerus for the tarso-metatarsal of a wader, and upon that occasion having pointed out the oval cicatrix as a certain character! Sir Charles Lyell concluded the meeting by a few complimentary remarks; and thus my labours have ended; and I cannot but ask myself, was it worth while to take so much trouble for such little purpose? There was a very large attendance, and the company seemed much gratified.

SAS Mantell

169. 1850, April 10

The following communication was read:

"On the Discovery, by Professor Lepsius, of Sculptured Marks in Rocks of the Nile Valley in Nubia, indicating that within the Historical Period the River flowed at a higher Level than in Modern Times", by Leonard Horner, Esq., F.G.S.

169a. Andrew Ramsay wrote in his diary:

Dressed & went to the Club. Capital meeting. Lyell in the chair, & present Lord Enniskillen, Lord Alfred Churchhill [Churchil], Sir

The Meetings

R Murchison, Sir Philipp Egerton, Smith of Jordanhill, Hopkins, Forbes, Prestwich, Capt. James, Sharpe, Austen, Prevost, Hamilton & self. I sat at the lower end among the jolly fellows & we all got into prodigious spirits. Went for a little to the Society.

IC Ramsay

170. 1850, April 24

The following communications were read:

"On the Boulder Clay of Wick", by John Cleghorn, Esq., communicated by the President.

"On the occurrence of Marine Shells in the Stratified Beds below the Till, near Airdrie", by James Smith, Esq., of Jordan Hill, F.G.S.

"On the New Red Sandstone of the Vale of Nith", by Robert Harkness, Esq., communicated by the President.

170a. Andrew Ramsay wrote in his diary:

Dined at the Geological Club, & sat at the lower end with Moore, Sharpe & ?Galton. I indulged in a "wild & extravagant gaiety", & we had roars of laughter long & loud. Spoke at night abt drift & opposed Murchison. Lyell supported me.

IC Ramsay

171. 1850, May 22

The following communications were read:

"On a Gap in the Greywacke Formation of the Eastern Lammermuirs, filled with Old Red Sandstone Conglomerate", by W. Stevenson, Esq., communicated by Sir R. I. Murchison, V.P.G.S.

"On the Stratified Formations of the Venetian Alps", by Signor Achille de Zigno, communicated by Sir R. I. Murchison, V.P.G.S.

"On the Limestone of Nash, Near Presteign, South Wales", by J. E. Davis, Esq., F.G.S.

Session 1849-50

171a. Gideon Mantell wrote in his diary:

Attended meeting and Council of the Geological Society. Prof. Sedgwick, Dr. Fitton, Sir R. Murchison, De la Beche present: Sir C. Lyell presided. Returned home with Reginald soon after twelve!

SAS Mantell

171b. Edward Forbes wrote to Andrew Ramsay on 23 May:

Last night was Geological meeting. We had a small but merry club party not remarkable for the propriety of the stories told. James (the Captain) was there...

It is about the Geological discussion I have chiefly to write. Davis's paper on Nash Scar was read. Aware of it in the morning I looked up my notes & set Salter to work to see to the lists of fossils. Davis attempted to show that the limestone was Wenlock L. & [?] infilled a blank between it & the Caradoc. He gave very copious & good lists of fossils. In his paper he remarked without much comment that the view he had taken was opposed to that advanced by Sedgwick & held by you & Aveline in your joint paper about Wales. The discussion brought down the whole Society, [?] Sharpe at the head on the Survey. Sedgwick was there & unfortunately wavered in his opinion & after making half a stand, gave it up. Murchison crowed on his old notions being right. Unluckily Sir Henry [De la Beche] had not made himself acquainted with the points & made a most unfortunate blustering speech commiting himself sadly in doctrines about organic remains. There was no stopping him. I took the first opportunity to follow, endeavouring to show that your view was founded entirely on purely geological & physical considerations & that Davis's own data went (as I still believe they do) to support that view. At the same time I granted that the Palaeontological features of the Nash Limestone were Wenlock & quite distinct from those of the Limestones at the top of the Caradoc about the Long Mynd. I called up Salter to speak to his own knowledge & he fairly showed that in all probability the Nash & the Woolhope must be regarded as equivalents & both at the base of the Wenlock series. It was difficult however to get people clear of the governor's speech & a strong impression went abroad that we stuck to our story because we were all of a clique ... One good result out of this. Much was said in the discussion about Survey evidence being quoted but never published. It told strongly against us in the fight & Sir Henry this morning gave in fully to the necessity of commencing the publication of catalogues of fossils from localities or districts.

IC Ramsay, f111

The Meetings

172. 1850, June 19

"On a Section of the Lower Greensand, at Seend, near Devizes", by William Cunnington, Esq., communicated by Joseph Prestwich, jun., Esq., F.G.S.

"On the Age and Position of the Fossiliferous Sands and Gravels of Farringdon", by R. A. C. Austen, Esq., F.G.S.

172a. Gideon Mantell wrote in his diary:

Council and meeting of Geological Sodety: a rambling paper on the Farringdon beds by Mr Austin [Austen]: in which there is not the slightest allusion to my account of them years ago. Professor Hitchcock attended.

SAS Mantell, quoted in Curwen 1940, p255

Notes, 1849-1850

1. Mantell's diary for the previous day records: 'Took the humerus of Pelorosaurus, and two cases of belemnites to the Royal Society for the evening meeting'. Curwen 1940, p250.
2. Buckland was starting to show symptoms of the mental illness which clouded the final years of his life. See Gordon 1894, pp267-271.
3. Minutes of the meeting show that Mr Tyler's name was withdrawn, and that Mr de Salis and Lieutenant D Galton were both elected to the Club.
4. The long-running dispute between Mantell and Owen over the moa bones from New Zealand is discussed in Rupke 1994, pp124-128.

Session 1850-1851

173. 1850, November 20

The following communications were read:

"Report on the occurrence of an Earthquake at Brussa", (forwarded from the Foreign Office, by order of Viscount Palmerston).

"Generalizations respecting the Erratic Tertiaries of Norfolk", by Joshua Trimmer, Esq., F.G.S.

"On the Erratic Tertiaries of the Valley of Gaytonthorpe", by Joshua Trimmer, Esq., F.G.S.

"On the Origin of the Soils of a part of Kent", by Joshua Trimmer, Esq., F.G.S.

"Description of the Limestone Quarry at Linksfield, Elgin", by Capt. T. R. L. Brickenden, F.G.S.

173a. Gideon Mantell wrote in his diary:

Council of the Geological Society; dined at the Athenaeum. To the evening meeting: defended a paper of Capt. Brickenden on the drift of Elgin. Returned with Mr Woodhouse to tea.

SAS Mantell

173b. Gideon Mantell wrote to Lambart Brickenden on 23 November:

Your paper was read last evening, and I write today to tell you of the ordeal it went through.[1] Lyell presided: Murchison, De la Beche, & many other good men were present. No one would believe the intercalated bed was boulder clay. Mr Prestwich produced notes he took some fifteen years ago, in which he showed what he averred was your boulder clay, to be a layer of red sand lying above & upon the old red, and a part of the regular series, the boundary line between the Devonian & Lias. Sharp [Sharpe] said the bed was nothing more than the upper layer of the Devonian, & that there had been a horizontal movement of the Lias beds upon it, hence the striae. Another suggested that if this boulder clay did contain boulders &c it was "boulder clay" of the Devonian epoch, in other words that the upper surface of the Devonian beds had suffered denudation and attrition before the deposit of the Liassic strata upon them. I objected that you stated rolled masses of both oolite & Devonian were in the clay, but this was overruled, that if so, probably the oolitic were only on the upper part & produced by the sliding of one series of beds over the other.

I entrenched myself as well as I could for I would not retreat; so I shall maintain my position till you reinforce the garrison, or command me to surrender. Sir H De la Beche gave me credit for being a true & valiant knight, & said if he wished to be defended in his absence he should select me!

NHM Brickenden, 27

174. 1850, December 4

The following communications were read:

"On the Geology of the Upper Punjaub and Peshaur", by Major N. Vicary, communicated by Sir R. I. Murchison, V.P.G.S.

"On the Silurian Rocks of Dumfriesshire and Kirkcudbrightshire", by R. Harkness, Esq., communicated by Sir R. I. Murchison, V.P.G.S.

"Description of the Graptolites of the Black Shales of Dumfriesshire", by Robert Harkness Esq., communicated by Sir R. I. Murchison, V.P.G.S.

"Report on the Coal Mines near Erzeroom", (forwarded from the Foreign Office, by order of Viscount Palmerston).

174a. Edward Forbes wrote to Andrew Ramsay on 7 December:

> We had a grand discussion on graptolites at the G.S. on Wednesday. De Barrande was there & spoke well: he has had a weeks work over our collection.
>
> IC Ramsay, f129

175. 1851, January 8

The following communications were read:

"On the Volcanic and Tertiary Strata of the Isle of Mull", by His Grace the Duke of Argyll, communicated by the President.

"On the Estuary Beds and the Oxford Clay of Loch Staffin, in the Isle of Skye", by Prof. E. Forbes, V.P.G.S.

175a. Andrew Ramsay wrote in his diary:

> Took John to the Geological Club. Lyell called me up & made me sit by him, which made Sir H. [De la Beche] uneasy. Pleasant party. Papers by Forbes & the Duke of Argyll. I spoke opposing Sir H. & Hopkins. They refine and give [?] physics that often mean nothing. Murchison Abich & Barrande approved of my view of the traps in question.
>
> IC Ramsay

176. 1851, January 22

The following communications were read:

"Memorandum respecting *Choristopetalum impar and Cyathophora (?) elegans*", by William Lonsdale, Esq., F.G.S.

"On the Superficial Accumulations of the Coasts of the English Channel, and the Changes they indicate", by R. A. C. Austen, Esq., F.G.S.

"On supposed Casts of Footsteps in the Wealden", by S. H. Beckles, Esq., communicated by the President.

176a. Gideon Mantell wrote in his diary:

Attended Council of the Geological Society and the evening meeting. Sir C. Lyell in the Chair. Murchison, De la Beche, Hopkins etc present. A paper by Mr Austen on elevated sea beaches etc. A very rambling and unsatisfactory affair. Mr Woodhouse returned home with me to supper.

SAS Mantell

177. 1851, February 5

The following communication was read:

"On the Silurian Rocks of the South of Scotland", by Sir R. I. Murchison, V.P.G.S. (commenced).

177a. Andrew Ramsay wrote in his diary:

Down to the Geological Club. Pleasant party. Lord Enniskillen proposed Lord Alfred Churchhill as a new member & Forbes proposed Mutabottom [?]. 2 The Duke of Argyll came to the meeting. Murchison read a paper on the Scotch Silurians. Sedgwick spoke but poorly. Sharpe, Sir Henry [De la Beche] & I followed. Murchison was pleased with what I said. He had the better part of the argument, but did not know the weight of evidence he had on his own side. I helped him thereby.

IC Ramsay

178. 1851, February 21

Annual General Meeting, at which Sir Charles Lyell read the Anniversary Address and William Hopkins was elected President.

The Meetings

178a. Gideon Mantell wrote in his diary:

Anniversary of Geol. Society at one ... Dined with the Geol. Society in the evening at Willis's Rooms.

SAS Mantell

178b. Andrew Ramsay wrote in his diary:

At the dinner, Forbes, Wilson, Aveline, Smyth, Sopwith, Captain James, Logan, and a few more of us got together. Hopkins, the new President, was in the chair. He was slow. Sedgewick [Sedgwick] made the great speech of the evening. By turns he made us cry and roar with laughter, as he willed. His pathos and his wit were equally admirable. Home at twelve.

IC Ramsay, and Geikie 1895, p177

179. 1851, February 26

The following communication was read:

"On the Silurian Rocks of Scotland", by Sir R. I. Murchison, V.P.G.S. (concluded).

179a. Andrew Ramsay wrote in his diary:

Hopkins assumed his place today as President. Sharpe made a very ill natured speech at the Society abt Murchison's metamorphic paper. When he can say an ill natured thing he does it. He said to me the other night at Forbes that the Geological Society had banished geology for 2 years (meaning Hopkins election). I had a snipe at his mechanical theory.

IC Ramsay

180. 1851, March 26

The following communications were read:

"On the Boulder Clay of Caithness", by John Cleghorn, Esq., communicated by Sir Charles Lyell, F.G.S.

"On the Erratic Tertiaries of Cheshire, and on the Scratched Boulders of the Till", by Joshua Trimmer, Esq., F.G.S.

"On the Sequence of Events during the Glacial or Pleistocene Period, as evinced by the Superficial Accumulations of North Wales", by Prof. A. C. Ramsay, F.G.S.

180a. Gideon Mantell wrote in his diary:

At 1/2 past 8 we [Benjamin Silliman and Mantell] went to the meeting of the Geological Society. Lyell, Murchison, De la Beche, Hopkins (presided), and a tolerable muster of old Fellows. The paper, a wild dream on glaciers and the glacial period by Prof. Ramsay: Prof. Silliman made a clever and kind comment on the paper. Left at twelve.

SAS Mantell, quoted in Curwen 1940, p266

180b. Andrew Ramsay wrote in his diary:

Read my paper at the Society. No man objected but Hopkins, who said little, however, being President, and he only objected to one point, and praised all the rest. Sir H. [De la Beche] made a capital speech, and I think made an impression on Hopkins on that very point that bothered him in my paper. Murchison, Lyell, and the rest scarce ventured to criticise my views, though they spoke well for the grasp and importance of the paper.

IC Ramsay, and Geikie 1895, p177

181. 1851, April 9

The following communications were read:

"On the Basement Beds of the Inferior Oolite in Gloucestershire", by the Rev. P. B. Brodie, F.G.S.

"On the Physical Geography of North America as connected with its Geological Structure", by Sir J. Richardson, M.D., communicated by Sir Charles Lyell, F.G.S.

"On the Erratics of Canada", by John J. Bigsy, M.D., F.G.S.

181a. Andrew Ramsay wrote in his diary:

I had him (Mr. Landsborough) to the Geological Club and afterwards to the Society. He sat besides Sir Phillip Egerton at dinner who conversed much with him, which I was very glad of. The old gentleman was much charmed. It will be an epoch in his life meeting so many scientific celebrities in one day.

IC Ramsay

The Meetings

182. 1851, April 30

The following communications were read:

"Notice of the Occurrence of an Earthquake at Carthagena", (forwarded from the Foreign Office, by order of Viscount Palmerston).

"On Fossil Rain Prints in the Recent, Triassic, and Carboniferous Periods", by Sir Charles Lyell, F.G.S.

"On the occurrence of a Track and Footprints of an animal in the Potsdam Sandstone of Lower Canada", by W. E. Logan, Esq., F.G.S.

"On the Footprints in the Potsdam Sandstone of Lower Canada", by Prof. Owen, F.G.S.

182a. Gideon Mantell wrote in his diary:

> Called at the Geological Society on our [Mr Woodhouse and Mantell's] way home: a poor attendance on Lyell "On Rain Drops"! Dreadfully fatigued and suffering very much.
>
> SAS Mantell

183. 1851, May 14

The following communications were read:

"On the Angular Flint Drift of the South-east of England, and on its distribution within and without the Wealden", by Sir R. I. Murchison, F.G.S.

"On a Deposit containing Osseous Remains of Mammalia at Folkestone", by Samuel J. Mackie, Esq., communicated by Sir R. I. Murchison, F.G.S.

183a. Gideon Mantell wrote in his diary:

> Council of the Geological Society. In the evening attended the meeting to hear Sir R. Murchison's paper on the Drift of Sussex. A very full attendance, and an animated discussion on the theory of Wealden denudation. Nothing came of it after all! A large

collection of Mammalian bones from diluvium of Folkestone; among them Irish Elk and Hyaena – Hippopotamus etc.

SAS Mantell

183b. Andrew Ramsay wrote in his diary:

Dined en famille with Reeks & then went to the Geological Society. Murchison had a paper on the denudation & drift of the Weald of Sussex. When the debating came he got what I considered a fearful thrashing. Lyell first spoke indifferently, unable to overcome the difficulties, but evidently feeling that Murchison's insane catastrophic solutions were the greatest difficulties of all. Then followed Sharpe who said that one would suppose from M's reasoning that Elephants were marine instead of terrestrial animals. Then came Mantell who in a most eloquent speech asked if the great Mammifers were anihilated by this catastrophe how is it that there bones are always found scattered & in fragments, would not the ligaments & skin keep them at least so far together that we would find the principal parts of the skeleton near. Then followed Forbes on the same tack, then Dr. Fitton asking for more facts and less theory, & then myself how little dependence was to be placed on angularity or non angularity of pebbles as a test of date. Every one came down hard on him. He was amazed, & he had filled the house. It was lucky for him that the prince did not come as he asked him to do. He thought he was to be rec'd with praise & every one opposed him. [3]

IC Ramsay

Notes, 1850-1851

1. Brickenden withdrew his paper from publication, and spoke again on the same subject on 25 June 1851, putting forward the same interpretation as before. This paper was published (Brickenden 1851). The Geological Survey Memoir on the Elgin district describes Upper Old Red Sandstone underlying a large Jurassic erratic, formerly considered to be *in situ*, in this quarry (Peacock *et al* 1968, p51).
2. The Dining Club minute book shows that Dr J Percy, Colonel J E Portlock and John Morris were proposed that evening, and all three elected on 25 February.
3. Murchison remained proud of this paper. He had his offprints elaborately bound in leather for presentation to his friends.

The Meetings

Session 1851-1852

184. 1851, November 5

The following communications were read:

"Notice of the Occurrence of an Earthquake at Chili", (forwarded from the Foreign Office, by order of Viscount Palmerston).

"On the Devonian and Cambrian Rocks of Cornwall and Devon", by the Rev. Professor Sedgwick, F.G.S.

184a. Adam Sedgwick wrote to Frederick McCoy on 9 November:

> We opened last Wednesday at Somerset House with my paper on N. Devon & Cornwall. It went off well. Murchison tried to make a stand up fight because I called the old rocks Cambrian & not Lower Silurian, but the President called to order saying that on a future day this point of nomenclature &c. wd. be discussed formally. De la Beche (the only man who knew the country well) was on my side on all the points.
> ML McCoy, microfilm M, frames 411-413

185. 1851, December 3

The following communications were read:

"On a curious Fossil Fern from the Coal at Cape Breton", by C. J. F. Bunbury, Esq., For.Sec.G.S.

"On the Cambrian and Silurian Rocks which appear at the base of the Carboniferous chain of Yorkshire, near the Craven Fault", by the Rev. Professor Sedgwick, F.G.S.

185a. Andrew Ramsay wrote in his diary:

> Thence to the Geological Society, where Sedgwick read rather a wearisome paper. I said nothing. Afterwards told Murchison of my coming marriage. [1]
> IC Ramsay

186. 1851, December 17

The following communications were read:

"Note on the Quader-formation of Germany", by Prof. Geinitz, communicated by Sir Charles Lyell, F.G.S.

"On the Causes of the Changes of Climate at different Geological Epochs", by William Hopkins, Esq., Pres. G.S.

"Notice of the Discovery of Reptilian Foot-tracks and Remains in the Old Red Sandstone of Moray", by Capt. L. Brickenden, F.G.S.

"Description of the *Telerpeton Elginense*, and Observations on supposed Fossil Ova of Batrachians in the Lower Devonian Strata of Forfarshire", by G. A. Mantell, Esq., LL.D., F.G.S. [2]

186a. Andrew Ramsay wrote in his diary:

Dined at the Geological Club. Darwin there. Went to the Society after. Hopkins had a grand paper. Sir H. [De la Beche] spoke nonsense. I was obliged in self defence to destroy one of his suppositions, but otherwise I spoke badly. Hopkins behaved crossly in interupting me, in a point that was against him, when I am sure I was right.

IC Ramsay

186b. Gideon Mantell wrote in his diary:

Council of the Geological Society: took the Devonian Reptile etc. In the evening attended the meeting; a very interesting paper by Mr Hopkins on temperature and climate: this paper and its discussion occupied the meeting till past eleven; and my Memoir was in consequence postponed!

SAS Mantell, quoted in Curwen 1940, p278

186c. Leonard Horner wrote to his daughter on 18 December:

Charles Darwin was at the Geological Society's Club yesterday, where he had not been for ten years – remarkably well, and grown quite stout.

Lyell 1890, 2, p195

The Meetings

186d. Gideon Mantell wrote to Lambart Brickenden on 20 December:

I deferred writing that I might have the pleasure of informing you of the result of last Wednesday's meeting when your paper and mine were to be read. I sent the specimen and fixed up a beautiful drawing of the respective parts, but unfortunately a previous paper by Mr Hopkins, the President, occupied the whole evening, and our papers were deferred till the next meeting. This delay has occasioned me much annoyance, for Prof. Owen, who came and examined my drawings and specimens, has sent a description published in today's Literary Gazette & most dishonestly assumes the right to name it ... [3]

NHM Brickenden, quoted in Spokes 1927, p236

187. 1852, January 7

The following communications were read:

"Notice of the Discovery of Boulders and Fossil Bones in clefts of the rock in Portland Island", by Mr A. Neale, communicated by J. C. Moore, Esq., Sec. G.S.

"On the Subescarpments of the Ridgeway Range, and their contemporaneous deposits in the Isle of Portland", by C. H. Weston, Esq., F.G.S.

187a. Gideon Mantell wrote in his diary:

A full attendance in the evening: Capt. Brickenden's paper was read by the Secretary, and I read a description of the <u>Telerpeton</u>, and an account of the presumed fossil ova from the Devonian shales of Forfarshire and the indications afforded by the organic remains of the latter having a fluvio-marine, if not a purely freshwater origin. Lyell, Murchison, Forbes, Carpenter, took part in the discussion. The President (Mr Hopkins of Cambridge) at the close of the discussion, emphatically announced that although my paper was read on this evening, it was published at the previous meeting Dec 17th, the title having then been declared by the Chairman, to ensure it precedence over any other description of the fossil. This announcement was warmly applauded, and so all ended well; Prof. O. [Owen] not having appeared! What a pity that a man of such ability should thus demean himself, as not dare to appear in such a meeting.

SAS Mantell

Session 1851-52

187b. Gideon Mantell wrote to Lambart Brickenden on 8 January:

The paper was read last evening to a very full meeting and passed off admirably. I had written to the Pres & Council to state the circumstances under which the specimen came into my hands, 4 & Prof. O.[Owen] I had found had written demanding that his account should supersede mine. The unanimous decision was, of course, in my favour, and the President announced from the chair most emphatically, that our paper was to all intents & purposes published at the former meeting, & must take precedence of any other. The Prof. did not appear; so of course every thing was agreable ...

There was of course all manner of doubts expressed as to the rock being Old Red Sandstone; & Sir R. Murchison talked about Oolite; & the possibility of the Spynie rock being an expansion from the Oolite on the opposite coasts. So also Prof. Forbes ridiculed the idea of the ova of Forfarshire being eggs of batrachians, & had no doubt they were molluscous: & yet not a shell or even a cast of a shell has been found in those beds ... I defended your Old Red manfully and did not give up my frogs & tritons; & I reminded the fellows that thirty years ago I had to defend myself from the charge of having mistaken teeth & bones of mammalia for those of unknown herbivorous reptiles, & the rock in which they occured for an ancient deposit, instead of being diluvium; & yet the Iguanodon & the Wealden were now admitted, & I had to substantiate my claim to the discovery. However, all was in good feeling, & nothing could be more satisfactory.

NHM Brickenden, part quoted in Spokes 1927, p239

187c. William Hopkins wrote to Richard Owen on 10 January:

... in the evening I privately intimated to Dr. Mantell that I could not as president admit from him a word of merely controversial nature between you. I am happy to say that not a word of this kind was said.

NHM Owen, XV/396

188. 1852, February 20

Annual General Meeting at which William Hopkins read the Anniversary Address and was re-elected President.

The Meetings

188a. Andrew Ramsay wrote in his diary:

> Geological Society Anniversary, Willis's Rooms. President pretty well supported – Goulbourne, Sir C. Lemon, Pusey, Sir. H. [De la Beche], Lyell, Murchison, etc. I observe our body annually creeps higher and higher up the table. We are now next the bigger wigs.
>
> Geikie 1895, p196

189. 1852, February 25

The following communication was read:

"On the Classification of the Lower Palaeozoic Rocks of Great Britain", by the Rev. Professor Sedgwick, F.G.S. [5]

189a. Andrew Ramsay wrote in his diary:

> Good scrimmage between Sedgwick and Murchison on the Lower Silurian and Cambrian question. It was not an enlivening spectacle. Sedgwick used very hard words. Murchison made a spirited and dignified reply. He appealed to me, and I aided in a speech giving a history of the survey of Wales.
>
> Geikie 1895, p197

189b. Sir Roderick Murchison wrote to Adam Sedgwick on 27 February:

> In enclosing you one of my cards for soirées, let me beg of you to prepare the abstract of your paper, so that there should be nothing in it which can be construed into an expression on your part that I had acted unfairly by you. This is the only point which roused my feelings the other night, and made me speak more vehemently than I intended. But I did intend to tell the meeting, in reverence to that very point (what I forgot to say) that I have over and over urged you to bring out your fossils and complete the subject you had undertaken.
>
> Clark and Hughes 1890, 2, p218; and Geikie 1875, 2, p140

189c. Adam Sedgwick wrote to Frederick McCoy on 8 March:

> My paper came on last Wednesday week. I think I made out a good case but I was so greatly fatigued, the hour was so very late, that I said little in reply – All who spoke were against me as a matter of course viz. Murchison, Ramsay (who has adopted

Murchison's names word for word), & Sharp. They said it was too late to change. I said no. I [?] presume the paper will be printed, & abstracts are out in the Lit Gazette & the Athenaeum.

ML McCoy, microfilm frames 181-183

190. 1852, March 24

The following communications were read:

"On the Foot Tracks in the Potsdam Sandstone of Lower Canada", by W. E. Logan, Esq., F.G.S.

"Description of the Potsdam Sandstone Foot Tracks (*Protichnites*)", by Prof. R. Owen, F.G.S.

190a. Gideon Mantell wrote in his diary:

Attended Council and meeting of the Geological Society ... The evening meeting was occupied by a paper on Silurian strata in Canada, bearing foot-tracks or supposed tracks by Logan: who read an account of the deposits: and followed by Prof. Owen who described the foot-prints – and gave them names: a very elaborate, and ingenious, and jesuitical paper, but very little to be depended on. The prints were assumed to be those of unknown crustaceans with 6 or 7 pairs of feet. I suggested that if the prints were really those of crustaceans then it was possible they might be those of Trilobites; animals which swarmed in those Silurian strata, and whose locomotive organs are not yet known: these may have resembled the paddles, or brachial-feet of Limulus, or Branchypus: and I exhibited a model of Isotelus grandis, 23 inches long, to prove that the magnitude of some Trilobites was more than sufficient to support such a hypothesis. The nature of the imprints is in my mind very uncertain.

SAS Mantell, quoted in Curwen 1940, p285

190b. Andrew Ramsay wrote in his diary:

Logan's paper and Owen's passed off well. Murchison made what Sedgwick called a speech characterised by a sort of bacchanalian joy at the tracks turning out not to be tortoise tracks, and Sedgwick himself rejoiced that the old resting-place of his mind was not disturbed by such a terrible innovation. He did not like to be too much disturbed. Lyell was <u>disappointed</u>, he said; then Forbes followed, and Owen rebuked him in his reply for entertaining any other feeling than that of joy at an error being corrected, and a scientific truth partly elucidated. [6] Mantell proposed that they were the tracks of great trilobites, but no one seconded him, or rather every one dissented, Burmeister's paper having gone so far to prove that trilobites had soft membranaceous appendages and no true feet. [7]

IC Ramsay, and Geikie 1895, p197

191. 1852, May 5

The following communications were read:

"On the Tertiary Formations of Belgium and their British Equivalents. Part I. On the Pliocene, Miocene, and Upper Eocene of Belgium", by Sir Charles Lyell, F.G.S.

"On the Geology of Catalonia", by Samuel Peace Pratt, Esq., F.G.S.

191a. Gideon Mantell wrote in his diary:

In the evening attended meeting of the Geological Society: Lyell a paper on the tertiary beds of Beligum: a very desultory, unsatisfactory affair!

SAS Mantell

191b. Charles Bunbury wrote in his diary:

We went into town to stay a week with the Lyells, and I attended the Geological Society. The Club very full. Sat between Charles Lyell and John Moore. Much pleasant talk, chiefly about geology. The evening meeting very good; an excellent paper by Edward Forbes, containing the results of his long and most elaborate examination (during the whole of last winter) of the tertiary formations of the Isle of Wight; very clear and satisfactory. He showed conclusively the existence there of several members of the tertiary series (upper Eocene and middle Eocene) that had before been entirely overlooked, and not known to exist in Britain; gave a methodical tabular arrangement, and pointed out the corresponding foreign types in France and Belgium.

Lyell 1906, 1, p362

Session 1851-52

192. 1852, June 16

The following communications were read:

"On the Silurian Rocks of the S. of Scotland, and on the Gold Districts of Wanlockhead and the Lead Hills", by Robert Harkness Esq., communicated by J. C. Moore, Esq., Sec.G.S.

"Description of some Graptolites from the South of Scotland", by J. W. Salter, Esq., F.G.S.

"On a protruded Mass of Ludlow Rock at Hagley Park, Herefordshire", by H. E. Strickland, Esq., F.G.S.

"On the Comparison of the Devonian Series of Belgium and England", by Daniel Sharpe, Esq., F.G.S.

"On the Comparison of the Tertiary Series of Beligum and England", by M. A. M. Dumont, For.M.G.S.

"On the meaning of the term 'Silurian System'", by Sir R. I. Murchison, F.G.S.

"Further Remarks on the Ornithoidichnites of the Weald", by S. H. Beckles, Esq., communicated by Sir Charles Lyell, F.G.S.
"Further Remarks on the Red Sandstone of Nova Scotia", by L. W. Dawson, Esq.; communicated by Sir Charles Lyell, F.G.S.

"Comparison of Bubble Marks and Rain Prints", by M. E. Desor, communicated by the President.

"On the Sections of the Lower Lias at Mickleton and Aston", by G. E. Gavey, Esq., F.G.S.

"On the Foot Tracks in New Red Sandstone", by Robert Rawlinson, Esq., communicated by the Earl of Ellesmere, F.G.S.

"On the Geology of the Lake of the Woods", by J. J. Bigsby, M.D., F.G.S.

"On the Geology of the Southern Portion of Cantyre", by Prof. J. Nicol, F.G.S.

192a. Edward Forbes wrote to Andrew Ramsay on 23 June:

At the last G.S. meeting Sharp [Sharpe] read a critical paper about the bearing of Dumont's classification of the Devonian upon our British arrangements. It gave rise to an interesting discussion, in which Jukes made a capital speech much to the purpose. J gave great satisfaction, the more so as old Griffith being present, Jukes took the opportunity, in very good taste, of pointing out Griffith's essential services to Irish geology. We have as usual had a very pleasant club dinner.

IC Ramsay, f160

Notes, 1851-1852

1. Ramsay married Miss Louisa Williams at Llanfairynghornwy on 20 July 1852.
2. The background to this paper, and to the continuing controversy over the Elgin reptiles, is given in Benton 1983.
3. Owen 1851. For palaeontologists *Leptopleuron*, the name Owen gave the reptile in his *Literary Gazette* paper of 20 December, has priority over Mantell's *Telerpeton*, in spite of the President's emphatic statement made at the following meeting.
4. Mantell's letter, which enclosed letters of Brickenden, Duff and Owen, was read to Council on 7th January, but has not survived.
5. The background to this important paper is given in Secord 1986, pp215-236.
6. Lyell was one of the chief opponents of the theory of the progression of life, and was keen to demonstrate the existence of reptiles in the Old Red Sandstone. Hence his disappointment when the tracks turned out to be Crustacean (Bowler 1976, pp74-75).
7. Burmeister 1846, p13. Mantell was, of course, correct.

Session 1852-1853

193. 1852, November 3

The following communication was read:

"On a Proposed Separation of the Caradoc Sandstone into two distinct Groups, viz. the May Hill Sandstone and the Caradoc Sandstone", by the Rev. Prof. Sedgwick, F.G.S. [1]

193a. Edward Forbes wrote to Andrew Ramsay on 4 November:

At the society Sedgwick came out with his story. The pith of it is that the Caradoc limestone of Phillips' district is not the Caradoc of the more northern localities & is Wenlock, or of Wenlock type. Sedgwick would therefore draw a line of separation among beds considered Caradoc. The argument was of course founded on fossils – the data supplied with McCoy. The impression left not only on my mind, but also on Strickland's, Austen, Sharpe, Morris & all I "conversed" with was that McCoy (who was there & spoke) had cooked 2 the fossil evidence to please Sedgwick & misled him. Salter spoke <u>very well</u> & from good data. His speech was very convincing & went to show that the Survey was justified in both cases. There was the usual spar between Murchy [Murchison] & Sedgwick about Cambrian. The discussion was lively & good.

IC Ramsay, f164, partly quoted in Secord 1986, p246

193b. Adam Sedgwick wrote:

I was battling at the Geological Society till near midnight.

A Sedgwick to unknown recipient, Clark and Hughes 1890, 2, p231

194. 1852, November 17

"Notice of the occurrence of an earthquake shock in the Azores", by T. Carew Hunt, Esq., H.M. Consul at St. Michael's.

"On the geology of South Africa", by G. A. Bain [A. G. Bain], communicated by the President.

194a. Charles Bunbury wrote in his diary:

Then to the evening meeting of the Geological Society; a very thin meeting, one of the thinnest I have ever seen. Mr. Bain's important paper on the "Geology of South Africa" was read, or rather a copious abstract of it by Rupert Jones. Murchison and Owen the principal speakers; the former on the Palaeozoic fossils, the latter on the gigantic reptilian remains.

Bunbury 1890-1891, 2, p105

The Meetings

195. 1853, January

The following communications were read:

"On the Remains of a Reptile (*Dendrerpeton Acadium*, Wyman and Owen) and of a Land Shell discovered in the Interior of an Erect Fossil Tree in the Coal Measures of Nova Scotia", by Sir Charles Lyell, F.R.S., V.P.G.S., &c and J. W. Dawson Esq.

"Notice of a Batrachoid Fossil in British Coal-shale", by Professor Owen, F.R.S., G.S. &c.

195a. Leonard Horner wrote to his daughter on 23 January:

Charles Lyell's paper last Wednesday at the Geological Society on the discovery he made in Nova Scotia, on the Bay of Fundy, of reptilian bones, and a land shell in the loose materials filling up the hollowed trunk of an upright stem of a sigillaria, in a bed of coal, excited a great deal of interest, as supplying the first instance of a *land* shell in a bed of coal belonging to the old coal formation, and another (the first in America) of the existence of animals of that advanced organization at so early a period.

Lyell 1890, 2, p208

196. 1853, March 9

The following communications were read:

"On the Albert Mine, Hilsborough, New Brunswick", by J. W. Dawson, Esq., communicated by Sir C. Lyell, V.P.G.S.

"Note on the Fossil Fish from Albert Mine", by Sir P. de M. G. Egerton, Bart., F.G.S., &c.

"On the Carcharodon and other Fish Remains in the Red Crag", by S. V. Wood, Esq., F.G.S.

196a. Charles Bunbury wrote in his diary:

Dined at the Geological Society's Club; a very full attendance. Murchison in the chair. Sat between Lyell and Daniel Sharpe; Austen opposite; Moore on the other side of Lyell. Meeting of the Geological Society. A curious paper by Mr. Dawson on the Albert Coal Mine in New Brunswick, followed by a very good discussion.

Bunbury 1890-1891, 2, p119

197. 1853, June 1

The following communications were read:

"On the Southern Termination of the Erratic Tertiaries; and on the remains of a Bed of Gravel on the Clevedon Down", by Joshua Trimmer, Esq., F.G.S.

"On the Origin of the Soils on the Chalk of Kent. Part III", by Joshua Trimmer, Esq., F.G.S.

"On the Geological and Glacial Phaenomena of the Coasts of Baffin's Bay and Davis' Strait", by P. C. Sutherland, M.D., communicated by Prof. A. C. Ramsay, F.G.S.

197a. Charles Darwin wrote to Charles Lyell on 7 June:

> I went up for a paper by the Arctic Dr. Sutherland on ice-action, read only in abstract, but I shd think with much good matter. It was pleasant to hear that it was written owing to the admiralty manual. [3] There was also a paper by Trimmer partly on the superficial deposits of Kent, Murchison urged his catastrophe view to account for the flints, so I gave your view of sub-glacial action & urged where on earth the flood, which divided France & England, could have found so vast a pile of almost clean flints. I stated that one of the arctic navigators, had informed you that the stones on the beach were angular in those countries: & on this head I asked Dr. Sutherland, & he <u>most strongly confirmed</u> this statement; & I thought you would like to hear this. Hopkins spoke, he admitted to a considerable extent, the force of my notion of (plastic) icebergs being driven by their momentum over considerable inequalities in an almost straight course. Chambers also spoke at length: have you seen his long & I must say interesting paper on glaciation in Edinb. New Phil. Journal: he actually reproduces Agassiz's notion of one continuous sheet of ice over the whole northern world, & treats all icebergians with the most supercilious contempt. [4]
>
> Burkhardt and Smith 1985-2003, 5, p141

Notes, 1852-1853

1. The background to this important paper is given in Secord 1986, chapter 8.
2. 'Cooked' replaces the words 'got up', which are deleted.
3. The *Admiralty Manual* (Herschel 1849) contains a chapter by Darwin on geology.
4. Chambers 1853.

Session 1853-1854

198. 1853, December 14

The following communications were read:

"On a Specimen of *Volkmannia Morrisii*, from the Glasgow Coal Shale", by J. D. Hooker, M.D., F.G.S.

"On the Structure of *Chonetes cornoides*", by Thomas Davidson, Esq., F.G.S.

"On a Batrachian Fossil from the Pictou Coal Field, Nova Scotia", by Prof. Owen, F.G.S.

"On Track-prints in the Lower Lingula Flags of North Wales", by J. W. Salter, Esq., F.G.S.

198a. T Rupert Jones wrote to Richard Owen on 15 December:

> Herewith I return the Drawings which with your permission were used in illustration of the Paper read last evening. Allow me to observe that the Paper gave rise to some lively & interesting remarks from Prof. Phillips & the President – & with Dr. Hooker's note on a conebearing piece of Volkmannia! from the Scotch Coal, – Mr Salter's note on some minute Crustaceous [?] (Entomostracous) tracks from the Lower Lingula Flags of Nth Wales, a note prepared at the Presidents request on the afternoon of yesterday – & with Mr Davidson's description of the structure of the Chonetes (Productus) Cornoides of the Mountain Limestone – afforded the Meeting a most instructive and pleasant evening.
> NHM Owen, 16/231

199. 1854, February 17

Annual General Meeting at which Edward Forbes read the Anniversary Address and William J Hamilton was elected President.

199a. Leonard Horner wrote to Charles Lyell on 22 February:

> The anniversary of the Geological Society went off very satisfactorily.[1] I think I wrote to you that we had given the Wollaston medal to Griffiths for his map of Ireland. I believe there

are few geological maps better executed or containing so much information. Forbes made a very good address to him, shewing how he had been an active promoter of geology in the field, for more than forty years.

We never had a more interesting or valuable address than Forbes has given us. His éloge of Von Buch was very good. As you may suppose, his main subject was the higher philosophy of the distribution of organic remains, and you will, I am sure, read it with interest and profit.

Lyell 1890, 2, p222

200. 1854, May 3

The following communications were read:

"On some intrusive Igneous Rocks in Cawsand Bay, near Plymouth", by Leonard Horner, Esq., F.G.S.

"On the May Hill Sandstone, and on the classification of the Palaeozoic Rocks of England and Wales", by the Rev. Prof. Sedgwick, F.G.S.

200a. John Salter wrote to Adam Sedgwick on 5 May:

I wish you could have been at the Society on Wednesday – to have given more life & meaning to the paper. Leonard Horner's paper on Devonshire occupied so much time, though but a small one, that it was impossible to read the whole of yours – & the discussion therefore turned on the sections you furnished, & the relations of the May Hill Sandstone. The place of this last as distinctly cut off from the Lower Group seems now admitted on all hands. but how could you support the view of the unconformity of the Caradoc of Wales to the Bala rocks. The Survey, on whose data, combined with your own the unconformity was first suggested have for some time given it up. Has not Jukes written you so? The pale slates (<u>pasty rock</u>, nobis) which everywhere underlies it & dips with it is, you know, the uppermost Bala rock. It is believed to be quite conformable in all but the faulted boundaries, though its fossils are those of the Upper Silurian. How strange it is that there are no Pentameri in it. Yet it cannot but be what you suggest, the May Hill Sandstone – our "Caradoc" & Murchison's "Upper Caradoc".

That I had to fight against you on the Onny section or rather the Buildwas & Severn section. The Olenus shales which you have placed just under the Pentamerus beds – are really in the shales at the bottom of the whole. [sketch] So that (as stated in our paper) if you take the section at the north you pass at once from the Cressage (Olenus) shales to the Pentam. beds – farther south you reach higher beds first & on the Onny all the strata known in the Caradoc section are exposed. I suppose M'Coy thought the Olenus beds immediately below the Pentam. beds, because they lie so at Malvern – But who knows if there is not as great a break at Malvern too?

I ventured on a proposition which will I fear please neither yourself nor Sir Roderick, & yet is both convenient with the general opinion – I think historically just, and is certainly geologically useful

D Upper Silurian
Middle Silurian ?Caradoc
C Lower Silurian (Murchison long ago)
B Upper Cambrian Lingula Flags (Sedgwick 1847)
A Lower Cambrian Longmynd Rock (M&S)

To the Lingula flags he has not the shadow of a claim, & it is – palaeontologically – more different (in Britain, N. America, Sweden, Bohemia) from C, than C is from D. There are no <u>species</u> in common & but few genera. Why should not the two Upper groups be what M claims them by priority of publication & why shd not you have the two lower – the whole being Lower Proterozoic – as you suggested long ago – The Tremadoc slate is the lowest member of C. with a general Bala type & several ident. species. [2]

CUL Sedgwick, IIIB, 68

200b. Samuel P Woodward wrote to Adam Sedgwick on 1 July:

There was a grand muster at the Geological on the night of your paper, & much disappointment that you were not there. I ought not to speak of what passed but great amusement was occasioned by our friend Salter offering to set things straight! When Sir Rod[k] [Murchison] signed my certificate he wrote that he was very happy to put his name once more beside yours. [3]

CUL Sedgwick, IIX, 81

200c. Edward Forbes's biographers wrote:

At the last evening meeting of the Society previous to his leaving for the north, a scene occurred showing how close and warm was the sympathy between the President and the Fellows. When the scientific business had been concluded, Sir Roderick Murchison rose, and after referring to Forbes's early connexion with the Society, and the numerous valuable papers and memoirs with which he had since enriched its Transactions, announced that before the return of another meeting their distinguished President would have entered upon another and distant sphere of labour. Sir Roderick, who had been among the first of the geologists to perceive and acknowledge the merit of his friend, dwelt gracefully on what was not the least remarkable feature in the connexion of Edward Forbes with the Society – his generous cordial intercourse with all, and his power of attaching every one to him. Forbes rose to reply, but his feelings overpowered him. "I thank you," followed by a gush of tears, told best his sense of the esteem in which his colleagues held him.

Wilson and Geikie 1861, p534

Notes, 1853-1854

1. Charles Lyell and his wife were visiting Madeira and the Canary Islands (Lyell 1881, 2, pp193-196).
2. Secord refers to this episode as 'The Battle of May Hill' (Secord 1986, p8).
3. Woodward's admission certificate No 1688, bears only eight signatures: Murchison, Darwin, Sharpe, Horner, Ramsay, Ansted, Morris and Salter. He was proposed on 1 February 1854 and elected on 8 March.

Session 1854-1855

201. 1855, January 3

The following communications were read:

"On a Submerged Forest at Fort Lawrence, Nova Scotia", by J. W. Dawson, Esq., F.G.S.

"On some additional small Reptilian remains from Purbeck", by Professor Owen, F.G.S.

"On a large Fossil Cuttle-fish, from the Kimmeridge Clay", by Professor Owen, F.G.S.

"On the Tertiary Beds of Hesse Cassel and its vicinity", by W. J. Hamilton, Esq., Pres.G.S.

201a. Andrew Ramsay wrote in his diary:

We went to the Geological Society after. I heard a slow paper by Hamilton. The attendance looked miserably meagre. All the old great ones were gone except Lyell. He Sharpe & Colonel Portlock alone occupied the front benches, & Lyell, Sharpe & Prestwich alone spoke. It looked wretched in the extreme.

IC Ramsay

201b. T Rupert Jones wrote to Richard Owen on 4 January:

The papers on Purb. [Purbeck] & Kim. [Kimmeridge] fossils were read last night, & gave rise to some little discussion. I have to tell Mr Brodie what will please him – that thanks were unanimously voted him for sending hither many fossils – at the same time the Socy acknowledged your kindness in describing them.

NHM Owen, 16/236

202. 1855 January 17

The following communication was read:

"On Vertical and Meridional Lamination of Primary Rocks", by Evan Hopkins, Esq., F.G.S.

202a. Andrew Ramsay wrote in his diary:

After lecture dined at the Geological Club. Sat next Lyell who bored me with heavy metamorphic talk. Evan Hopkins read an insane paper on the crystalline rocks. We all talked. Smyth pitched in heavily, & Hopkins thick skinnedly bore it all; nothing affects his self conceit.

IC Ramsay

203. 1855, January 31

The following communications were read:

"Additional observations on the Silurian and Devonian rocks near Christiana in Norway", by Sir R. I. Murchison, V.P.G.S., &c., &c.

"On the causes producing foliation in rocks, and on some observed causes of foliated structure in Norway and Scotland", by David Forbes Esq., F.G.S., A.I.C.E.

203a. David Forbes wrote to H C Sorby on 24th March:

> Although I have not the pleasure of your personal acquaintance I have to thank you for your valuable paper which you kindly sent me through Mr. Jones [1] – I have read it with great pleasure and am a perfect adherent of your views and have expressed myself strongly to that effect in a paper on Foliation at the G.S. which when printed I shall be most happy to send you – Mr. Sharpe and myself had a sharp discussion on the subject – he being your opponent but I hope to convince even him some of these days and I believe he is rather staggered in his notions. I am anxious to prove cleavage Mechanical – and that Cleavage and Foliation are two distinct processes as these two points affect seriously all my subsequent resoning on the subject and prevent me going on with my observations until I have got a somewhat settled issue of the question – as I have been working on the subject for a considerable time and have a number of results of observations – and also Synthetical.
>
> SCA Sorby, SLPS 51-49, printed in Higham 1963, p45

204. 1855, February 16 [2]

Annual General Meeting, at which W. J. Hamilton read the Anniversary Address and was re-elected President.

204a. Andrew Ramsay wrote in his diary:

> Anniversary of the Geological. Hamilton read a good address, especially doing good justice to the memory of old Greenough, & in less degree to that of Sir Henry [De la Beche]. Logan got the medal at which I was well pleased, but I got exasperated when I heard Hamilton congratulate the geologists on Sir Roderick's [Murchison] appointment to the Geological Survey, and <u>because</u> he would direct our still lingering labours in Siluria, and because he

would direct our Permian & New Red subdivision, that I left the room, but thinking better of it ere I passed the library I walked in immediately at the other door & spoke to ?Twalmley. However afterwards I spoke to Sir Roderick about it at the Athenaeum & also to Hamilton after dinner & I hope it will be set straight. The dinner was a failure. There were few distinguished persons there (of science) no ambassadors & no bishops, & Sharpe in his address knuckled the table and mumbled miserably to the cloth. I sat between Dr. Bigsby & Austen & Colonel James & Mr. Smith of Jordanhill were close by. Rogers made a good speech & so did Colonel Portlock. Reeks got Muzzy rather & when we had got Hamilton Austen James & all the rest into the smoking room after, he slightly evinced it, & <u>sent for</u> Sir Roderick. Percy however prevented it by stepping out & bringing him in & there we all sat & were jolly for an hour. Home at 1.

IC Ramsay

205. 1855, February 21 [3]

The following communication was read:

"Evidences of the Occurrence of Glaciers and Icebergs in the Permian Period", by Andrew Ramsay, F.G.S.

205a. Andrew Ramsay wrote in his diary:

Went to the Geological Council where Sharpe made but a seedy appearance in the chair. not much better at the club dinner, and worst of all at the Society in the evening.

IC Ramsay

206. 1855, May 30

The following communications were read:

"Notice of the Occurrence of a Bore at Port Lloyd, Bonin Islands", by P. W. Graves, Esq., H. M. Consul-General for the Sandwich Islands, forwarded by the Foreign Office.

"On the probable Extension of the Coal-Measures beneath the South-eastern Parts of England", by R. Godwin-Austen, Esq., F.G.S.

206a. William Pengelly wrote to his wife:

I must now give you my promised account of my visit to the Geol. Soc. There were probably about forty persons present, which

I believe is considered a good attendance. We were rather late, and found on our arrival that a paper was being read descriptive of Manna Loa, the volcano in Owhyee [Hawaii]. At its close Austen, a well-known geologist, who once lived at East Ogwell, read a paper on the 'Probability of Coal existing at workable depths near London', ... A discussion followed the paper, in which the author was by no means spared, as the various speakers expressed themselves freely. This part was extremely interesting, not only on account of the remarks made, but also because it gave me an opportunity of seeing and hearing many eminent men, as Lyell, Murchison, Col. Portlock, Sharpe, Smyth, Prestwich, Morris, etc. Daubeny and Percy were also there, but did not speak. Lyell is a merry-looking fellow, very bald, and, according to C.Hanbury, junior, like me in a 'general way'. C.Hanbury introduced me to a few persons. I seemed to get on best with Morris, the author of the great Catalogue. [4] After the meeting we got into a tea-room, and did ample justice to the good things there spread, in leaving the Geological the author of the paper on Manna Loa came out with me, and appeared very sociable; he told me he was seven days in reaching the top of the mountain, which is about two and a half miles, and that the cold was so intense that he could not sleep a wink ...

Pengelly 1897, p54

Notes, 1854-1855

1. Probably a copy of Sorby 1853.
2. Ramsay's diary gives 15 February, a Thursday, while the Society's *Quarterly Journal* gives 16, a Friday.
3. Ramsay's diary gives 20 February, a Tuesday, while the Society's *Quarterly Journal* gives 21, a Wednesday.
4. Morris 1854.

Session 1855-1856

207. 1856, January 9

The following communications were read:

"On the Physical Geography of the Tertiary Estuary of the Isle of Wight", by H. C. Sorby, Esq., F.G.S.

"On the probable Permian Character of the Red Sandstones of the South of Scotland", by E. W. Binney, Esq., F.G.S.

The Meetings

207a. One of his friends wrote to Henry Sorby in January:

> I have intended for some days to write to you to say I was at the meeting of the Geological Society on the 19th & heard your paper read – it was very interesting & most successful production & the discussion that followed proved it to be considered such. Sir C. Lyell, Major James and Mr. D.Sharp [Sharpe] were the most prominent speakers, & they all appeared to regret that you were not present. Mr Prestwich read the paper & not well. I thought it lost some good points in its delivery – you really ought to have been present, to have explained away a few apparent discrepancies & to have taken the lead in a very animated & learned discussion.
> SCA Sorby, SLPS 51-66,partly quoted in Higham 1963, p46

208. 1856, March 19

The following communications were read:

"On some Organic Remains from the Bone-bed at the base of the Lias at Lyme Regis", by the Rev. Mr. Dennis, communicated by Sir C. Lyell, V.P.G.S.

"On the Valenciennes Coal-basin", by MM. Degousée and Laurent, Civil Engineers, in a letter to, and communicated by, A. Tylor Esq., F.G.S.

"On the Sandstones and Breccias of the South of Scotland of an age subsequent to the Carboniferous Period", by R. Harkness, Esq., F.G.S., Professor of Geology and Mineralogy, Queen's College, Cork.

208a. Andrew Ramsay wrote in his diary:

> Dined at the Geological Club & sat between Sir Phillip [Egerton] & Galton, who is a gentleman of great good humour & small capacity.[1] Jukes was there as Sir Roderick's [Murchison] guest & Sir Charles Lyell also had another, a country parson who afterwards read a paper on some supposed Mammalian bones from the Lias, & whom Owen regularly "chewed up" after. Harkness also had a paper on the Permians of the S. of Scotland feebly done. I spoke twice, once in opposition to one of Sharpe's crotchets that these S. of Scotland breccias had been formed in lakes.
> While Owen was demolishing the clergyman it was curious to see Lyell winking and blinking & feeling ashamed of his protegé.[2]
> IC Ramsay

209. 1856, April 9

The following communications were read:

"Notes on the Geology of the Neighbourhood of Sydney, Newcastle, and Brisbane, Australia", by Mr. James S. Wilson, Geologist to the North Australian Expedition, communicated by Sir R. I. Murchison, F.G.S.

"On the Lowest Strata of the Cliffs at Hastings," by S. H. Beckles, Esq., F.G.S.

"On the Palaeontological and Stratigraphical Relations of the so-called 'Sands of the Inferior Oolite'", by Thomas Wright, M.D., F.R.S.E., communicated by Professor Ramsay, F.G.S.

"On the Probable Origin of the English Channel by means of a Fissure", by Ami Boué, For.Mem.G.S.

209a. Andrew Ramsay wrote in his diary:

At the Museum & Geological Club. A paper at the Geological Society by Dr. Wright on the sand of the I.O. [Inferior Oolite] proving it to be Lias. It did not meet with perfect favor by any means altho' I think he had the right sow by the ear. I defended it. So did Woodward. Morris rather attacked it.

IC Ramsay

210. 1856, May 28

The following communications were read:

"On the Silurian Rocks of Wigtownshire", by J. C. Moore, Esq., F.G.S.

"On the Action of Ocean-currents in the Formation of the Strata of the Earth", by C. Babbage, Esq., F.G.S., communicated by W. H. Fitton, M.D., F.R.S., F.G.S.

210a. William Pengelly wrote to his wife on 29 May:

... and then to Somerset House to attend the meeting of the Geological Society. Two papers were read, one by Mr. Moore on the rocks of Wigtonshire, etc., which was discussed by Col. Portlock, Murchison and Salter; the other was by the famous Babbage, on the formation of sedimentary outliers, etc., which called up Portlock, Lyell, Salter, Stephenson, the engineer, Prof. Tyndall,

The Meetings

Huxley etc. It was a magnificent meeting, and made me wish for a town residence. Whilst we were 'coffeeizing' I renewed my acquaintance with many old friends.

Pengelly 1897, p57

211. 1856, June 19

The following communications were read:

"On a Section near Mont Blanc", by Major S. Charters, F.G.S.

"Further Notice of the Recent Eruption from the Volcano of Mauna Loa in Hawaii (Owhyhee)", by W. Miller, Esq., H.M. Consul-General for the Sandwich Islands.

"On the Geology of Varna and its Vicinity, and of other parts of Bulgaria", by Capt. Spratt, R.N., F.R.S., F.G.S.

"On the Geology of Trinidad", by H. G. Bowen, Esq., F.G.S.

"On the Fossils found in the Chalk-flints and Greensand of Aberdeenshire" by J. W. Salter, Esq., F.G.S.

"On the Correlation of the Middle Eocene Tertiaries of England, France and Belgium", by J. Prestwich, Esq., F.R.S., Treas.G.S.

211a. Charles Bunbury wrote in his diary:

I had some geological talk with Murchison, who gave me an account of the discussion at the Geological Society last night on the nummulitic fomation. He contends (and I think with great reason) that the vast formation of nummulite limestone in Asia and South Europe is only <u>in part</u> represented by the beds which Prestwich and Lyell consider as its equivalents in middle Europe, and that it corresponds to the Lower Eocene <u>as well</u> as the Middle Eocene of England, &c.

Bunbury 1890-1891, 2, p413

Notes, 1855-1856

1. This was the Douglas Galton who Ramsay had attempted to blackball on 27 February 1850.
2. Mammals in the Liassic would have fitted in with Lyell's minority views on the non-progression of life (Bartholomew 1976).

Session 1856-1857

212. 1857, February 20

Annual General Meeting at which Colonel J. E. Portlock read the Anniversary Address and was re-elected President.

212a. Leonard Horner wrote to his wife on 21 February:

> The Geological Society's dinner went off well. We had a very good speech from Owen, and also an excellent one from Lord Panmure on the importance of better educating the officers of the army in science, and describing what has been done and what is still doing towards that end, and highly approving of appointments being given by competitive examinations and not from patronage as heretofore. I was not at home till half past eleven.
> Lyell 1890, 2, p269

213. 1857, April 22

The following communications were read:

"Description of a new Fossil Crustacean (*Tropifer laevis*, C. Gould) from the Lias bone-bed", by Charles Gould, Esq., B.A.

"Description of a new Crustacean (*Pygocephalus Cooperi*, Huxley) from the Coal Measures", by Professor Huxley, F.R.S., F.G.S.

"On the Geology of Strath, Skye", by A. Geikie, Esq., of the Geological Survey of Great Britain. With "Descriptions of some fossils from Skye", by T. Wright, M.D., F.R.S.E., communicated by Professor Ramsay, F.G.S.

213a. Archibald Geikie wrote in his autobiography:

> Professor Ramsay, who communicated the paper, sent me a gratifying account of its reception at the meeting, where Murchison, Lyell, Egerton, and Leonard Horner were among the auditors.
> Geikie 1924, p65

Session 1857-1858

214. 1857, December 2

The following communication was read:

"On some Peculiarities in the Microscopical Structure of Crystals, applicable to the Determination of the Aqueous or Igneous Origin of Minerals and Rocks", by H. C. Sorby, Esq., F.R.S., F.G.S.

214a. Charles Bunbury wrote in his diary:

> Dined at the Geological Club. Dr. Livingstone was there as a guest, but did not talk much.[1] I had some good talks with Murchison, Douglas Galton, and Colonel James of the Ordnance Survey. Murchison asked me about the fossil plants of the Rothliegendes or Lower Permian of Germany, of which he said Goppert had sent him a list, showing them to be with a few exceptions (Neuropteris Loshii one of the exceptions) specifically distinct from those of the coal formation, though of the same genera. (But I am not sure whether Brongniart's genus, Callipterus is found in the true coal). He said that Beyrich is, he believes, the only geologist who refers the Rothliegendes to the Carboniferous period. He told me that Pander, a very accurate and painstaking Russian naturalist, has found reason to melt down fourteen of Agassiz's genera of fossil fish into one.
>
> Bunbury 1890-1891, 3, p61

215. 1858, April 28

The following communications were read:

"On some Vegetable Remains from Madeira", by Charles J. F. Bunbury, Esq., F.R.S., F.G.S.

"On a Section of a part of the Fifeshire Coast", by the Rev. Thomas Brown, communicated by Sir R. I. Murchison, V.P.G.S.

"On the Lower Coal-measures, as developed in British America", by J. W. Dawson, LL.D., F.G.S, Principal of McGill College, Montreal.

"Some Observations on *Stigmaria ficoides*", by E.W. Binney, Esq., F.R.S., F.G.S.

Sessions 1857-58, 1858-59

"On a species of Fern from the Coal-Measures of Worcestershire", by John Morris, F.G.S.

215a. Charles Bunbury wrote in his diary:

> Attended the meeting of the Geological Society (for which indeed I had come to town). Read my paper on the fossil leaves from Madeira, which was very well received. Lyell gave a clear and satisfactory account of the geological relations of the bed.
> Bunbury 1890-1891, 3, p86

Note, 1857-1858

1. Dr. Livingstone's name is recorded as a visitor on this day in the Club minute book (GSC M3), but he apparently did not go on to the Society meeting afterwards. He was presumably introduced by Murchison, who was also present. David Livingstone was in England for 1857 and the first part of 1858.

Session 1858-1859

216. 1859, January 5

The following communications were read :

"On Fossil Plants from the Devonian Rocks of Canada", by J. W. Dawson, LL.D., F.G.S., Principal of McGill College, Montreal.

"On some Points in Chemical Geology", by T. Sterry Hunt, Esq. of the Geological Commission of Canada, communicated by Prof. A. C. Ramsay, F.R.S., F.G.S.

216a. Charles Bunbury wrote in his diary:

> Dined at the Geological Club; present, John Phillips (president), Lord Enniskillen, Mr. Horner, John Moore, William Hamilton, Prestwich, Prof. Miller of Cambridge, Mr. Mylne, Dr. Bigsby, and one or two others. Pleasant talk. Lord Enniskillen is a very good fellow and a thorough Irishman. He made us all laugh by saying of the famous fossilist Count Münster, that he was very stingy and unfair, always <u>making exchanges and giving nothing in return</u>.

The Meetings

Hamilton said that when he was in Asia Minor, Europeans could travel with safety through most parts of the country; <u>now</u> the whole country swarms with <u>Greek</u> robbers, so that no one can travel without a strong escort, and these bandits infest even the immediate neighbourhood of Smyrna, where he was able to ramble alone with perfect safety.

Evening meeting of the Geological Society.

There was a rather interesting discussion between C. Lyell, W. Hamilton, and Prof. Miller, on the question whether serpentine is always a metamorphic rock or sometimes intrusive; the author of the Paper had maintained the first doctrine, Lyell and Hamilton held the other.

Bunbury 1890-1891, 3, p125

217. 1859, January 19

The following communications were read :

"On the Gold-fields of Ballarat and Creswick Creek", by H. Rosales, Esq., in a letter to W. W. Smyth, Esq., Sec.G.S.

"Description of Two Species of Cephalaspis", by John Harley, Esq., communicated by Prof. T. Huxley, F.G.S.

217a. Charles Bunbury wrote in his diary:

Dined at the Geological Club. At the evening meeting of the Society was read a paper by Mr. Rosales on the gold field of Ballarat in Victoria; not very interesting in itself, but it gave occasion to a good discussion, branching out into a variety of topics in which Murchison and Lyell took the most prominent part. Among other things the author of the paper alluded to the great streams of basalt or lava overlying the auriferous drift, and to the occurrence of vegetable remains, and in particular of a cone of the "she-Oak" (Casuarina) under the basalt. This gave me occasion to speak of the vegetation, recent and fossil, of Australia, and especially of the Banksia cones now in Joseph Hooker's possession. [1] By the way, Murchison says that those cones were found in the Colony of Victoria, not in New South Wales. Murchison was very copious and instructive on the subject of the gold deposit, and of the occurence of gold in general. [2]

Bunbury 1890-1891, 3, pp130-131

Notes, 1858-1859

1. Hooker describes fossil Araucarian cones and Banksia wood from Norfolk Island and Chobham in a letter to Charles Darwin, 22 December 1858. Burkhardt and Smith 1985-2003, 7, p219 and in Hooker 1859.
2. For Murchison's position as 'the leading expert on the world's gold supply' see Stafford 1989, p19 and Chapter 2.

Session 1859-1860

218. 1859, November 30

The following communications were read :

"On some Bronze Relics found in an Auriferous Sand in Siberia", by T. W. Atkinson, Esq., F.G.S., F.R.G.S.

"On the Volcanic Country of Auckland, New Zealand", by Charles Heaphy, Esq., Provincial Surveyor, &c., communicated by the President.

"On the Geology of a part of South Australia between Adelaide and the River Murray", by T. Burr, Esq.

"On some Tertiary Rocks in the Colony of South Australia", by the Revd. Julian E. Woods, F.G.S.; with "Notes on the Fossil Polyzoa and Foraminifera", by G. Busk, Esq., F.R.S., F.G.S., W. K. Parker, Esq., Mem. M.S. and T. Rupert Jones, Esq., F.G.S.

218a. Charles Bunbury wrote in his diary:

> Dined at the Geological Club – a scanty attendance, owing to the anniversary meeting of the Royal Society on the same evening; but I had some pleasant talk with John Moore.
> Evening meeting of the Geological Society. The first paper, a notice by Mr. Atkinson, the Siberian traveller, on some <u>bronze</u> ornaments found in the auriferous drift of Eastern Siberia – a pretty good discussion on this curious subject – much more curious and extraordinary if the fact be well ascertained, than the flint knives or hatchets in the European drift, as articles made of bronze imply a much higher stage of civilization than those of flint. In reality it is most probable that these Siberian bronze articles are of much later date than the auriferous drift, whatever

might be the accident by which they were brought into the midst of it. I was glad to have the opportunity of seeing Atkinson, whose travels I have read with interest.

The second paper was a good account, by a Roman Catholic priest, of the volcanic cones and craters near Auckland in New Zealand; a district in which these volcanic phenomena seem to come uncommonly thick.

Last two papers on certain geological characteristics of a part of south Australia.

Bunbury 1890-1891, 3, pp197-198

219. 1860, May 30

The following communications were read:

"On certain Rocks of Miocene and Eocene age in Tuscany, including Serpentine, accompanied by Copper-ore, Lignite, and Alabaster", by W. P. Jervis, Esq., F.G.S.

"On the Ossiferous Caves of the Peninsula of Gower, in Glamorganshire, South Wales", by H. Falconer, M.D., F.R.S., F.G.S. with an Appendix by J. Prestwich, Esq., F.R.S., Treas.G.S., "On a Raised Beach in Mewslade Bay, and the occurence of the Boulder-clay on Cefn-y-bryn, in Gower"; the reading of this paper was begun.

219a. William Pengelly wrote to his wife on 31 May:

Then came the Geological Club Dinner, which I attended as Lyell's guest. I was well received by all; many of them were old friends. Amongst them were Horner, Murchison, Lyell, Percy, Godwin-Austen, Smyth, Lubbock, Prestwich, and Falconer. It went of capitally. I sat by Lyell, who told me spontaneously he would gladly vote for me as F.R.S.![1] My lecture was much and well spoken of.[2] Then to the Geological Society, where two papers were read by Falconer on the Gower Caves. There was nothing new on the question of human chronology. A good discussion followed, in which Lyell, Austen, Prestwich, and I took part.

Pengelly 1897, p98

219b. Hugh Falconer wrote to Joseph Prestwich on 2 June:

You know what a fierce onslaught was made on me by Lyell and Austen.[3] I thought the latter was going to eat me up. The whole subject will be up again at the next meeting, when the main brunt of the battle will fall on you. There is no wavering on the mammalian evidence – it is coming out stronger than ever, as I can show you when you happen to pass this way.

Prestwich 1899, p152. See also Boylan 1977, p45

219c. William Pengelly wrote to his son on 7 June:

On Wednesday I dined with the Geological Club; we were about thirty, including some of the most eminent geologists. After dinner we went to the Geological Society, where a paper was read by Dr. Falconer descriptive of some ossiferous caverns near Swansea; he made the astounding statement that between ten and eleven hundred antlers <u>of the Reindeer</u> had been taken out of ONE cavern. There is no manner of doubt about its correctness.

Pengelly 1897, p104

Notes, 1859-1860

1. William Pengelly was elected a Fellow of the Royal Society on 4 June 1863, chiefly due to canvassing by Lyell.
2. Pengelly had lectured on 26 May at the Royal Institution of Great Britain on Devonian fossils.
3. An account of this dispute, which related to the relative ages of the fossil bones, the raised beach and the boulder clay, is given in Prestwich 1899, pp149-153.

Session 1860-1861

220. 1860, December 5

The following communication was read:

"On the Structure of the North-west Highlands, and the Relations of the Gneiss, Red Sandstone, and Quartzite of Sutherland and Ross-shire", by Professor James Nicol, F.G.S. [1]

220a. Roderick Murchison wrote to Archibald Geikie on 6 December:

As the Nicollian <u>Onslaught</u> was most carefully illustrated by numerous diagrams which covered a large space of the Great Hall in Burlington House [2] & as the memoir was admirably read by Warrington Smyth it was manifest that without a good hearty rejoinder & emphatic denial of his faults & twists the impression on the greater part of the worthies who come to our meetings would have been very detrimental. For, granting the supposed data as pitted against what N called the 'theory of his opponents which never could be permitted to overthrow all the good old Scottish Geology', the logic of our adversary is good enough.

Until you get a copy of the diagrams & an abstract of the memoir, you will scarcely be able to understand what we have to grapple with & defeat; [?] Jones has promised to let me have copies of the diagrams. Those selected for exhibition were chiefly those which actually cut to pieces my sections as published after my visit with Ramsay. One of these represent what I told you before the twisting round underground of all the formations & bringing ref the western gneiss so as to clap it caponally on (& near the surface only) upon the Quartz rock & limestone. This is the Eribol section & the fact (if one) that the annelid tubes are overturned in what I call Upper Quartz & which he says is the overturned Lower Quartz was sure to make some impression. [3] But I begged leave to doubt the fact in primus, & next I contended that neither there nor at Loch Maree (of which he had a section) was it physically possible to wrench underneath the lower gneiss & changing both its strike & its mineral character to convert it into micaceous, flaggy quartzose rock & lay it conformably on the Quartz Rock & limestone.

I read parts of your letter, particularly that part which gives such clear proofs of transition along the tract between Loch Maree & Loch Broom & I cannot doubt that this independent evidence must have had its weight. But notwithstanding all that I did (& they tell me I fought well & manfully) there is too much reason to fear that Nicol's concern will produce a very adverse effect.

GSL Geikie

221. 1861, January 23

The following communications were read:

"On the Gravel and Boulders of the Punjab", by J. D. Smithe, Esq., F.G.S.

"On *Pteraspis Dunensis* (*Archaeoteuthis Dunensis*, Roemer)", by Prof. T. H. Huxley, F.R.S., Sec.G.S.

"On the 'Chalk-rock' lying between the Lower and the Upper Chalk in Wilts, Berks, Oxon, Bucks, and Herts", by W. Whitaker, Esq., B.A., F.G.S.

221a. Andrew Ramsay wrote in his diary:

Dined at the Geol: Club and sat between Lord Enniskillen & Sir H James. Lyell opposite. Horner in the Chair. Papers by Captn. Smyth, Huxley & Whitaker after. Spoke twice, and in explaining Austen's theory of the Upper Greensand, was complimented after by Lyell for my remarkably lucid explanation of a difficult subject.

IC Ramsay

222. 1861, February 6

The following communication was read:

"On the Altered Rocks of the Western and Central Highlands", by Sir R. I. Murchison, F.R.S., V.P.G.S. and A. Geikie, Esq., F.G.S.

222a. Andrew Ramsay wrote in his diary:

At the Geol: Soc. Sir R [Murchison] & Geikie spoke a paper on the Highlands. They took 2 hours & exhausted the audience. But for Harkness & I, I think few of them would have understood what it was about.

IC Ramsay

223. 1861, February 15

Annual General Meeting at which Leonard Horner read the Anniversary Address and was re-elected President.

223a. Andrew Ramsay wrote in his diary:

At the Museum & the Geol: Soc: to assist at the anniversary. In the Evening at the Freemason's Tavern at the Anniversary Dinner. Horner in the Chair. Gladstone & Whewell there, Scrope, Lyell, Sir R [Murchison] &c. Sat between Scrope & William Longman.

IC Ramsay

224. 1861, February 20

The following communications were read:

"On the Coincidence between Stratification and Foliation in the Crystalline Rocks of the Highlands", by Sir R. I. Murchison, V.P.G.S. and A.Geikie, Esq., F.G.S.

The Meetings

"On the Rocks of portions of the Highlands of Scotland South of the Caledonian Canal, and on their equivalents in the North of Ireland", by Professor R. Harkness, F.R.S., F.G.S.

224a. Andrew Ramsay wrote in his diary:

He [Howell] & I went to the Geological Society. Paper by Sir R [Murchison] & Geikie on the foliated rocks of the Highlands. They quoted me for Arran & Anglesey, & then in the debate Tyndal rose & spoke, & said the very things I had been quoted for as if they were his own on the spur of the moment. They referred to the Coincidence of foliation & bedding that I had [?] united the half of that 20 years ago & the remainder 5 or 6. He had not been listening. So I put the saddle on the right horse & [?] the audience.

IC Ramsay

225. 1861, March 4

The following communications were read:

"On the Succession of Beds in the Hastings Sand in the Northern portion of the Wealden Area", by F. Drew, Esq., F.G.S., of the Geological Survey of Great Britain.

"On the Permian Rocks of the South of Yorkshire; and on their Palaeontological Relations", by J. W. Kirby, Esq., communicated by T. Davidson, Esq., F.G.S.

225a. Andrew Ramsay wrote in his diary:

Went with him [Hutton] to the Geol Society to hear Drew's paper. Good but dry. Spoke thereon.

IC Ramsay

226. 1861, March 20

The following communications were read:

"On a Collection of Fossil Plants from the Nagpur Territory, Central India", by Sir C. Bunbury, Bart., F.R.S., F.G.S.

"On the Age of the Fossiliferous thin-bedded Sandstones and Coalbeds of the Province of Nagpur, Central India", by the Rev. Stephen Hislop, communicated by the President.

"On the Geological Age of the Coal-bearing Rocks of New South Wales", by the Rev. W. B. Clarke, F.G.S.

"On some Reptilian Remains from North-western Bengal", by Prof. T. H. Huxley, F.R.S., Sec.G.S.

226a. Andrew Ramsay wrote in his diary:

Dined at the Geol Club, & went to the Society after. Lectured on Silurian rocks.

IC Ramsay

226b. Charles Bunbury wrote in his diary:

Geological Society's meeting. My paper on the "Fossil Plants from Nagpore", (which has hung on my hands two years!) was read. Then Huxley gave us, not a paper, but a *viva voce* account, in his clear and spirited manner, of the remains of the Dicynodon, and of a fish called Ceratodus, which he had determined in specimen from the Burdwan coal formation; and he showed the inference to be, (though not with certainty) that the formation is Triassic.

Bunbury 1890-1891, 3, p254

227. 1861, April 10

The following communications were read:

"On the Geology of the Country between Lake Superior and the Pacific Ocean (between 48 and 55 parallels of latitude), explored by the Government Exploring Expedition under the command of Captain J. Palliser (1857-1860)", by James Hector, M.D., communicated by Sir R. I. Murchison, V.P.G.S.

"On the Elevations and Depressions of the Earth in North America", by Dr. Dr. A. Gesner, F.G.S.

227a. Andrew Ramsay wrote in his diary:

At the Museum & the Geological Club to dinner. At the Society in the evening. Dr Hector's paper on N. American exploring expedition.

IC Ramsay

227b. Charles Lyell had written to Roderick Murchison the previous week:

> I am not allowed though much recovered to be at the Council today & regret it as I find the President is to bring before you the question of going back to Somerset House which I regret as I think the effect of our move has been in two ways successful: first it has increased the number of visitors not being members of the Society & so far rendered our <u>meetings</u> more useful; <u>secondly</u>: the decline of the attendance of fellows has not been at so rapid a rate annually as it was <u>during</u> the last years before our move to Burlington House; <u>thirdly</u>: we hear better now than at first since the curtains were added & this would improve as the attendance increased; <u>fourthly</u> if we go back to the East and then find our meetings decrease in number as I fully expect we shall not find the rooms at Burlington House free to take us back on Wednesdays; <u>fifthly</u> the popularity of geology with the public is not diminishing as some pretend, but as the sale of elementary works & periodicals like the Geologist which I am told sells nearly a thousand copies, and the crowds at the Geol. Section at the British Association prove is increasing, and if our terms are getting more technical, the public proportionately is becoming more educated. All that is wanted gradually to ensure larger meetings is that some of the leading men should have more faith in the popularity of their subject and a desire to educate the public and not to make the meetings merely places where a few adepts may exchange opinions.
> C Lyell to R I Murchison, 8 April 1861, GSL Murchison, L17/39

228. 1861, June 19

The following communications were read:

"On the Lines of Deepest Water around the British Isles", by the Rev. R. Everest, F.G.S.

"On the Old Red Sandstone Rocks of Forfarshire", by James Powrie, Esq., F.G.S.

"On the Ludlow Bone-Bed and its Crustacean Remains", by J. Harley, M.B.Lond., communicated by Prof. Huxley, Sec.G.S., &c.

"On the Outburst of a Volcano near Edd, on the African Coast of the Red Sea", by Capt. R. L. Playfair, Officiating Political Resident, Aden, communicated by Sir R. I. Murchison, V.P.G.S.

"Notice of the Occurence of an Earthquake on the 20th of March, 1861, in Mendoza, Argentine Confederation, South America", by C. Murray, Esq., communicated by the President.

"On the Increase of Land on the Coromandel Coast", by J. W. Dykes, Esq., from a Letter to Sir C. Lyell, F.G.S.

228a. Charles Bunbury wrote in his diary:

I attended the Council of the Geological Society and dined at the Club where there was a good muster. I sat between Sir Roderick Murchison and Huxley; had some talk with the former on African discovery, and much with the latter on various topics.

Huxley is an exceedingly clever man, and rather an agreeable one: and I believe a good man, but I cannot take very cordially to one entirely without veneration.

At the evening meeting of the Geological Society (the concluding one of the session) several short papers were read; the most interesting to me was a notice of the breaking out of a new volcano on the African coast of the Red Sea, not far from the Straits.

Bunbury 1890-1891, 3, pp276-277

Notes, 1860-1861

1. The background to this paper is given in Oldroyd 1990, p6.
2. Ordinary Meetings of the Society were opened to wives and daughters of fellows from November 1860, and were transferred from Somerset House to Burlington House in anticipation of increased attendance. This increase never materialised, and in February 1863 the meetings returned to Somerset House and the invitation to ladies was withdrawn (Woodward 1907, pp 242-244).
3. Nicol used the shape of the annelid burrows to determine whether the strata were the right way up or overturned. Murchison here brushes the evidence aside.

The Meetings

Session 1861-1862

229. 1861, November 6

The following communications were read:

"Note on the bone-caves of Lunel-Viel, Herault", by Monsieur Marcel de Serres, Professor at the 'Faculté des Sciences', Montpellier.

"On the Petroleum-Springs in North America", by Abraham Gesner, M.D., F.G.S.

"Notice on the discovery of additional remains of land animals in the Coal-Measures of the South Joggins, Nova Scotia", by J. W. Dawson, LL.D., F.G.S, Principal of McGill College.

"On a volcanic phenomenon witnessed in Manilla", by John G. Veitch, Esq.

229a. J J Bigsby wrote to J W Dawson on 6 November:

> Your paper on the Dendrerpeton &c come on tonight before a very large audience in Burlington House Piccadilly, Sir R. M. [Murchison] in the chair, and all the leading geologists present – Prestwich, Falconer, Austen, Ramsay, Lyell &c &c. Not being very well, I did not stop to hear it, but I can say that the illustrating pictures and diagrams were very good. At the Club dinner Prof. Huxley gave a very clever summary of your discoveries; and with Murchison & Lyell pointed out their important bearing on philosophical geology.
>
> MGA Dawson

230. 1862, February 5

The following communications were read:

"On some Volcanic Phenomena lately observed at Torre del Greco and Resina", by Signor Luigi Palmieri, Director of the Royal Observatory on Vesuvius, in letters addressed to H. M. Consul at Naples, and dated December 17th, 1861 and January 3rd, 1862 sent from the Foreign Office by order of Earl Russell.

"On the Recent Eruption of Vesuvius", by M. Pierre de Tchihatcheff, communicated by Sir R. I. Murchison, V.P.G.S.

"On Isodiametric Lines as a means of representing the Distribution of Sedimentary (clay and sandy Strata), as distinguished from Calcareous Strata, with especial reference to the Carboniferous Rocks of Britain", by E. Hull, Esq., B.A., F.G.S. of the Geological Survey of Great Britain.

230a. Andrew Ramsay wrote in his diary:

> I took him [Johnes] to the Geol: Club. No Vice being present I was put in the chair. Vesuvian paper by Hull at night. Sir R [Murchison] in the chair. Sir R praised him not knowing what he was saying & Morris Salter & I partially pitched into him.
>
> IC Ramsay

231. 1862, February 21

Annual General Meeting at which Thomas Huxley read the Anniversary Address and Andrew Ramsay was elected President. [1]

231a. Sir Charles Bunbury wrote in his diary:

> Attended the anniversary meeting of the Geological Society. Mr. Horner, the out-going President being abroad, [2] Murchison, Vice-President, was in the chair. Ramsay was elected the new President. Murchison himself gave us an obituary notice of Dr. Fitton, and did it very well. Then the other notices of the deceased members were read by Warrington Smythe. Then Huxley gave us, in lieu of a presidential address, a most admirable and striking discourse on the present state and relations of palaeontology; beginning with noticing the great advantage, in all branches of knowledge, of taking from time to time, a general review of our progress and of the results actually gained. Applying this to palaeontology, he pointed out that, while our real advance in knowledge was very great, there was a tendency to exaggerate the actual gain, and to place too much reliance on it in certain points. He applied this particularly to the conclusions which have been drawn from palaeontology as to the origin of organic life, and as to the successive appearance of higher foms of life. He dwelt much on the insecurity of negative evidence in researches of this sort, ingeniously comparing the case to that of proving by negative evidence the innocence of a prisoner in a court of justice. He expatiated also on the meaning of geological synchronism, or

contemporaneity, as deduced by organic remains, with contemporaneity in the ordinary sense.

An important and very instructive and interesting part of his discourse was devoted to showing that, great as the difference between the present organic world and that of any remote geological time may appear, the resemblances are much greater and more important. He mentioned numerous instances of organic types, even of genera, which had come down unchanged from the palaeozoic times to our own: and showed in detail the comparatively small (surprisingly small) amount of difference, as to orders and larger groups, between the organic beings of the present day and those of all previous geological periods. On the whole, I have rarely listened to a scientific discourse more calculated to suggest thought and enquiry, to excite the faculties or to provoke controversy.

Anniversary dinner of the Geological Society at Willis' rooms – I sat by Charles Lyell. The Duke of Argyll and Monckton Milnes were present as guest, and both spoke – and spoke well.

Bunbury 1890-1891, 3, pp335-337, and Lyell 1906, 2, p171

231b. Andrew Ramsay wrote in his diary:

Anniversary of the Geological Society. I was elected President of the Society. Mr Horner previous Pres: being at Florence Sir R [Murchison] occupied the chair & Smyth &. Huxley read (& composed) the anniversary address.

I took the chair at the anniversary dimer at Willis' rooms, the Duke of Argyll as my right & Lord Ducie on my left. There were 87 present, nearly twice as many as last year, & among them Monckton & Milner Mr Pugh & Mr Heywood Mr P.s Dr Williams Principal of Jesus, Sir C Lyell Sir E Bunbury Sir R Murchison Henry Cole, General Portlock, Sir H James, all my Survey colleagues almost, <illegible> & Charles, Smyth &c &c. Some good speeches were delivered. When over, Huxley came running round & said Ramsay you spoke gloriously. The Duke of Argyll gave my health.

IC Ramsay

231c. Charles Lyell wrote to Leonard Horner on 23 February:

I must send you a few words on the anniversary, which went off very well. Murchison read your letter [3] which was well received, and he then delivered an appropriate complimentary address to Godwin Austen on presenting the medals. Austen, who was remarkably gratified by the honour, replied at length, and said he should work much harder in future. The chairman then gave a biographical account of the late Dr. Fitton, which he had got up with much pains, and which was a just tribute to one who had taken so active a part in the Society as well as in our science. After which Huxley delivered a brilliant critical discourse on what palaeontology has and has not done, and proved the value of negative evidence, how much the progressive development system has been pushed too far, how little can be said in favour of Owen's more generalised types when we go back to the vertebrata and invertebrata of remote ages, the persistency of many forms high and low throughout time, how little we know of the beginning of life upon the Earth, how often events called contemporaneous in Geology are applied to things which instead of coinciding in time, may have happened ten millions of years apart, &c. &c., and a masterly sketch comparing the past and present and almost every class in zoology, and something of botany cited from Hooker, which he said he had done because it was useful to look into the cellars and see how much gold there was there, and whether the quantity of bullion justified such an enormous circulation of paper. I never remember an address listened to with such interest or received with such applause, though there were many private protests against some of his bold opinions.

The dinner at Willis's was well attended; I should think eighty or more present. The Duke of Argyll made an excellent speech on proposing Ramsay's health. Monckton Milnes made a happy and humerous speech in reply to 'Members of the House of Commons'. I was requested to give the 'Universities', which I coupled with Dr. Williams, Principal of Jesus College, with whom we stayed at Oxford, who spoke fluently in reply. Lord Ducie, Sir Phillip Egerton, Sir H. James, most of the Council, and a full representation of Jermyn Street were there. The Duke of Argyll having talked of Scotland as a specific centre from which so many geologists had come, Warrington Smyth stood up for other centres of creation south of the Tweed, and late in the evening Huxley made them merry by a sort of mock-modest speech. I sat between Charles Bunbury and Dr. Williams, and had a pleasant time of it, and was pleased to think how much life there is coming on in the Society, when all of us who are above sixty are added to the extinct organisms.

Lyell 1881, 2, p356

231d. Ramsay's biographer wrote:

So at the Anniversary, on the 21st February, he [Ramsay] was duly elected President – an honour well earned by twenty-one years of continuous devotion to geology, and the large part taken by him in the work of the Geological Survey. In the evening he began his duties by presiding at the annual dinner of the Society, where, with the Duke of Argyll on his right, and Lord Ducie on the left, and most of the leaders of the geological science around him, he had the satisfaction of seeing a company of nearly ninety assemble to celebrate the foundation of the oldest geological society. Those of that company who still survive will remember the admirable way in which the new President spoke. Never before had he so distinguished himself in the difficult art of post-prandial oratory. In returning thanks for his health he showed a quiet dignity and simplicity, with touches at once of humour and pathos, which went straight to the heart of the listeners, and called forth many rounds of applause.

Geikie 1895, p271

232. 1862, March 5

The following communications were read:

"On the Glacial Origin of certain Lakes in Switzerland, Scotland, Sweden, and North America", by A. C. Ramsay, F.R.S., President of the Geological Society. [4]

232a. Andrew Ramsay wrote in his diary:

> Presided at Club & Soc. evg meeting. Spoke my paper on origin of Swiss lakes. "Damned with faint praise" by Lyell & vigorously opposed by Falconer who showed singular ignorance of glacier laws. Admirably defended by Huxley, & afterwards spoke myself. It was a very lively meeting & one sitting next Reeks said it was like the old days of Buckland & Sedgwick once again. It was said on the whole the sense of the meeting went with me, but I am uncertain of this.
>
> IC Ramsay, partly quoted in Geikie 1895, p271

232b. Roderick Murchison wrote to Louis Agassiz a few days later:

> In a paper read to the Geological Society Professor Ramsay has made stronger demands on the power of ice than you ever did. He imagines that every Swiss lake north and south (Geneva, Neuchatel, Como etc.) has been scooped out, and the depressions excavated by the abrading action of the glaciers ...
>
> Agassiz 1885, 2, p574

232c. Andrew Ramsay wrote to Mrs Cookman later in the year:

> I do not suppose you will find fault with the paper on the ground that it wants boldness. When it was read Dr. Falconer of Indian-fossil-elephant celebrity made an onslaught on it of forty minutes. I observe that most of the men older than myself repudiate it, while most of the younger bloods accept it. Lyell rejects, but then I have Darwin, Hooker, Sir William Logan, Jukes and Geikie.
>
> 9 Dec 1862, in Geikie 1895, p272

232d. Charles Lyell wrote to Roderick Murchison in 1864:

> Now I have heard that he [Falconer] claims to have played a great part at the G.S. on 5 of March 1862, but on that evening I spoke at equal length against Ramsay's views mentioning the non-existence of a great lake at Ivrea, having shortly before surveyed that ground with Gastoldi, & also contending that unequal movements of upheaval & depression had caused the lakes & not ice; an argument repeated by me a year afterwards in the Antiquity Page 316, 317, 318 &c. wh. I have seen nowhere else brought forward. [5]
>
> 24 June 1864, GSL Murchison, L17/41

233. 1862, May 21

The following communications were read:

"On the Metamorphic Rocks of the Banffshire Coast, the Scarabins, and a portion of East Sutherland", by Prof. R. Harkness, F.R.S., F.G.S.

"On the Geology of the Gold-fields of Nova Scotia", by the Rev. D. Honeyman, communicated by the President.

"On some fossil Crustacea from the Lower Coal-measures of Nova Scotia; on *Eurypterus*; and on some Tracks of Crustacea in the Lower Silurian Rocks", by J. W. Salter, Esq., F.G.S.

233a. Roderick Murchison wrote to Archibald Geikie on 29 June:

> I was quite ashamed when the memoir of Harkness was read the other day to see merely the old map (mss) of Sharp [6] with all

its errors suspended with Sir W Logan sitting in front of it & calling for me to point out the great changes which have been made.

GSL Geikie, f56

Notes, 1861-1862

1. Huxley's address caused Darwin some uneasiness, with its emphasis on the persistence of animal types rather than their progression (Desmond 1982, pp85-88).
2. Horner left England in September 1861 and arrived in Florence in October. His wife, Anne, died in Florence in May 1862, and he returned to England in June (Lyell 1890, 2, pp307-308).
3. No reference to this letter is made in the official minutes of the meeting.
4. The background to this paper is given in Davies 1969, pp303-309.
5. C Lyell 1863.
6. This map, prepared by Daniel Sharpe in 1852, is in the Geological Society's archives (LDGSL 702). It was replaced sometime in 1862 by a large manuscript based on the work of Murchison and Geikie (LDGSL 703).

Session 1864-1865

234. 1864, November 23

The following communications were read:

"On the occurrence of Organic Remains in the Laurentian Rocks of Canada", by Sir W. E. Logan, LL.D., F.R.S., F.G.S. Director of the Geological Survey of Canada. [1]

"On the Structure of certain Organic Remains found in the Laurentian Rocks of Canada", by J. W. Dawson, LL.D., F.R.S., F.G.S. with a Note by W. B. Carpenter, M.D., F.R.S., F.G.S.

"On the Mineralogy of certain Organic Remains found in the Laurentian Rocks of Canada", by T. Sterry Hunt, Esq., M.A., F.R.S., of the Geological Survey of Canada, communicated by Sir W. E. Logan, LL.D., F.R.S., F.G.S.

234a. William Logan wrote to a relative the following day:

Last evening our papers (my own, Dawson's, Hunt's, and Carpenter's) were read before the Geological Society, and I think we had a success.

W E Logan to J Logan, 24 Nov 1864, in Harrington 1883

235. 1865, April 26

The following communications were read:

"On the Character of the Cephalopodous Fauna of the South Indian Cretaceous Rocks", by Dr. F. Stoliczka, communicated by the Assistant-secretary.

"On the growth of Flos Ferri, or Coralloid Aragonite", by W. Wallace, Esq., communicated by W. W. Smyth, Esq., F.R.S., Sec.G.S.

"Notes on presenting some rhomboidal specimens of ironstone, &c.", by Sir J. F. W. Herschel, Bart., K.C.H., F.R.S., F.G.S., &c. with a Note by Captain T. Longworth Dames, communicated by Sir C. Lyell, Bart., F.R.S., F.G.S.

235a. Charles Lyell wrote to John Herschel on 28 April:

The discussion on your & Capt Dame's notes came off at the G.S. on Wednesday when Professor Ramsay, Messrs Hull & Forest of the Government Survey & others gave their opinions, sufficiently diverse to make a good debate & to show how useful it is to have the theory of cleavage & jointed structure & sun-cracks from shrinkage & dessication well agitated. It seemed to me that the favourite notion was, that the sides of the rhomboids being produced by two sets of parallel joints & the top & bottom of the box being the planes of lamination or stratification, the hydrous per-oxide of iron was originally disseminated equally through the mass of ferruginous and then separated, going to the exterior, leaving the centre discoloured, & causing an outer ferruginous coat. That this is the case in some analagous instances of spheroidal concretions seemed tolerably well made out. Your specimens were much admired & I have no doubt the subject will fructify in the brains of some of the speakers. To the repeated assertion of one speaker after another that they could match the phenomena by specimens of rocks of every age, I & others asked 'but how do you explain such cases?' and everyone had a different answer. Those who advocated weathering were somewhat posed by the bottom of the box being so like the lid.

RS Herschel, HS, 11, f439

Note, 1864-1865

1. The background to this group of papers is given in O'Brien 1970.

Session 1867-1868

236. 1868, February 5

The following communication was read:

"On the Geological Structure of Argyllshire", by His Grace the Duke of Argyll, K.T., D.C.L., F.R.S., F.G.S., &c. [1]

236a. Roderick Murchison wrote to Archibald Geikie on 6 February:

We had the grandest meeting last night which has been known in Somerset House for many a year !!! The Duke's paper (which I never saw till it came out of his pocket) was a piece of hard & stout reasoning upon what he considered as to inconsequences [?] of your inferences from the very clear facts which you yourself lay down as postulates.

It is in short an effort, & I think as I said a successful one, to vindicate the dignity of the Highland crystalline rocks, which, as they assume their present forms when in a hard state, have from that day to this given the principal relief to all the Scottish scenery. In other words that subterranean emery has left its outlines which have never been eradicated.

You know that this is my Creed whether in the Alps or the Highlands. I made your apology and said with the much candour you had in dedicating to me your attractive work it [?] assumed that you too I did not enhance [?embrace] all your views. [2]

At the same time I spoke of you as the one of all others who had [?] & would ?observe well & honestly & that when the Survey came to be extended to Argyllshire I had no doubt you would look carefully to all the data & if necessary modify any opinion founded upon your first rapid sketches [3] ...

P.S. When the Duke finished his long oration Lyell first spoke. He did not grapple with the main points, either for or against you but by the stories he told of recent changes he had seen in America (all loose gaily [?]) & which gave such an ?obviously fixed duration to certain water beds &c he seemed rather to favour the Duke's view. But the application was very obscure.

<u>Ramsay</u> Then up rose '<u>Vini plenum</u> [4]' & first literally <u>assaulted</u> Lyell for abandoning <u>all the principles</u> he had been successfully advocating for years – This was done in his <u>too fierce</u> way. He then went on as far as he was able, to defend your views; but he got into a muddle about the Upper Silurian & Old Red Sandstone, of neither of which are there traces in the Highland counties alluded to by the Duke. In short I am compelled to tell you that he made out a very bad case & I deeply regretted your <u>absence</u> and his <u>presence</u>. This is strictly entre nous, for I really love Ramsay & am pained when he makes a mistaken expression of this sort. The rooms laughter let my friend loses <u>caste</u> [?]

Then I harangued away as you can imagine.

David Forbes also strongly supported the Duke's view. Little Jones also strengthened the Duke's case by the proofs of splits & valleys opened by old fissures around the Weald & this brought out Sir Jn Lubbock who was about to strengthen your side by a discourse on the Weald & as it was then 1/2 past 10 clock I deduced, that if he opened out that sermon I must claim to speak for 1/2 an hour that ... much laughter & Sir Jn was stopped in his in daylight.

Two Scotsmen spoke one <u>pro</u> & the other <u>con</u> one shewing great effects for old subterranean rocks the other great proofs of denudation irrespective of internal movements.

Then, just at the close, Tyndall threw in what he called 'a pebble' & tried to show what water was really doing now in the Alps; but he is so notoriously ignorant of subterranean ... forces & the true state of the subsoil, that his observation went for little.

Prestwich & Evans both spoke in favour of your general views.

The Duke's reply was prompt & eloquent & he was (both afer the reading of his paper & at the end) more loudly applauded than I ever recollect any talk to have been in my time.

There were 130 persons present.

GSL Geikie, f129

236b. Roderick Murchison wrote again to Archibald Geikie two days later:

I lose not a post to assure you, that nothing could have been more divested of personality than the paper of the Duke. Besides, both before he read it & afterwards, he distinctly explained that it was against the too wide extension of the new views that he was crying [?], & that he merely took up your work as his theme, because it had so attracted public attention & was so popular.

8 Feb 1868, GSL Geikie f130

Notes, 1867-1868

1. The background to this paper is given in Oldroyd 1990, p6, although the paper itself is not mentioned.
2. Geikie's *Scenery of Scotland* (Geikie 1865) was dedicated to Murchison in spite of the divergence of their views on the subject. Oldroyd, 1990, pp152-153 gives some revealing drafts of the dedication from the Geikie papers at Haslemere, while Murchison's own copy of the book is described in Thackray 1983.
3. Geikie did not modify his opinion until 1884, when he give up the Murchisonian interpretation of the structure of the northwest Highlands altogether (Oldroyd 1990, p9).
4. 'full of wine'.

Bibliography

Adams, F D, 1938. *The birth and development of the geological sciences*. London, Bailliere, Tindall and Cox.

Agassiz, E C, 1885. *Louis Agassiz: his life and correspondence*. London, Macmillan.

Agassiz, J L R, 1840. *Études sur les glaciers*. Neuchâtel & Soleure.

Allen, D E, 1976. *The naturalist in Britain, a social history*. London, Allen Lane.

Anon, 1896. 'The Palaeontographical Society of London', *Geological Magazine* 33: 385-388.

Austen, R A C, 1845. 'On the coal beds of Lower Normandy', *Quarterly Journal of the Geological Society* 2: 1-6.

Babbage, C, 1830. *Reflections on the decline of science in England, and on some of its causes*. London.

Babbage, C, 1837. 'On impressions in sandstone resembling those of horses' hoofs', *Proceedings of the Geological Society of London* 2: 439.

Bartholomew, M, 1976. 'The non-progress of non-progressionism: two responses to Lyell's doctrine', *British Journal for the History of Science* 9: 166-174.

Benton, M J, 1983. 'Progressionism in the 1850s: Lyell, Owen, Mantell and the Elgin fossil reptile *Leptopleuron (Telerpeton)*', *Archives of Natural History* 11: 123-136.

Bowler, P J, 1976. *Fossils and progress: paleontology and the idea of progressive evolution in the nineteenth century*. New York, Science History Publications.

Boylan, P J, (ed) 1977. *The Falconer papers, Forres*. Leicester, Leicestershire Museums, Art Galleries and Records Service.

Brickenden, L, 1851. 'On the occurrence of boulder clay in the limestone quarry, Linksfield, Elgin, N.B.', *Quarterly Journal of the Geological Society* 7: 289-292.

Buckland, W, 1817. 'Description of a series of specimens from the Plastic Clay', *Transactions of the Geological Society of London* 4: 277-304.

Buckland, W, 1823. *Reliquiae Diluvianae*. London.

Buckland, W, 1825. 'Reply to Dr Fleming's remarks on the distribution of British animals', *Edinburgh Philosophical Journal* 12: 304-319.

Buckland, W, and De la Beche, H T, 1835. 'On the geology of the neighbourhood of Weymouth and adjacent parts of the coast of Dorset', *Transactions of the Geological Society of London*, second series 4: 1-46.

Bunbury, F, 1890-1891. *Memorials of C. J. F. Bunbury, middle life*. Mildenhall, privately printed. Three volumes.

Bunbury, F, 1891. *Memorials of C. J. F. Bunbury, early life*. Mildenhall, privately printed.

Burke, E, 1759. *A philosophical enquiry into the origin of our ideas of the sublime and beautiful*. 2nd ed. London.

Burkhardt, F and Smith, S (eds), 1985-2003. *The Correspondence of Charles Darwin*. Cambridge, Cambridge University Press. Twelve volumes.

Burmeister, H C, 1846. *The organization of trilobites, deduced from their living affinities*. London, Ray Society.

Burt, R, 1977. *John Taylor, mining entrepreneur and engineer*. Buxton, Moorland Publishing Co.

Chambers, R, 1853. 'On glacial phenomena in Scotland and parts of England', *Edinburgh New Philosophical Journal* 54: 229-281.

Charlot, M, 1991. *Victoria, the young Queen*. Oxford, Blackwell.

Cheney, C R, (ed) 2000. *A handbook of dates: for students of British history*. Royal Historical Society guides and handbooks, 2nd ed. Cambridge, Cambridge University Press.

Chorley, R J, Dunn, A J and Beckinsale, R P, 1964. *The history of the study of landforms or the development of geomorphology*. Volume 1. London, Methuen.

Clark, J W and Hughes, T McK, 1890. *The life and letters of the Reverend Adam Sedgwick*. Cambridge, Cambridge University Press. Two volumes.

Cook, E T and Wedderburn, A, (eds), 1909. *The Letters of John Ruskin*. London, G Allen. Two volumes.

Curwen, E C, (ed), 1940. *The journal of Gideon Mantell, surgeon and geologist*. Oxford, Oxford University Press.

Dana, J D, 1845. 'Observations on pseudomorphism'. *American Journal of Science and Arts* 48: 81-92, 397.

Daubeny, C G B, 1826. *A description of active and extinct volcanos*. London.

Davies, G L, 1969. *The earth in decay, a history of British geomorphology, 1578-1878*. London, Macdonald.

Dearman, W R, and Turner, S, 1983. 'Models illustrating John Farey's figures of stratified masses', *Proceedings of the Geologists Association* 94: 97-104.

De Chabriol, J S D, & Bouillet, J B, 1827. *Essai géologique et minéralogique sur les environs d'Issoire*. Clermont-Ferrand.

De la Beche, H T, 1822. 'Remarks on the geology of the south coast of England', *Transactions of the Geological Society of London*, second series 1 : 40-47.

Desmond, A J, 1982. *Archetypes and ancestors: palaeontology in Victorian London 1850-1875*. London, Blond & Briggs.

Desmond, A J, 1989. *The politics of evolution: morphology, medicine and reform in radical London*. Chicago and London: University of Chicago Press.

Evans, J, and Whitehouse, J H, (eds) 1835-1847. *The diaries of John Ruskin. Part 1: 1835-1847*. Oxford, Clarendon.

Fitton, W H, 1828. [Presidential Address] *Proceedings of the Geological Society of London* 1: 50-62.

Geikie, A, 1865. *The scenery of Scotland viewed in connexion with its physical geology*. London, Macmillan.

Geikie, A, 1875. *The life of Roderick I. Murchison.* London, John Murray. Two volumes.

Geikie, A, 1895. *Memoir of Sir Andrew Crombie Ramsay.* London, Macmillan.

Geikie, A, 1924. *A long life's work: an autobiography.* London, Macmillan.

Gordon, Mrs E O, 1894. *The life and correspondence of William Buckland.* London, John Murray.

Greene, M T, 1982. *Geology in the Nineteenth Century, changing views of a changing world.* Ithaca and London, Cornell University Press.

Greenough, G B, 1820. *A geological map of England and Wales.* London, Geological Society.

Greenough, G B, 1840. 'The Memoir to accompany the second edition of the geological map of England and Wales', *Proceedings of the Geological Society of London* 3: 180-185.

Harcourt, E W (ed), [1880-1905]. *The Harcourt papers.* Private circulation. Thirteen volumes.

Harrington, B J, 1883. *The Life of Sir W. E. Logan, etc.* London, Sampson Low & Co.

Henslow, J S, 1822. 'Geological description of Anglesea', *Transactions of the Cambridge Philosophical Society* 1: 359-452.

Herschel, J F W, (ed), 1849. *A manual of scientific enquiry: prepared for the use of Her Majesty's Navy and ... travellers in general.* London, Admiralty.

Higham, N, 1963. *A very scientific gentlemen. The major achievements of Henry Clifton Sorby.* Oxford, Pergamon Press.

Hooker, J D, 1859. *On the flora of Australia, its origin, affinities, and distribution; being an introductory essay to the flora of Tasmania.* Reprinted from pt 3 of *The botany of the Antarctic Expedition, Flora Tasmaniae,* vol 1. London.

Horrebow, N, 1758. *The natural history of Iceland.* London.

Hutchinson, P O, 1843. *The geology of Sidmouth and of south-eastern Devon*. Sidmouth, John Harvey.

Laudan, R. 1976. 'William Smith: stratigraphy without palaeontology'. *Centaurus* 20: 210-216.

Lyell, C, 1863. *The geological evidences of the antiquity of Man, with remarks on theories of the origin of species by variation*. London, John Murray.

Lyell, K, (ed), 1881. *Life, letters and journals of Sir Charles Lyell, Bart*. London, John Murray. Two volumes.

Lyell, K, (ed), 1890. *Leonard Horner*. London: Women's Printing Society. Two volumes.

Lyell, K, (ed), 1906. *The life of Sir Charles J. F. Bunbury, Bart*. London, John Murray. Two volumes.

MacEnery, J, 1859. *Cavern researches ... edited from the original manuscript notes, by E. Vivian*. London, Simpkin, Marshall and Co.

Morris, J, 1854. *A catalogue of British fossils ... with reference to their geological distribution and to the localities in which they have been found*. 2nd ed. London.

Moxon, C, (ed) 1842. *The Geologist, being a record of investigations and discoveries in geology, mineralogy, etc*. London. Two volumes.

Murchison, R I, 1826. 'Geological sketch of the north western extremity of Sussex, and the adjoining parts of Hants and Surrey', *Transactions of the Geological Society of London*, second series 2: 97-108.

[Northmore, T], 1825. 'Organic remains in Kent's Hole and Chudleigh Cave'. *The Monthly Magazine or British Register* 59: 190-191.

O'Brien, C F, 1970. '*Eozoon Canadense*: the dawn animal of Canada', *Isis* 61: 206-223.

Oldroyd, D R, 1990. *The Highlands controversy. Constructing geological knowledge through fieldwork in nineteenth-century Britain*. Chicago, University of Chicago Press.

Olmsted, J M D, 1944. *François Magendie, pioneer in experimental physiology and scientific medicine in XIX century France*. New York, Schuman's.

Owen, R, 1840. 'Fossil Mammalia', Part 1 of Charles Darwin (ed), *The Zoology of the Voyage of H M S Beagle*. London, 1838-1840.

Owen, R, 1851. 'Vertebrate air-breathing life in the Old Red Sandstone'. *Literary Gazette and Journal of Science and Art* 20 December 1851, no 1822, p900.

Owen, R S, 1894. *The life of Richard Owen*. London, John Murray. Two volumes.

Peacock, J D, Berridge, N G, Harris, A L and May, F, 1968. *The geology of the Elgin district*. Memoirs of the Geological Survey, Scotland.

Pengelly, H, (ed) 1897. *A Memoir of William Pengelly, of Torquay, F.R.S., geologist, with a selection from his correspondence*. London, John Murray.

Phillips, J, 1836. *Illustrations of the Geology of Yorkshire, Part II. The Mountain Limestone District*. London.

Phillips, J, 1841. *Figures and descriptions of the Palaeozoic fossils of Cornwall, Devon and West Somerset*. London, Longman, Brown, Green & Longman.

Playfair, J, 1802. *Illustrations of the Huttonian theory of the Earth*. Edinburgh.

Prestwich, Mrs [G A], 1899. *Life and letters of Sir Joseph Prestwich*. Edinburgh and London, William Blackwood and Sons.

Prévost, C, 1828. 'Les continents actuels, ont-ils été, a plusieurs reprises submerges par la mer?', *Memoires de la Société d'Histoire Naturelle de Paris* 4: 249-346.

Rudwick, M J S, 1963. 'The foundation of the Geological Society of London: its scheme for cooperative research and its struggle for independence', *British Journal for the History of Science* 1: 325-355.

Rudwick, M J S, 1985. *The Great Devonian Controversy*. Chicago, University of Chicago Press.

Rupke, N A, 1983. *The great chain of history: William Buckland and the English school of geology (1814-1849)*. Oxford, Clarendon.

Rupke, N A, 1994. *Richard Owen: Victorian naturalist*. New Haven, Yale University Press.

Scrope, G P, 1825. *Considerations on volcanos*. London.

Secord, J A, 1986. *Controversy in Victorian geology: the Cambrian-Silurian dispute*. Princeton, Princeton University Press.

Sedgwick, A, and Murchison, R I, 1829. 'On deposits contained between the Primary rocks and the Oolitic Series in the North of Scotland', *Transactions of the Geological Society of London*, second series 3: 125-160.

Sedgwick, A, and Murchison, R I, 1839. 'Classification of the older stratified rocks of Devonshire and Cornwall', *Philosophical Magazine and Journal of Science*, series 3, 14: 241-260.

Sorby, H C, 1853. 'On the origin of slaty-cleavage', *Edinburgh New Philosophical Journal* 55: 137-148.

Sowerby, J [and Sowerby, J de C], 1812-1846. *The Mineral Conchology of Great Britain*. London. Seven volumes.

Spokes, S, 1927. *Gideon Algernon Mantell, LL.D., F.R.C.S., F.R.S., surgeon and geologist*. London, Bale & Danielsson.

Stadler, E A (ed), 1972. *Journey through a part of the United States of North America in the years 1884 to 1846 by Dr Albert C Koch*. Carbondale, Southern Illinois University Press.

Stafford, R A, 1989. *Scientist of empire. Sir Roderick Murchison, scientific exploration and Victorian imperialism*. Cambridge, Cambridge University Press.

Stanley, A P, 1879. *Memoirs of Edward and Catherine Stanley, edited by their son*. London, John Murray.

Thackray, J C, 1983. 'Geikie's *Scenery of Scotland* 1865', *Newsletter, Society for the History of Natural History* 20: 6.

Tickell, C, 1995. *Mary Anning of Lyme Regis*. Lyme Regis, Lyme Regis Philpot Museum.

Torrens, H, 1995. 'Mary Anning (1799-1847) of Lyme; "the greatest fossilist the world ever knew"', *British Journal for the History of Science* 28: 257-284.

Turner, S, and Dearman, W R, 1979. 'Sopwith's geological models', *Bulletin of the International Association of Engineering Geology* 19: 331-345.

Van Riper, A B, 1993. *Men among the mammoths, Victorian science and the discovery of human prehistory.* Chicago, University of Chicago Press.

Verneuil, 1847. 'Note sur le parallélisme des roches des dépôts Paléozoïques de l'Amerique Septentrionale avec ceux de l'Europe, suivie d'un tableau des espèces fossiles', *Bulletin de la Société Géologique de France* 2nd series 4: 646-710.

Walford, E, [ca 1875]. *Old and new London.* London. Six volumes.

Whittet, T D, 1983. 'The Crown and Anchor and the arts and sciences', *Pharmaceutical Historian* 13 (3&4), unpaginated.

Wilson, L G, 1972. *Charles Lyell, the years to 1841: the revolution in geology.* New Haven, Yale University Press.

Wilson, G, and Geikie, A, 1861. *Memoir of Edward Forbes.* Cambridge, Macmillan.

Woodward, H B, 1907. *The history of the Geological Society of London.* London, Geological Society.

Young, G, 1817. *A history of Whitby and Streoneshalh Abbey.* Whitby. Two volumes.

Name Index

All references are to paragraph numbers. *'As eye witness'* refers to writers of the eye witness reports; *'as author'* refers to authors of those papers read at the evening meetings which were noticed by the eye witnesses; *'other refs'* includes all those noted as present at meetings, including those taking part in discussions, with a few other references.

Abich, H 175a
Ackland, T 58a
Adair, Lord 82a
Agassiz, J R L *as eye witness* 95b; *as author* 61, 93, 94; *other refs* 95a
Albert, Prince Consort 162a
Ansted, D T 128b
Argyll, Duke of *as author* 175, 236; *other refs* 177a, 231a-d
Ashburnham, Mr 97a
Athenaeum as eye witness 38a, 39a
Atkinson, T W *as author* 218
Austen see Godwin-Austen
Aveline, W T 141a, 178b

Babbage, C *as author* 59, 72, 210
Babington, W 45a
Bailey 7a,
Baily, F 66a, 141a
Bain, A G *as author* 194; *other refs* 115b
Bakewell, R 54a
Bancroft, G 143a, 143c
Barclay, Mr 87a, 98a
Barrande, J 174a, 175a
Bartlett, T O 34a
Bayfield, Captain T *as author* 118
Bayley 82a
Beechey, Admiral 36a
Bensted, Mr 109a
Bigsby, J J *as eye witness* 229a; *other refs* 204a, 216a
Bilton, W *as eye witness* 88b, 89a
Binney, E W *as author* 133
Bland, W *as author* 46
Bowerbank, J S *as author* 101; *other refs* 124b, 142a, 142c
Brickenden, T R L *as author* 173, 186, 187; *other refs* 156a

Bristow, H W 152b, 153a, 160b
Broderip, W J 27b, 41a, 43a, 45a, 46a, 82a, 87a, 98a
Brodie, P B *as eye witness* 108a; *as author* 108, 136, 164
Brongniart, A 7a
Brown, R *as author* 133, 161; *other refs* 3a, 17a, 18a
Brunel, I K 159a
Brunnow, Baron 104a-c
Buckingham, Duke of *as author* 18
Buckland, W *as eye witness* 3a, 20b; *as author* 3, 9, 17, 23, 30, 72, 75, 94, 95, 101; *other refs* 1a, 4a, 5a, 6a, 7a, 8a, 10a, 14b, 15a, 16a, 17b, 18a, 21a, 22a-c, 27a, 28a, 28b, 31a, 32a-c, 33a, 36a, 44a, 44b, 49a, 54a, 56a, 58a, 61b, 66a, 69a, 72a-b, 73a, 75a, 77c, 79a-b, 82a, 87a, 88a, 91a, 93a, 97a, 98a, 100a-b, 101a, 105a, 106a, 107a, 112a, 115c, 118a, 119a-b, 123a-c, 124a, 129a, 130c, 132c, 133a, 135b, 147b, 151b, 152a, 153a, 154a, 155a, 156a, 160a-c
Buckland and De la Beche *as authors* 34, 35
Buddle, J 79a, 101a
Bunbury, C J F *as eye witness* 68a, 68b, 77a-b, 99a, 115b, 116a, 117b, 118a, 119b, 123a, 123d, 124b, 126b, 127b, 128a, 129b, 130c, 131b, 132c, 133a-b, 138a, 145a, 146a, 147b, 191b, 194a, 196a, 211a, 214a, 215a, 216a, 217a, 218a, 226b, 228a, 231a; *as author* 123, 138, 145, 215, 226; *other refs* 231c
Bunbury, C J F, see also Dawson and Bunbury
Bunbury, E *as eye witness* 102a; *other refs* 231b
Bunbury, Mr 101a, 161a
Burlington, Lord 82a
Burnes, A 66a

Caldcleugh, A *as author* 73
Carpenter, W B 154a, 187a
Cavendish, Lord 49a
Chambers, R 143a, 197a
Chantrey, F L 7a, 31a
Chassereau 54a
Charlesworth, E 73a, 105a, 154a
Christie, T *as author* 43
Churchill, Lord A 169a, 177a
Clerke, Major T H S 82a, 93a, 98a, 100b, 106a
Clift,W *as author* 51; *other refs* 6a, 41a, 54a, 82a
Cole, H 231b
Cole, W W, Earl of Enniskillen 46a, 66a, 75a, 79a, 82a-b, 87a, 93a, 104b, 107a, 169a, 177a, 216a, 221a
Conybeare, W D *as eye witness* 3a; *as author* 3, 27, 28; *other refs* 16a, 17b, 23a, 47a, 48a, 49a, 50a, 110a-b, 128a
Cook, E *as author* 45

Crawfurd, J 14a
Crichton, A *as author* 8; *other refs* 5a, 66a
Cully, M 28a
Cumming, J *as author* 127
Cuvier, Baron G 15a, 16a

Dames,T L *as author* 235
Darwin, C *as eye witness* 84a, 85a, 197a; *as author* 68, 73, 83, 131; *other refs* 73b, 77a-b, 82a, 130c, 138b, 143a, 152a-b, 153a, 186a, 186c
Daubeny, C G B 12a, 95a, 112a
Davidson,T *as author* 198
Davis, J E *as author* 171
Davy, H 5a
Dawson, Mr 106a
Dawson, J W *as author* 196, 229
Dawson, see also Lyell and Dawson
Dawson, J W and Bunbury, C J F *as authors* 126
Dechen, H von 10a
De la Beche, H T *as author* 19, 20, 63, 67, 153, 160; *other refs* 6a, 33a, 37a, 41a, 44a, 45a, 46a, 48a, 50a, 56a, 58a, 67a, 79a-b, 81a, 83a, 87a, 88a-b, 89a, 95a, 98a, 109a, 115a, 115c, 116a, 119b, 123a-b, 124b, 128b, 129a, 130c, 132c, 133a-b, 134b, 135b, 138b, 141a, 143a, 150a-b, 155a, 156a, 165a, 166a, 168a, 171a, 171b, 173b, 175a, 176a, 177a, 180a-b, 184a, 185a, 186a, 188a
De la Beche, see also Buckland and De la Beche
De Montlosier, Count *as author* 44
De Serres, M *as author* 5
Dennis, Rev Mr *as author* 208
Donkin, Sir R 79a
Drew, F *as author* 225
Drinkwater 66a
Ducie, Lord 231b-d
Duncan, P M 66a
Dunn, J *as author* 44

Edwards, Dr (of America) 134a
Egerton, P de M G *as author* 67, 69; *other refs* 75a, 82a, 87a, 106a, 107a, 168a, 169a, 181a, 208a, 213a, 231c
Emmerson, the American 154a
Evans, Sir J 236a
Everest, R *as author* 103

Falconer, H *as eye witness* 219b; *as author* 219; *other refs* 146a, 164a, 229a, 232a, 232c-d
Faraday, M 156a

Farey, 197a
Featherstonhaugh, G W 88a, 93a, 99a, 100a, 106a, 107a, 116a
Ferguson, Mr 87a
Ferguson of Raith 49a
Fitton, W H *as eye witness* 40a; *as author* 24, 114; *other refs* 1a, 5a, 12a, 13a, 14a, 15a, 17b, 20a, 22a, 26a, 28a, 41a, 43a, 44a, 44b, 45a, 46a, 48a, 49a, 54a, 58a, 64a, 66a, 69a, 75a, 79a, 82a, 83a, 88a, 99a, 100b, 102b, 151b, 171a, 183b
Fitzallan, Lord 87a
Forbes, D *as eye witness* 203a; *as author* 203; *other refs* 236a
Forbes, E *as eye witness* 111b, 115c, 135b, 137a, 138b, 142c, 148b, 149a, 151b, 171b, 174a, 192a, 193a; *as author* 175, 191, 199; *other refs* 93a, 100b, 113a, 114b, 122c, 130c, 133a, 139a, 141a, 142a, 142c, 143a, 154a, 158a, 160b, 164a, 167b, 168b, 169a, 177a, 178b, 183b, 187a-b, 190b
Forbes, E, biographer: *as eye witness* 200c
Forbes, J 162a
Forest 235a
Franklin, J *as author* 18

Galton, D 170a, 208a, 214a
Geikie, A *as eye witness* 213a; *as author* 213
Geikie, see also Murchison and Geikie
Gilbert, D 14a, 69a
Gilbert, Mr 106a
Gladstone, W E 223a
Godwin-Austen, R A C *as eye witness* 80a, 90a, 98b; *as author* 62, 80, 118, 172, 176, 206; *other refs* 81a, 128b, 160b, 167b, 169a, 193a, 196a, 204a, 219a, 229a, 231c
Goulbourne 188a
Grant, R E *as author* 107, *other refs* 86a
Grantham, R B *as author* 141
Graves, P W *as author* 206
Graves, Captain 164a
Gray, J E 5a, 94a
Greenough, G B *as eye witness* 63a, 70a; *as author* 57, 91; *other refs* 4a, 5a, 8a, 12a, 13a, 17a, 17b, 18a, 19a, 20a, 21a, 22a, 22b, 22c, 26a, 27a, 28b, 38a, 41a, 43a, 44a, 44b, 46a, 48a, 49a, 50a, 57, 58a, 59a, 63a-c, 64a, 65a, 66a, 68b-c, 73a, 75a, 77a-b, 79a, gla, 82a, 83a, 85a, 87a, 88a-b, 94a, 95a, 97a, 98a, 99a, 100b, 102b, 104b, 106a, 107a, 117a-b, 122a, 148b, 150a
Griffith, Sir R 192a, 199a
Guillemard 4a
Gurney, H 69a

Haliburton, Mr 87a
Hall, Captain B 36a, 43a, 93a-b, 98a
Hall, J 93a, 97a, 98a, 101a, 106a
Hallam, H H 49a, 66a, 82a, 104b, 106a, 141a
Hamilton, W J *as author* 87, 201, 204; *other refs* 82a, 93a, 97a, 122c, 130c, 169a, 216a
Hanbury, C jun 206a
Harding, Major W 81a
Harkness, R *as author* 174, 208, 233; *other refs* 222a
Heaphy, C *as author* 218
Hector, J *as author* 227
Henslow, J S 47a
Herschel, J F W *as author* 40; *other refs* 12a, 14a, 24b-d, 49a
Heywood, Mr 231b
Hitchcock, E 172a
Hoffman, F *as author* 45
Hooker, J D *as author* 198; *other refs* 138a
Hopkins, E *as author* 202
Hopkins, W *as eye witness* 187a; *as author* 186; *other refs* 141a, 169a, 175a, 176a, 178b, 179a, 180a-b, 187a, 197a, 198a
Horner, L *as eye witness* 103a, 104b, 105a, 122b, 122c, 139a, 141b, 142b, 186c, 195a, 199a, 212a; *as author* 45, 58, 128, 200; *other refs* 75a, 98a, 141a, 150a, 213a, 216a, 219a, 221a, 223a
Horsfield, T 32b
Howell, H H 224a
Hull, E *as author* 230; *other refs* 235a
Humboldt, Baron A von 3a
Hunt, Consul *as author* 103
Hunt, T Sterry *as author* 216
Hutton, R 79a
Hutton 225a
Hutton, W *as author* 46, 55
Huxley, T H *as author* 221, 226, 231; *other refs* 210a, 228a, 229a, 232a

Ibbetson, Captain L L B 93a, 115a, 141a, 143a
Ingham, R 66a, 93a, 98a

James, Captain H 126c, 160b, 169a, 169a, 171b, 178b, 204a, 207a, 214a, 221a, 232b-c
Johnes 230a
Johnston, J 49a, 58a
Johnstone, Sir J 104b
Jones, Prof 82a
Jones, T R *as eye witness* 198a, 201b; *other refs* 194a

Jukes, J B *as eye witness* 104a; *as author* 148; *other refs* 143a, 151a, 167b, 192a, 208a
Jukes, J B and Selwyn, A R C *as authors* 155

Keyserling, Count 106a
Kingdon, J *as author* 6
Koch, A 105a, 122c

Lambert, J *as author* 93
Landsborough, Mr 181a
Lansdowne, Marquis of 56a, 66a, 104a-c
Lemon, Sir C 49a, 66a, 87a, 93a, 101a, 106a, 188a
Lindley, J *as author* 25
Lockhart, J S 49a
Logan, W E *as eye witness* 234a; *as author* 190, 234; *other refs* 178b, 204a, 233a
Longman, W 223a
Lonsdale, W 66a, 80a, 88a-b, 128a
Lorne, Marquis of 106a
Lubbock, Sir J W 66a, 82a, 219a, 236a
Lyell, C *as eye witness* 1a, 2a, 4b, 14a, 15b, 22c, 24c, 24d, 27a, 27b, 28a, 28b, 30a, 32c, 35a, 36a, 41b, 42a, 43a, 44a, 45a, 46a, 47a, 48a, 49a, 51a, 53a, 55b, 58a, 59a, 61a, 63c, 66a, 67a, 73b, 82a, 83a, 143c, 160d, 227b, 231c, 232d, 235a; *as author* 4, 95, 96, 110, 116, 122, 131, 145, 163, 182, 191; *other refs* 5a, 6a, 11a, 25a, 26a, 32a, 33a, 37a, 44b, 50a, 54a, 56a, 58a, 62a, 63a, 63b, 69a, 73a, 77c, 88a, 94a, 97a, 98a, 99a, 100a-b, 101a, 118a, 119b, 122c, 135a-b, 137a, 141a, 144a-b, 147b, 150a, 155a, 156a, 158a, 160a-c, 168b, 169a, 170a, 171a, 173b, 175a, 176a, 180a-b, 183b, 187a, 188a, 190b, 196a, 201a, 202a, 206a, 207a, 208a, 210a, 213a, 216a, 217a, 219a, 221a, 223a, 229a, 231a-b, 232a, 236a
Lyell, C and Dawson *as authors* 195
Lyell, C and Murchison *as authors* 21, 22
Lyell, M *as eye witness* 96a

McCoy, F 160b
Mackenzie, C 45a
Mackintosh, C 100a
Mackintosh, A F *as author* 119
McLauchlan, H 115a
McNeil, Sir J 101a
Magendie, F 46a
Mallet, R 152b
Mantell, G A *as eye witness* 7a, 11a, 31a, 33a, 54a, 54b, 107a, 109a, 110a, 111a, 114a, 120a, 121a, 122a, 123b, 123c, 124a, 125a, 126a,

130b, 132a, 134a, 135a, 136a, 143b, 144a, 147a, 148a, 152a, 156a, 157a, 159a, 160a, 160c, 162a, 167a, 168b, 171a, 172a, 173a-b, 176a, 178a, 180a, 182a, 183a, 186b, 186d, 187b-c, 190a, 191a; *as author* 10, 17, 54, 67, 104, 120, 123, 125, 152, 156, 168; *other refs* 18a, 32a, 57a, 87a, 122c, 124b, 126b, 133a, 147b, 183b, 190b
Mantell, R N *as author* 168; *other refs* 167a, 171a
Mantell, Mr 87a
Malcolm, J 49a
Martin, P J *as author* 13; *other refs* 167a
Mitchell, J *as eye witness* 55a, 57a, 60a, 61b, 69a, 71a, 72b, 74a, 76a, 77c; *other refs* 69a, 73b, 94a
Martin, P J 167a
Miller, W H 216a
Milman 82a
Milnes, M 231a-d
Milton, Lord 49a
Mitchell, Sir T 93a, 148a-b
Moore, Sir J 128a
Moore, J C *as author* 210; *other refs* 154a, 170a, 191b, 196a, 216a, 118a
Morpeth, Lord 49a, 143a, 143c
Morris, J *as author* 74, 133; *other refs* 119b, 126b, 168a, 193a, 206a, 209a, 230a
Morrison, Mr 5a
Moxon, C *as eye witness* 102b
Mudge, Col 87a, 93a, 98a
Munch, P A 164a
Murchison, R I *as eye witness* 4a, 5a, 6a, 8a, 9a, 10a, 12a, 13a, 21a, 22a, 24a, 24b, 32b, 34a, 41a, 43b, 44b, 56a, 64a, 65a, 72a, 75a, 81a, 88a, 90b, 91a, 104c, 134c, 220a, 232b, 233a, 236a-b; *as author* 10, 26, 32, 49, 50, 56, 65, 104, 111, 132, 134, 135, 140, 157, 159, 162, 166, 177, 179, 183; *other refs* 20a, 25a, 27a, 33a, 37a, 43a, 45a, 46a, 49a, 50a, 58a, 63a, 63b, 69a, 70a, 73a, 77a, 79a-b, 82a, 87a, 88b, 94a, 95a-b, 97a, 98a, 99a, 100a, 102b, 106a, 107a, 118a, 119b, 126a, 128a-b, 130a, 130c, 139a, 140a, 146a, 158a, 160a-c, 169a, 170a, 171a, 173b, 176a, 180a-b, 184a, 187a, 188a, 189a, 189c, 190b, 194a, 196a, 197a, 200b-c, 204a, 206a, 208a, 210a, 211a, 213a, 214a, 217a, 219a, 228a, 229a, 230a, 231a-c
Murchison and Geikie *as authors* 222, 224
Murchison and Verneuil *as authors* 99, 100
Murchison, Verneuil and Keyserling *as authors* 106
Murchison, see also Lyell and Murchison
Murchison, see also Sedgwick and Murchison
Murray of Simprin 36a
Mylne, J 216a

Napier, Sir C 130c
Nasmyth, Mr *as author* 141
Necker de Saussure, L A 44a, 94a
Nicol, J *as author* 150, 220
Northampton, Marquis of, 87a, 88a, 99a, 100a, 106a, 112a

Oersted 2a
Oeynhausen, K von 10a
Oldham, T 141a, 151a
Otter, Captain 140a
Own, Mrs C *as eye witness* 79b, 86a
Owen, R *as eye witness* 82b, 136b; *as author* 86, 98, 103, 105, 113, 124, 136, 190, 198, 201; *other refs* 54a, 82a, 98a, 100b, 103a, 107a, 123a, 168a-b, 190b, 194a, 208a, 212a

Panmure, Lord 212a
Parish, W *as author* 51; *other refs* 69a
Peel, Sir R 160a-d
Pentland, J B *as author* 25; *other refs* 16a, 107a
Percy, J 143a, 204a, 219a
Phillips, J 83a, 87a, 95a, 100b, 115a-b, 198a, 216a
Phillips, Sir T [?Phillipps] 30a
Playfair, J 58a,
Playfair, L 117a, 143a, 153a, 160b
Playfair, R L *as author* 228
Pengelly, W *as eye witness* 206a, 210a, 219a, 219c
Portlock, Colonel J E 201b, 204a, 206a, 210a, 231b
Pratt, S P 126b, 141a
Prestwich, J *as eye witness* 50a; *as author* 129, 142, 165, 211; *other refs* 69a, 154a, 160b, 169a, 173b, 201a, 206a, 207a, 219a, 229a, 236a
Prévost, C 150a, 169a
Pringle, Captain 43a, 87a, 93a, 100a, 101a
Pugh, Mr 231b
Pusey, P 188a

Ramsay, A C *as eye witness* 100a, 100b, 113a, 114a, 115a, 117a, 118b, 119a, 125b, 126c, 126d, 127a, 128b, 129a, 130a, 131a, 132b, 140a, 141a, 142a, 143a, 144b, 150a, 150b, 151a, 152b, 152b, 153a, 154a, 155a, 158a, 160b, 161a, 163a, 164a, 165a, 166a, 167b, 168a, 169a, 170a, 175a, 177a, 178b, 179a, 180b, 181a, 183b, 185a, 186a, 188a, 189a, 190b, 201a, 202a, 204a, 205a, 208a, 209a, 221a, 222a, 223a, 224a, 225a, 226a, 227a, 230a, 231b, 232a, 232c; *as author* 155, 180, 232; *other refs* 126e, 189c, 213a, 229a, 230a, 235a, 236a
Ramsay, A C biographer: *as eye witness* 231d
Randon, Lord 104b

Reeks, T 117a, 143a, 153a, 160b, 168a, 204a, 232a
Renouard 94a
Richardson, W *as author* 60
Richmond, Duke of 104a-b
Rodgers, H 157a
Rogers 204a
Rosales, H *as author* 217
Rose 69a
Rosthorn of Wolfsberg 75a
Ruskin, J *as eye witness* 73a, 93b, 109b, 110b, 112a
Russell 69a

Salter, J W *as eye witness* 126e, 130d, 133c, 134b, 200a; *as author* 135, 198; *other refs* 135b, 149a, 150a, 200a, 210a, 230a
Sanders 115a, 141a, 154a
Scott, Archdeacon T H *as author* 42
Scouler, J *as author* 71
Scrope, G P *as eye witness* 22b; *as author* 12, 41; *other refs* 5a, 22a, 22c, 223a
Sedgwick, A *as eye witness* 17b, 62a, 79c, 92a, 111c, 184a, 191b, 193b; *as author* 9, 16, 33, 41, 48, 53, 85, 92, 102, 117, 125, 126, 139, 152, 184, 185, 189, 193, 200; *other refs* 1a, 10a, 14a, 22a, 22c, 23a, 24a-d, 26a, 27a, 28a, 28b, 31a, 37a, 38a, 40a, 47a, 48a, 49a, 66a, 67a, 69a, 71a, 77a-b, 79a-b, 82a, 87a, 98a, 100b, 119b, 122a, 122c, 132c, 147b, 151b, 153a, 155a, 160a-d, 171a-b, 177a, 178b, 190b
Sedgwick and Murchison *as authors* 17, 30, 72, 79, 89
Selkirk, Lord 154a
Selwyn, A R C 150a
Selwyn, see also Jukes and Selwyn
Sharpe, D *as author* 138, 149, 192; *other refs* 109a, 126b, 126e, 135b, 141a, 146a, 164a, 169a, 170a-b, 173b, 177a, 179a, 183b, 189c, 193a, 196a, 201a, 203a, 204a, 205a, 206a, 207a
Silliman, B 180a
Smith, Dr 87a
Smith, J [FRS] 27b
Smith, J of Jordanhill 95a, 141a, 169a, 204a
Smith, W 41a
Smithe, J D *as author* 221
Smyth, W W 141a, 153a, 160b, 178b, 202a, 206a, 220a, 230a, 231b
Somerville, Dr W 68a-b
Sopwith, T *as eye witness* 79a, 87a, 93a, 97a, 98a, 101a, 106a; *as author* 97; *other refs* 100b, 115a, 128b, 178b
Sorby, H C *as author* 207
Sotherby 49a
Sowerby, ?J de C 18a

Spratt, Lieut T A B *as author* 137
Stanley, E 143c
Stephenson, R 210a
Stokes, C *as author* 69, 72; *other refs* 17a, 26a, 43a, 46a, 66a, 69a, 75a, 79b, 82b, 97a, 98a
Strickland, H E *as author* 64, 70; *other refs* 108a, 128b, 193a
Strutt, Mr 41a
Sumner, Archbishop 160a-d
Sutherland, P C *as author* 197
Symonds 104b

Tagart, E *as author* 130
Taylor, J 3a, 58a, 79a, 87a, 93a, 97a, 100a-b, 101a, 141a
Taylor, R C *as eye witness* 14b, 15a, 16a, 17a, 18a, 19a, 20a, 23a, 26a, 32a, 37a
Tennant, C 100a
Tennant, J 97a
Thomson, T 100a
Thomson, P 5a
Tomsend, J 6a
Trevelyan, J 101a
Turner, E *as eye witness* 63b, 68c; *other refs* 45a, 50a, 58a, 63a
[?] Twamley 204a
Twiss 112a
Tyler 160b, 168a
Tyndall, J 210a, 236a

Underwood, T R 2a
Ure, Dr 100a

Van de Weyer 66a, 160b-d
Van Voorst, J 167b
Vicary, Captain N *as author* 130, 146
Vigors, N A 41a
Vine, Mr 34a
Vivian, E *as author* 147
Von Buch, Baron 106a
Vyvyan, R A 49a

Walton 132b
Warburton, H 4a, 5a, 15a, 21a, 22a, 22c, 66a, 88a, 111b, 118a-b
Weaver, T *as author* 37, 81,
Webster, T 17a
Weekes 54a
Weston, C H *as author* 158

Whewell, W *as author* 141; *other refs* 49a, 76a, 77a-b, 79a-b, 82a, 83a, 94a, 95a-b, 101a, 106a, 223a
Whishaw 45a
Whitaker, W W *as author* 221
Widdrington, Captain *as author* 112
Wilberforce, S 155a
Williams, D *as author* 77, 88, 90; *other refs* 72a, 81a,
Williams, G 141a, 154a
Williams, Dr 231b-c
Wilson 178b
Wollaston, W H 1a
Woodhouse, Mr 173a, 176a, 182a
Woods, Mr [of Exeter] *as author* 6
Woodward, S P *as eye witness* 94a, 95a, 200b; *other refs* 105a, 209a
Wright, T *as author* 209

Yates, J *as author* 38; *other refs* 41a, 63a

Subject Index

All references are to paragraph numbers. A highly selective subject index, concentrating on subjects of controversy.

Amber and its fossils 124
Basalt, origin of 8
Cambrian-Silurian controversy 56, 85, 102, 104, 117, 125, 126, 134, 135, 139, 140, 171, 184, 189, 193, 200
Caves and cave geology 1, 5, 9, 147, 219
Coal and coal geology 55, 145, 161, 206
Concretions 235
Devonian controversy 63, 64, 72, 79, 80, 81, 88, 89, 90, 91, 99, 184
Diluvialism 4, 14, 15, 27, 28, 35
Drift and drift deposits 132
Earthquakes 68, 103, 124
Elevation 59, 62, 68, 72, 73, 77, 83
Erosion and denudation 21, 22, 27, 28, 164, 183
Evolution and palaeontology 231
Fossil amphibians 98
Fossil birds 124, 125, 130, 152, 168
Fossil fish 61
Fossil human bones 147
Fossil insects 108
Fossil invertebrates 133, 149, 154, 164, 174
Fossil mammals 1, 3, 14, 15, 16, 32, 51, 86, 105, 107, 122, 208
Fossil plants 3, 17, 123, 126, 133, 138, 145, 161, 214, 215, 226
Fossil reptiles 3, 6, 16, 23, 30, 34, 44, 54, 103, 123, 124, 125, 130, 156, 195
Fossil tracks 41, 190
Freshwater formations 5, 8, 17
Glaciation and glacial theory 93, 94, 95, 96, 119, 162, 180, 197, 205, 232
Gold 217
Metamorphic structures 138, 202, 203, 216
Meteorites 118
Microscopy 120
Mining geology 3, 93
Models 97
Palaeontographical Society 142
Scotland, including Highland controversy 4, 10, 16, 150, 173, 177, 186, 187, 213, 220, 222, 224, 233, 236
Volcanoes and volcanic geology 12, 44, 45, 83, 122, 206, 230

BSHS MONOGRAPHS

The BSHS Monographs series aims to promote the study of the history of science and technology by publishing works of value that might not otherwise become available. it is a non-profit making venture, producing titles to high scholarly standards. Previous titles in the series are:

No 1: L J Jordanova & R Porter: *Images of the Earth: Essays in the History of Environmental Sciences* - 2nd revised and enlarged edition. 1997. 293pp [ISBN 0-906450-12-8]

No 2: D Outram: *The Letters of Georges Cuvier: A Summary Calendar of the MS and Printed Materials Preserved in Europe, the United States of America and Australasia.* 1980. 102pp [ISBN 0-906450-05-5]

No 3: B Wynne: *Rationality and Ritual: The Windscale Inquiry and Nuclear Decisions in Britain.* 1982. 222pp [ISBN 0-906450-02-0]

No 4: M Hunter: *The Royal Society and its Fellows, 1660-1700: The Morphology of an Early Scientific Institution* - 2nd Edition, 1994. 291pp [ISBN 0-906450-09-8]

No 5: G Rees & C Upton: *Francis Bacon's Natural Philosophy: A New Source. A Transcription of MS Hardwick 72A with Translation and Commentary.* 1984. 197pp [ISBN 0906450-04-7]

No 6: P Morris & C Russell: *Archives of the British Chemical Industry.* 1988. 273pp [ISBN 0-0906450-06-3]

No 7: S Sheets-Pyenson: *Index to the Scientific Correspondence of John William Dawson.* 1992. 275pp [ISBN 0-906450-07-1]

No 8: M Shortland (ed): *Science and Nature.* 1993. 291pp [ISBN 0-906450-08-X]

No 9: M Crosland: *In the Shadow of Lavoisier: the 'Annales de Chimie' and the Establishment of a New Science.* 1994. 354pp [ISBN 0-906450-10-1]

No 10: J Lester (ed P J Bowler): *E Ray Lankester and the Making of Modern British Biology.* 1995. 219pp [ISBN 0-906450-11-X]

No 11: J V Field & Frank A J L James: *Science in Art: Works in the National Gallery that illustrate the History of Science and Technology.* 1997. 110pp, 60 illustrations [ISBN 0-906450-13-6]